DYNAMIC STILL LIFE FOR ARTISTS

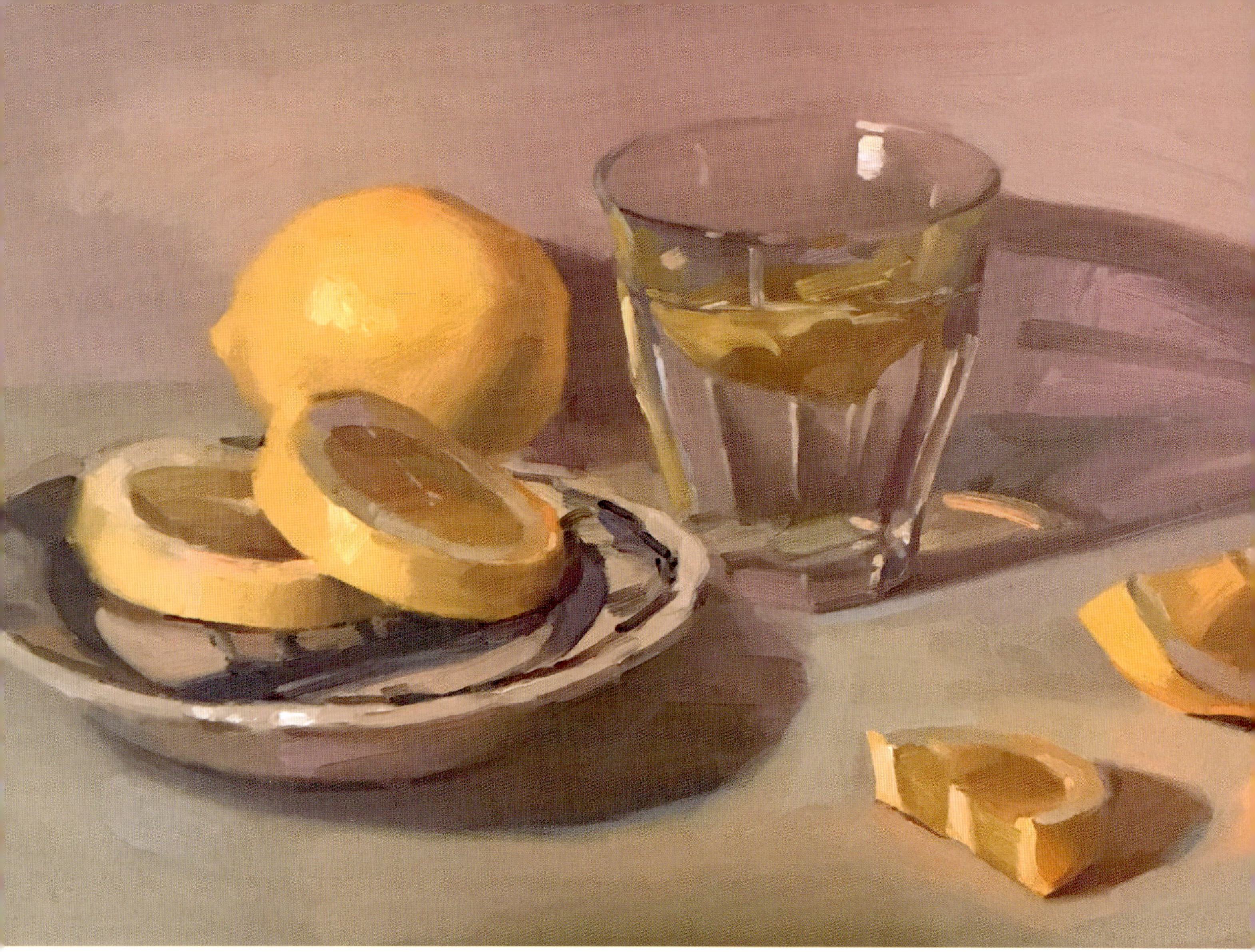

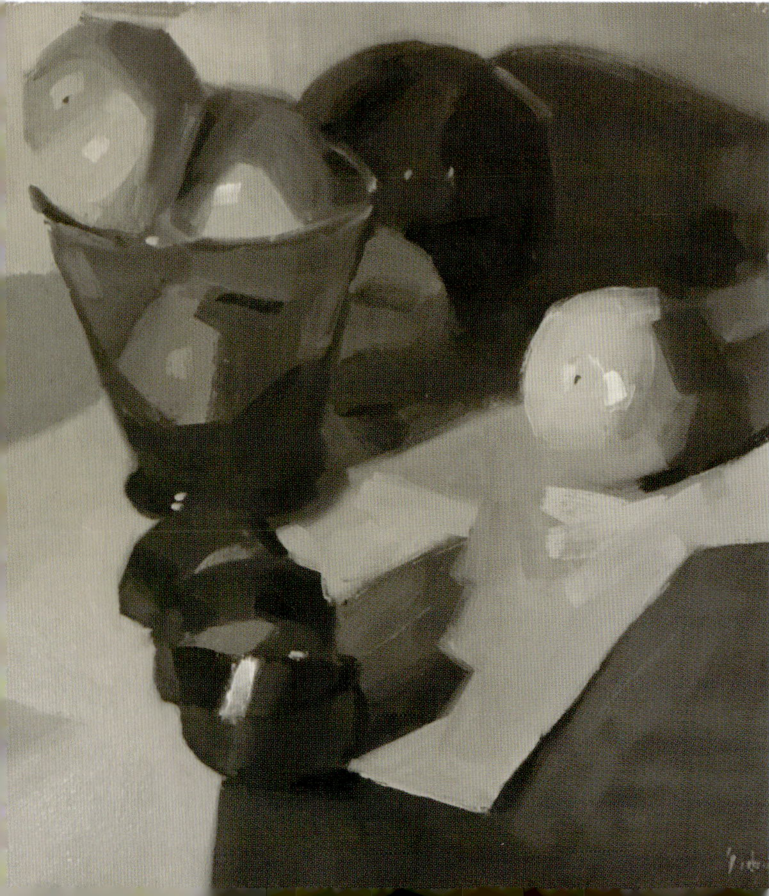

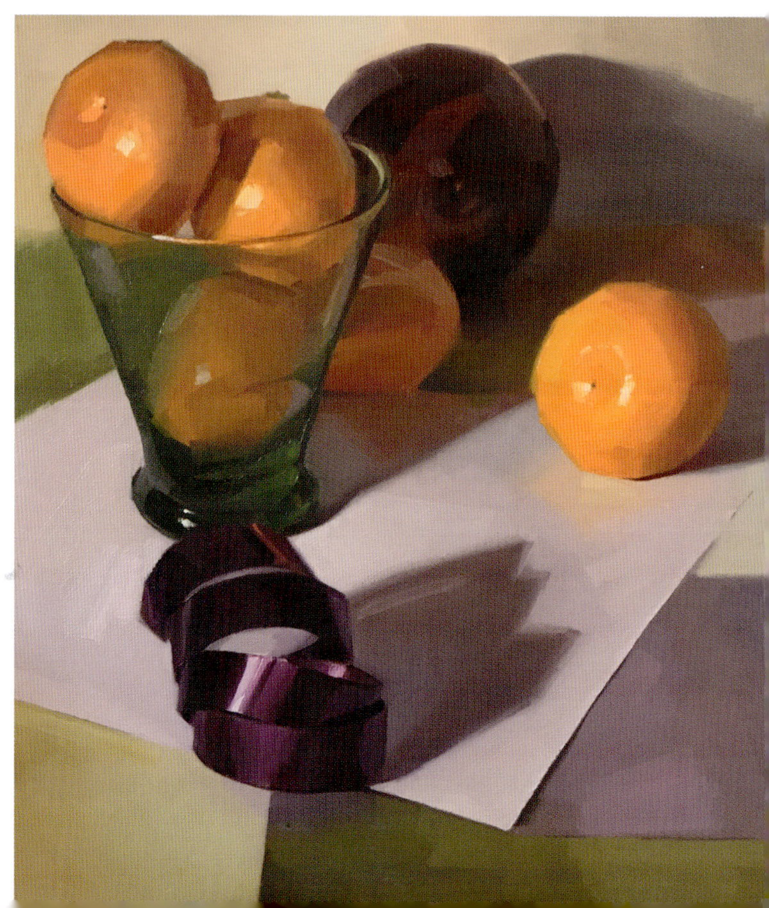

SARAH SEDWICK

DYNAMIC STILL LIFE FOR ARTISTS

A Modern Guide to Essential Concepts and Techniques

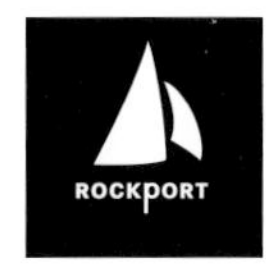

ROCKPORT

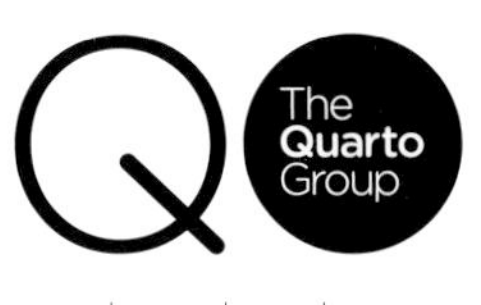

Brimming with creative inspiration, how-to projects, and useful information to enrich your everyday life, quarto.com is a favorite destination for those pursuing their interests and passions.

First published in 2023 by Rockport Publishers, an imprint of The Quarto Group,
100 Cummings Center, Suite 265-D, Beverly, MA 01915, USA.
T (978) 282-9590 F (978) 283-2742 Quarto.com

10 9 8 7 6 5 4 3

ISBN: 978-0-7603-7700-0

Digital edition published in 2023
eISBN: 978-0-7603-7701-7

Library of Congress Control Number: 2022940609

Cover Images: Sarah Sedwick except backcover third image from right Robert Williams
Design and Page Layout: Megan Jones Design
Photo credits: All images by Sarah Sedwick unless other artist listed and photography on pages 16, 18, 20, 21, 23, 24, 26, 27, 29, 31, 40, 49, 63, 88, 89, 98–101, 115–117, and 155 by Robert Williams

Printed in China

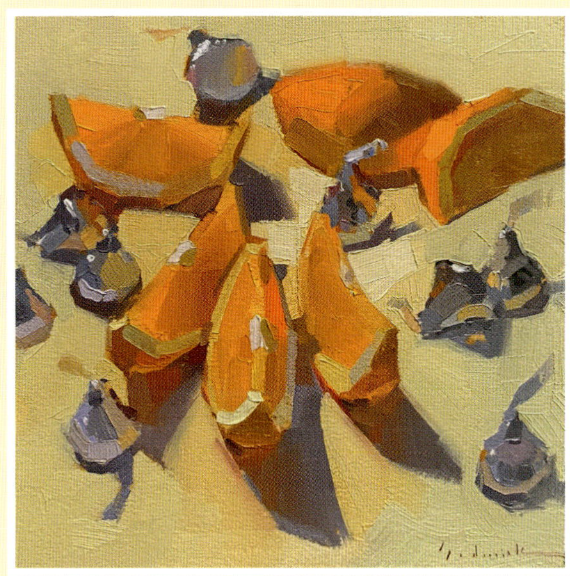

For Eleanor

Sarah Sedwick, *Vitamin C* color study, 8" × 8" | 20.3 × 20.3 cm

CONTENTS

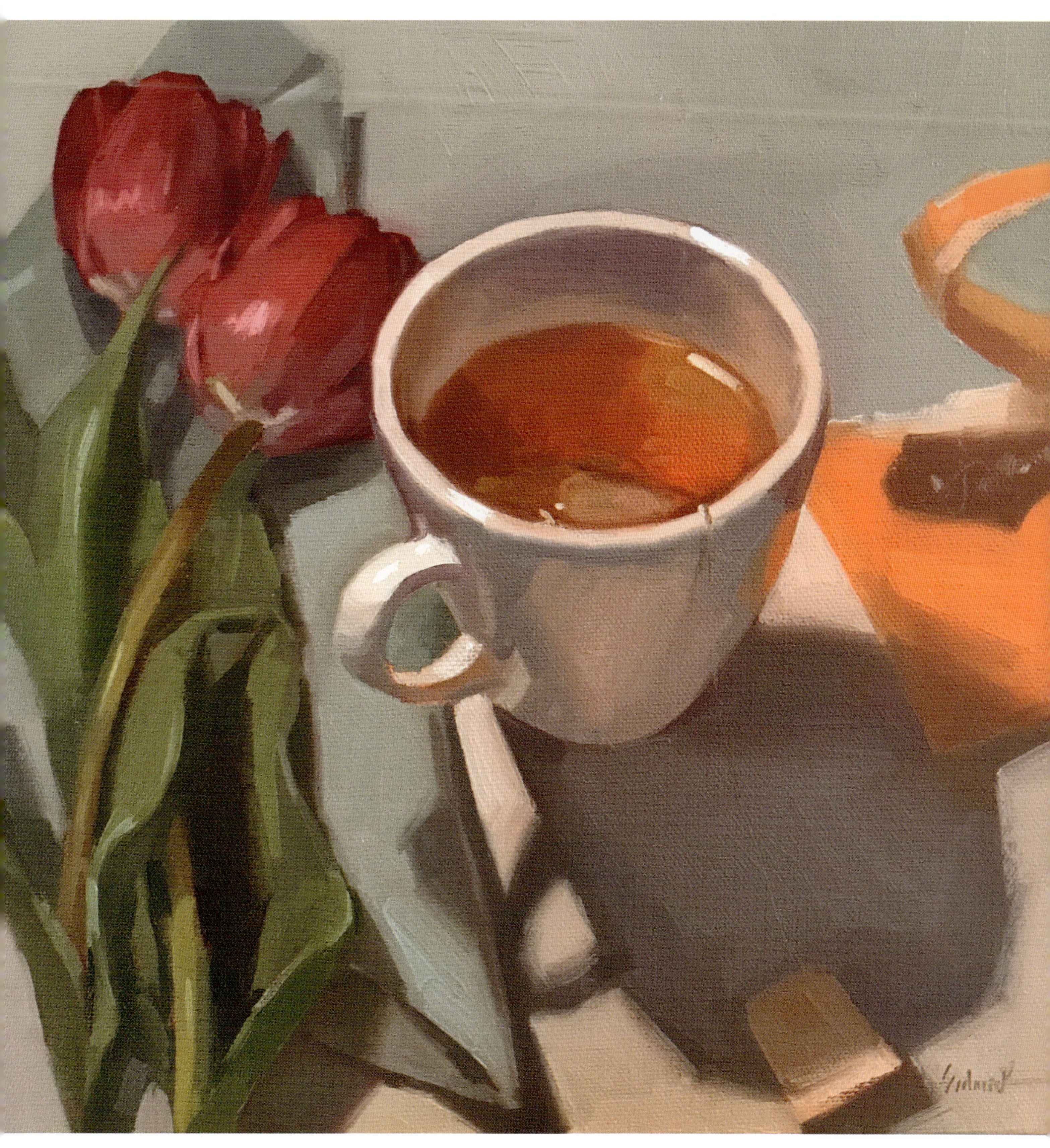

Sarah Sedwick, *Tulips and Tea*,
oil on canvas, 10" × 10" | 25.4 × 25.4 cm

INTRODUCTION: WELCOME TO DYNAMIC STILL LIFE FOR ARTISTS

Painting is a journey, with many paths and endless avenues of study. It's something to do for a lifetime—you never run out of things to learn and explore! Still life has captivated me for many years and has helped me strengthen the fundamentals that apply to every other type of painting. Whether you have been painting for a while or are just taking the first steps on your art journey, it's never too early—or too late—to discover how a still life painting practice can improve your work in any genre!

Is "dynamic still life" an oxymoron? After all, "dynamic" implies something in motion, or constantly changing. In the past, still life painting may have been perceived at best as merely academic—a way to study form, the action of light—and at worst, as dusty, boring, and antiquated. Contemporary still life has injected exuberant color, lively brushwork, and outside-the-box subject matter into this time-honored genre, my favorite to explore and teach.

Welcome to *Dynamic Still Life for Artists*! Thank you for joining me on this journey.

WHY STILL LIFE?

Still life is a laboratory where all the fundamentals of painting can be studied, and in a controlled environment. The light doesn't change, the wind doesn't knock the easel over, the model doesn't take a break. It's a low-cost, accessible way to practice working from life—from direct observation—which is the best way to improve your results when photo reference has to be used.

Still life is a great option for artists who work in small spaces or don't even have a dedicated painting space. I started my art journey at the dining room table. The setup requirements for still life are minimal, and chances are, some great subject matter is already lurking on your kitchen counter. And speaking of subjects, *color* is the inspiration for so many of my paintings. I love spending time thinking about and experimenting with color combinations—and with still life, unlike landscape and figure painting, the color possibilities are endless. If you can see it and it's inanimate, it can be part of a still life. You can even create your own still life subjects by sculpting with clay, folding origami paper, potting a plant in a lovely container, or baking a cute cupcake!

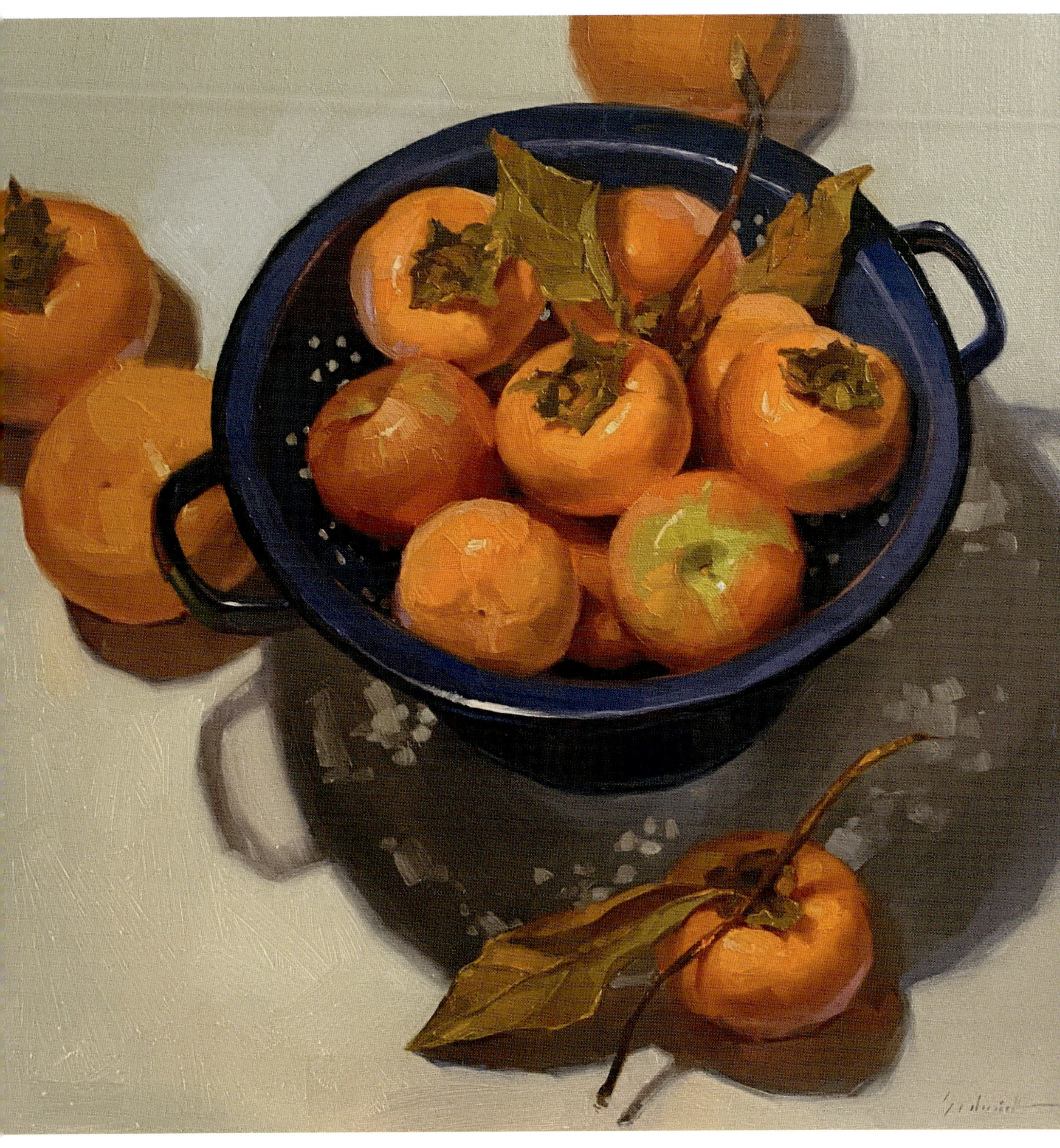

Sarah Sedwick, *Abundance*,
oil on canvas, 18" × 18" | 45.7 × 45.7 cm

So what exactly are the fundamentals of painting that still life enables us to work on in a targeted way? First, observing and depicting value relationships. When learning to paint, we think we are practicing what happens between our hand, the brush, and the canvas, when really we are honing the skill of *seeing like an artist*. Conveying how light moves across a form creates the illusion of three-dimensionality on a two-dimensional surface, the essence of realistic, representational painting. Even if the style of painting is loose and expressive—even if the colors used are whimsical or exaggerated—there is only one way to create the illusion of roundness, or sharpness, or gravity on a canvas, and that's to capture the value relationships you're observing.

With still life, it's easy to create clear lighting scenarios—a straightforward way to observe lights and darks, squinting to simplify what we see, and comparing values to each other. How quickly or slowly light transitions into shadow not only shows us form—think of the difference between a sharp corner and a rounded curve—but it also conveys texture, whether that texture is happening on a lemon, a tree trunk, or a cheekbone!

Still life is also a great way to study design and composition, experimenting with vantage point and cropping to create interesting designs on the canvas. And unlike portraiture, where the convention is a vertical rectangle, or landscape, which is often horizontal, a wide variety of formats work well in still life, from square to tall and skinny or round!

I think of the painting planning process outlined in this book—setting up a still life, sketching, examining values and value *relationships*, and considering the concepts that make a composition click—like planning a party. Go over the details carefully ahead of time so that when the day of the party arrives—or you finally put paint to canvas—you can relax and enjoy the fun.

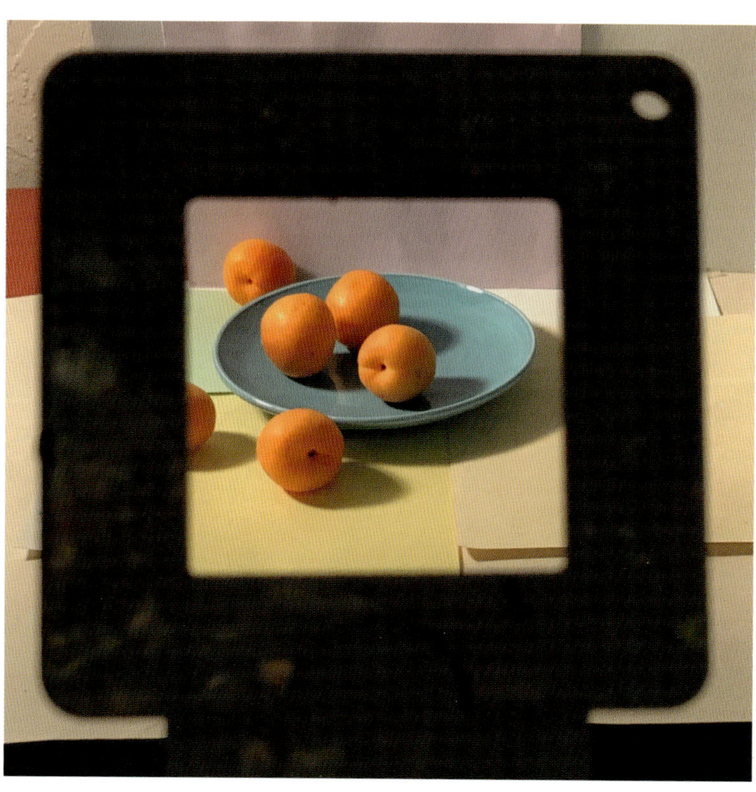

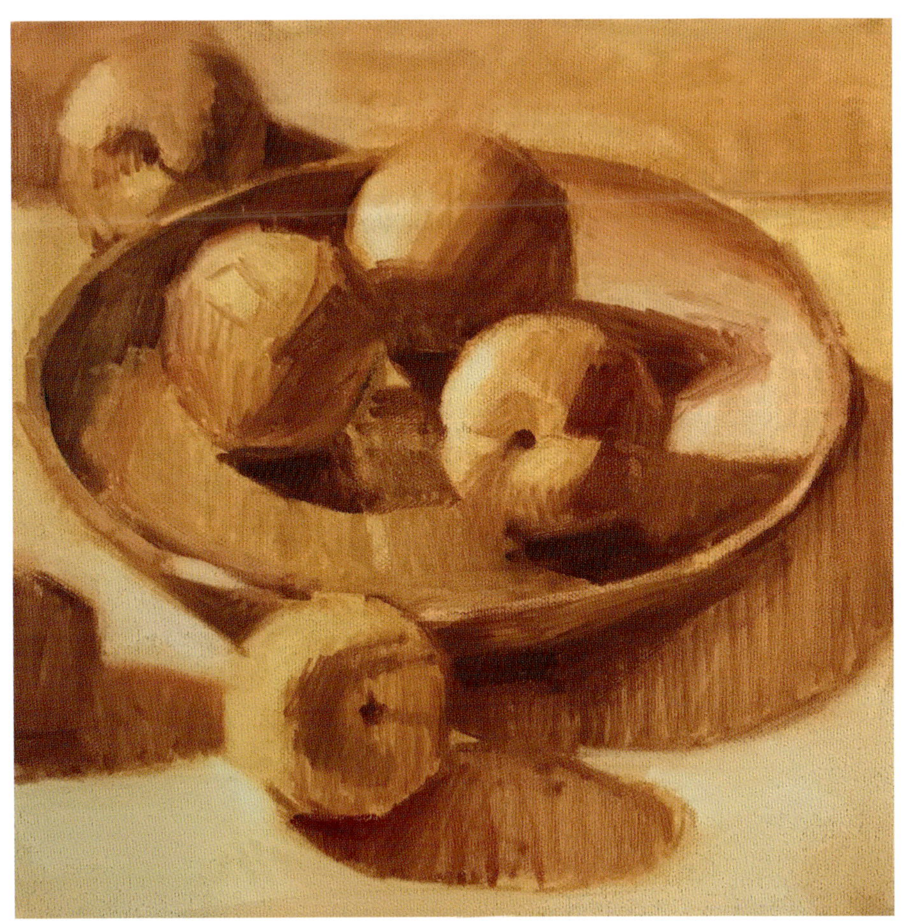

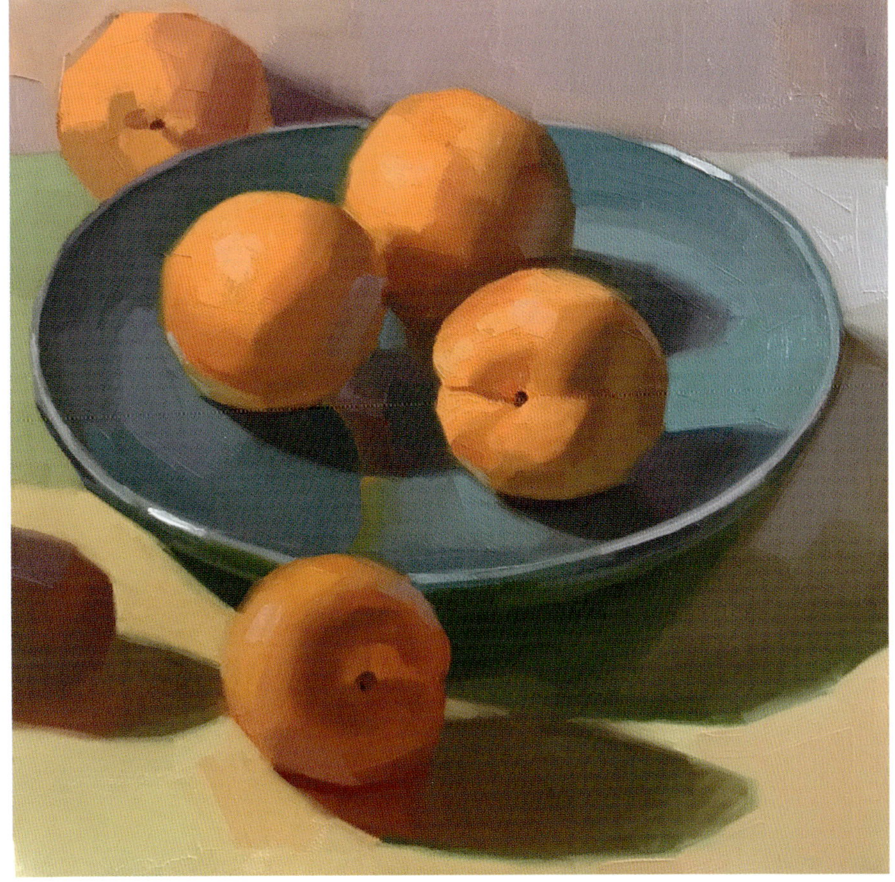

Sarah Sedwick,
Apricots on Blue,
oil on canvas,
10" × 10" | 25.4 × 25.4 cm

MY ART JOURNEY

The art journey can begin at any time in life. For me, it started early. My mother claims I could draw a perfect circle at the age of one! This story *may* be exaggerated by maternal pride, but I do remember being obsessed with mark-making from the time I could hold a pencil. I was blessed to grow up in a family that supported my passion.

The decision to attend art school was a tough one, and one I have never regretted. To this day, I lay out my palette the way I was taught to in Painting 101—and that's just one of many art school lessons that still serve me well! I attended Maryland Institute College of Art in Baltimore and studied illustration, mistakenly thinking that this would result in a "career" come graduation. The program was extremely interesting and valuable, but I found that my interests lay outside of commercial illustration—especially because by the time I graduated in 2001, the field was shifting toward digital media in a big way, and I wasn't too interested in computers. If the old me could see me now!

Also at that time, social media barely existed, and the commercial gallery system still felt like the only way to gain exposure or sales as a fine artist. Bewildered by

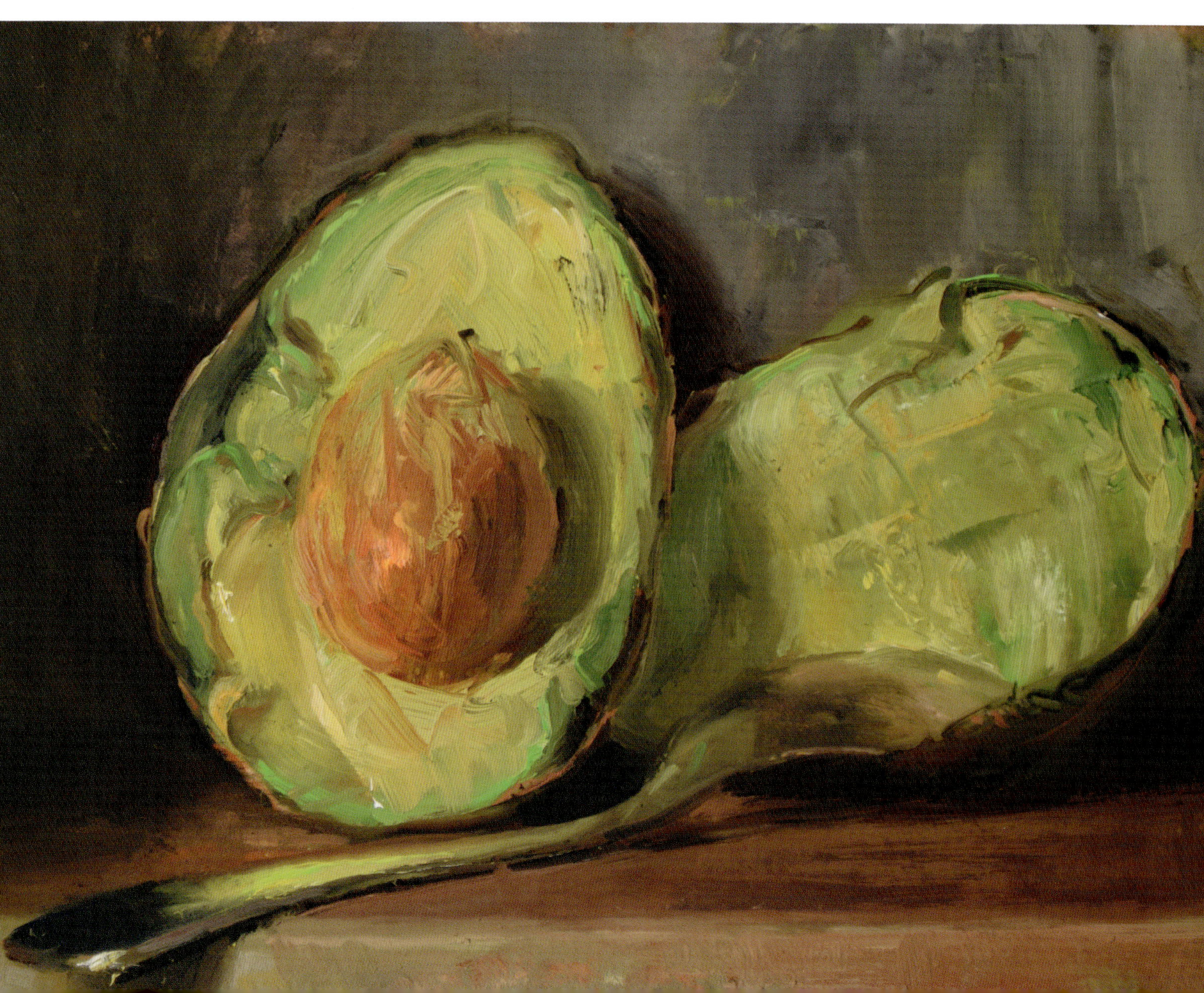

the prospect of approaching a gallery, as I believed that to be valued, my art had to be *big* and *important*, I had what I call my "quarter life crisis" and stopped painting for several years, struggling with my fears and misconceptions. During that time, I worked in restaurants and a bookstore, and as a plant lady (watering office plants—a fun job!), and eventually the thought came: "Maybe being an artist is just not going to happen." That felt very sad.

And then I discovered the Daily Painting movement. I had begun reading art blogs, and Daily Painting, which was started by Duane Keiser and popularized by artists like Karen Jurik and Carol Marine, was all about blogging. Posting small paintings—mostly still life—each day and auctioning them on eBay for a fraction of what "real" fine art might cost in galleries, these artists inspired me to pick up a brush, and I haven't stopped since!

After a few years of Daily Painting, I started working larger, had shows locally, and began to teach painting—really just to find out whether I enjoyed teaching or not. Well, I *loved* it, and the path of my art journey forked in a big way. Today, it is my life's mission to help people get back into painting—or discover it for the first time—in a way that is non-intimidating. Painting is not EASY—there are a lot of things to learn—but it can be SIMPLE. And after all, if it was easy, it wouldn't be so very rewarding!

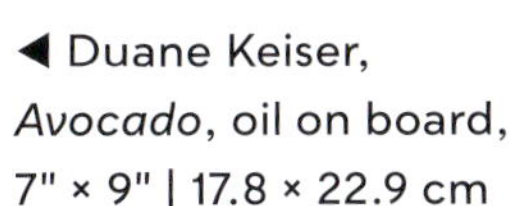

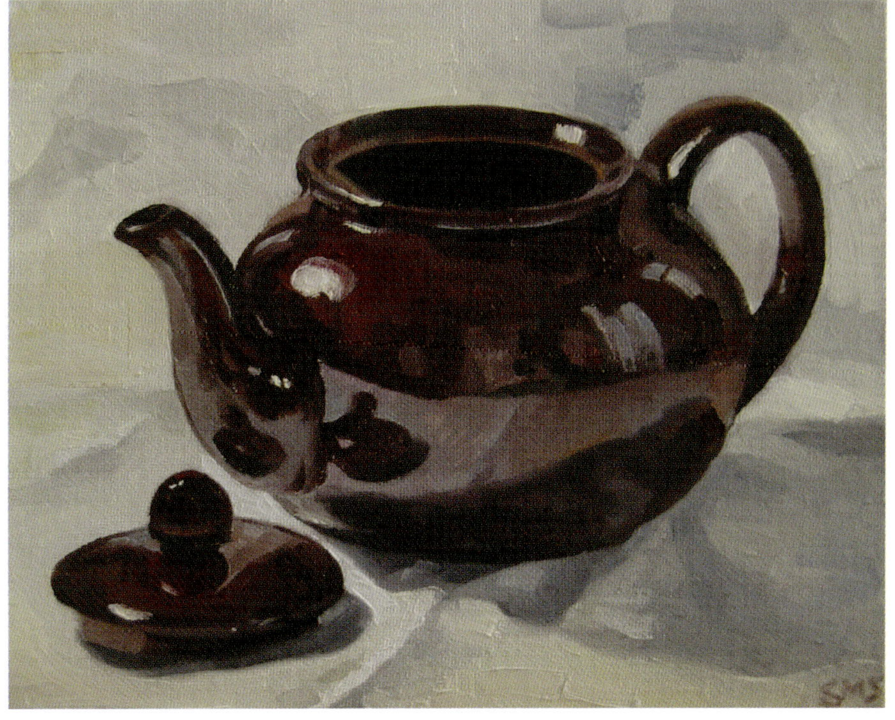

◀ Duane Keiser, *Avocado*, oil on board, 7" × 9" | 17.8 × 22.9 cm

▶ Sarah Sedwick, *English Teapot*, oil on canvas, 8" × 10" | 20.3 × 25.4 cm

My first daily painting, and first blog post. February 21, 2008.

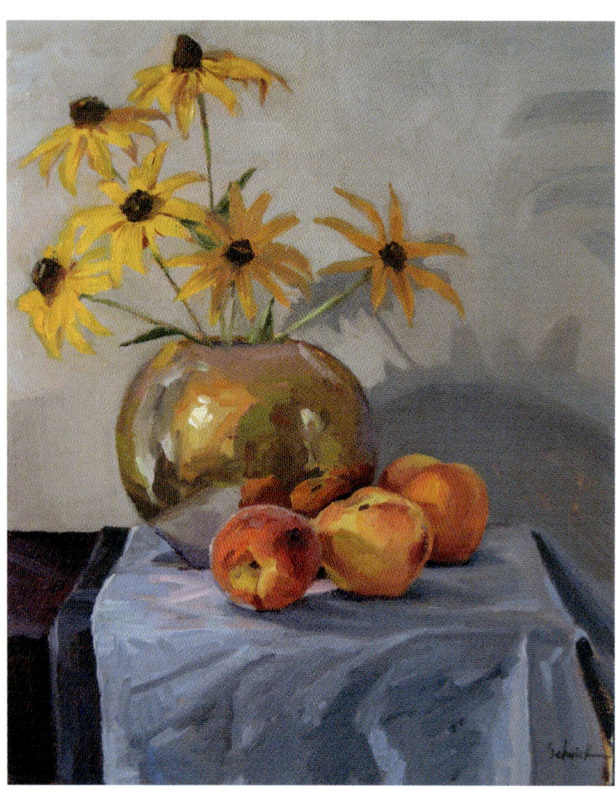

Sarah Sedwick, *Black-Eyed Susans and Peaches* (2010), oil on canvas, 8" × 10" | 20.3 × 25.4 cm

YOUR ART JOURNEY

The best thing about teaching art is the wide variety of people I get to work with. No matter their age or background, my students have several things in common. First, passion—sometimes passion that has been put on hold for half a lifetime while family and career took precedence, sometimes passion that has taken them in many different art making directions before bringing them to the study of painting. And second, their goals.

"I want to get better at painting" is something I hear a lot. It's something I think to myself a lot too! "Better" implies comparison, and hopefully the comparison is to ourselves, the painters we were a year, two years, twenty years ago. I suggest that the improvement you'll experience may not show up first in the work itself, but in the *feeling* you have while you're working. More confidence, more ideas, more enthusiasm—all as a result of the growth that comes from consistent practice—from showing up! As Picasso famously said, "Inspiration exists, but it has to find you working."

It's never too late to begin painting. It's never too late to improve. Whether your goal is to share, show, and sell your art, or you never want another soul to see it, you can experience the passion and achieve the fulfillment of painting. The only mistake we can make as artists is not to make our work. Maybe you've learned that the hard way, as I did in the years after art school.

There's a lot of art to look at in the world these days. We've gone from dusty bookshelves to shiny smartphones, and new technology has exponentially grown the number of amazing artists in our view. The feeling may emerge that the world doesn't need another artist, doesn't need what we have to offer. And that is not the case! Your vision is valuable. The way you see the world is a gift to your viewers. A gift only you can give!

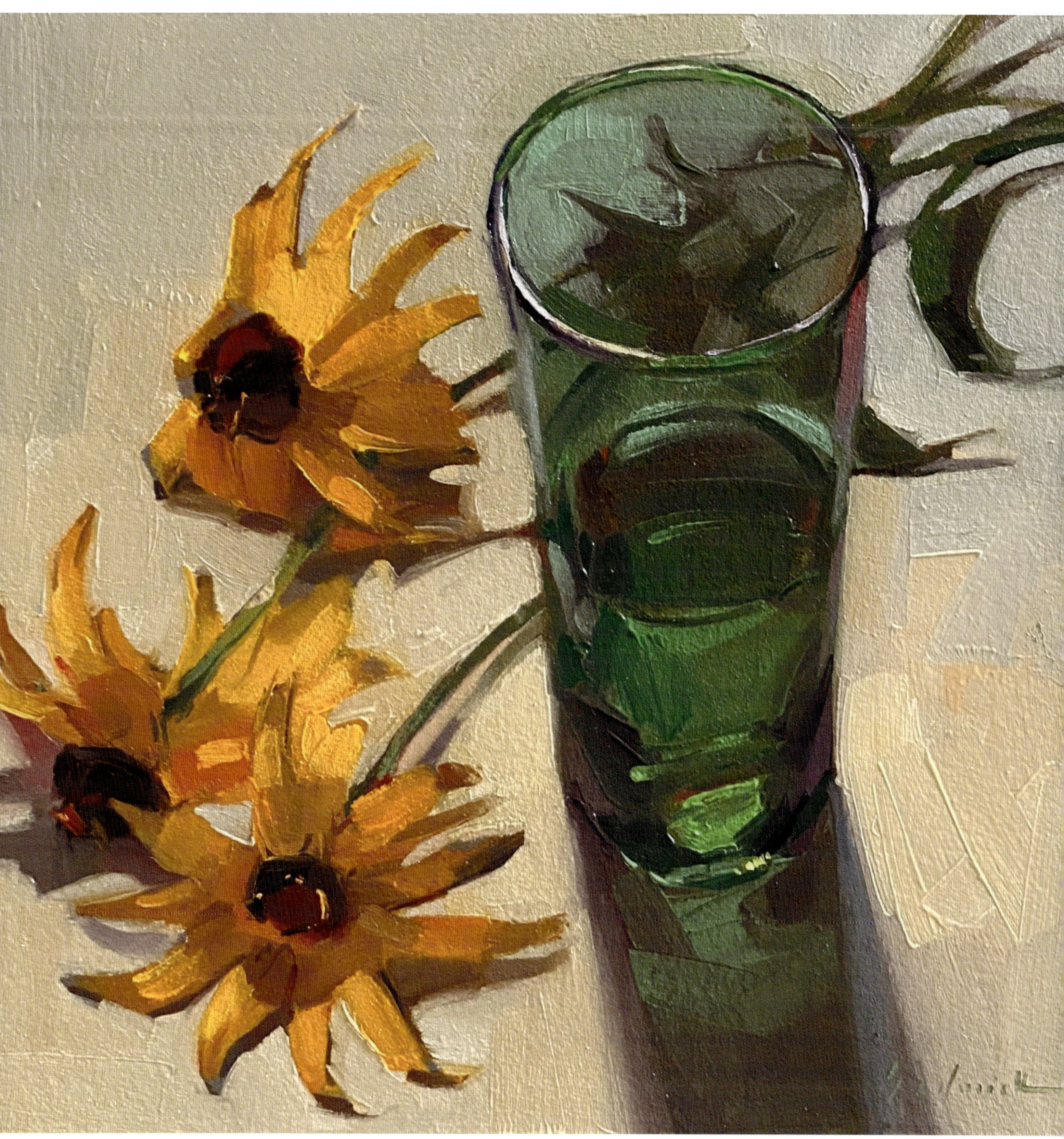

Sarah Sedwick, *Out of Water* (2021), oil on canvas, 8" × 8" | 20.3 × 20.3 cm

The same subject, with eleven years of easel time in between them!

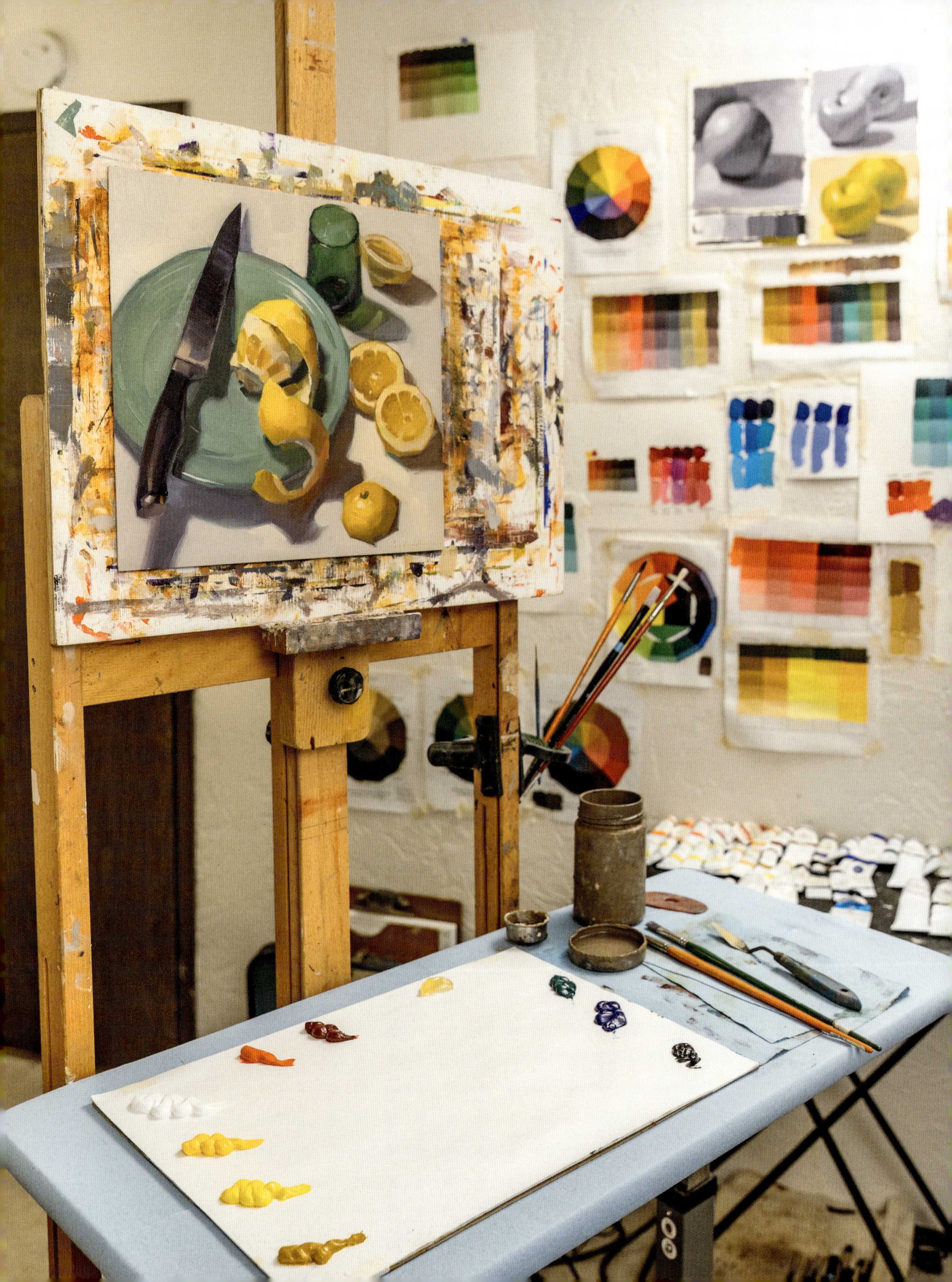

1

PAINTING SPACES AND STUDIOS

One of the keys to improving your painting is painting *a lot*. And it's much easier to paint a lot when your materials are organized and accessible. If you have to dig up and arrange your materials each time you paint, even getting started will feel like an uphill battle.

Of course, we don't all have the luxury of a dedicated room in which to make our art or an unlimited art supply budget—and the good news is, we don't need either! It doesn't take much to get started with still life or practice it in a new way. In this chapter, I'll introduce some simple ideas to economize space and share the core materials I consider "must haves" and "good to haves."

◀ My home studio. When I paint on canvas panels, I use folded-over masking tape to adhere the panels to a backing board. Over time, the board becomes a piece of abstract art!

DIFFERENT ARTISTS, DIFFERENT SPACES

From the dining room table to deep in the woods, painters work in all kinds of spaces, and they need different gear, depending. Still life offers an easy way to work from life with a low barrier to entry and without leaving the (climate-controlled) comfort of home! You don't need fancy props, expensive lights, or a large workspace to get started. For the outdoorsy, still life painting en plein air is a wonderful way to explore the colors of sunlight at different times of day. Easels that work both in the studio and out in the field are a great option when space is tight. They can be taken out in the landscape, used anywhere in the house, and packed in a suitcase for travel—and compactly stored when not in use. Strada Easel, Prolific Painter, and my favorite, the LederEasel, are a few (of the *many*) good options when space is tight—or when adventure calls.

Keeping materials pared down to the essentials and using creative storage ideas can really help when working in small spaces. Rolling carts and taborets keep an impressive amount of art supplies organized and can be stowed under a table or in a corner when not in use. Tabletop easels fold up compactly and can be raised to standing height by placing them on a box. Storage for paintings—especially wet ones—can also be an opportunity for creative solutions. Shallow shelves made of strips of crown molding are great for drying and displaying paintings on canvas or panel, and office desk organizers can provide compact storage for several wet paintings.

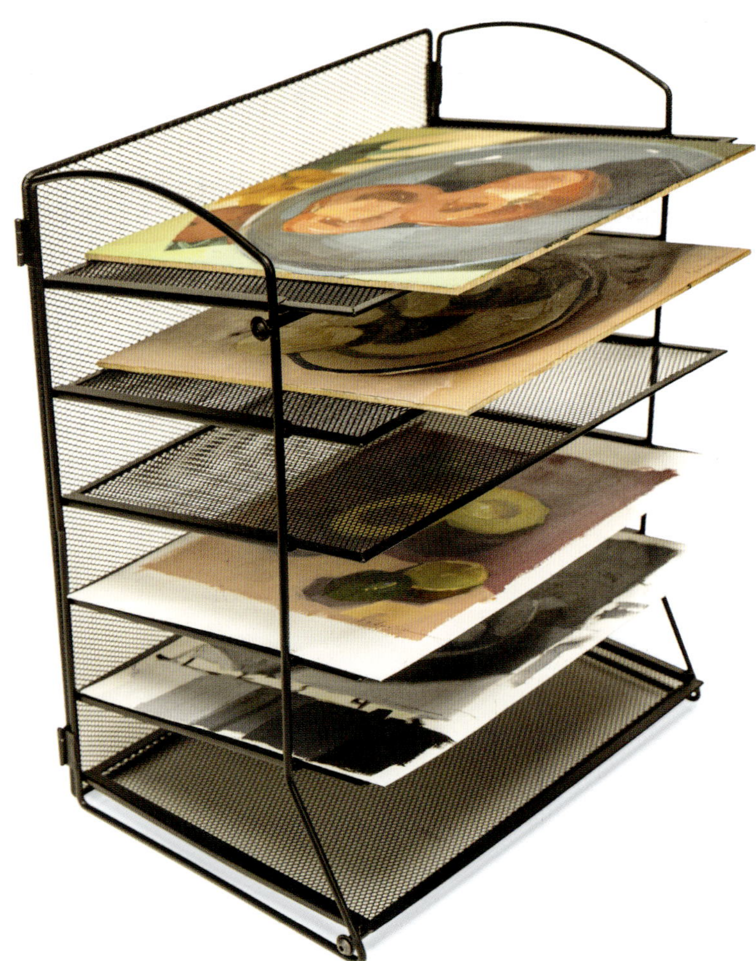

For space-saving studio solutions, office supply stores are a great resource! A desktop file organizer makes a great drying rack for paintings on canvas, panel, or paper.

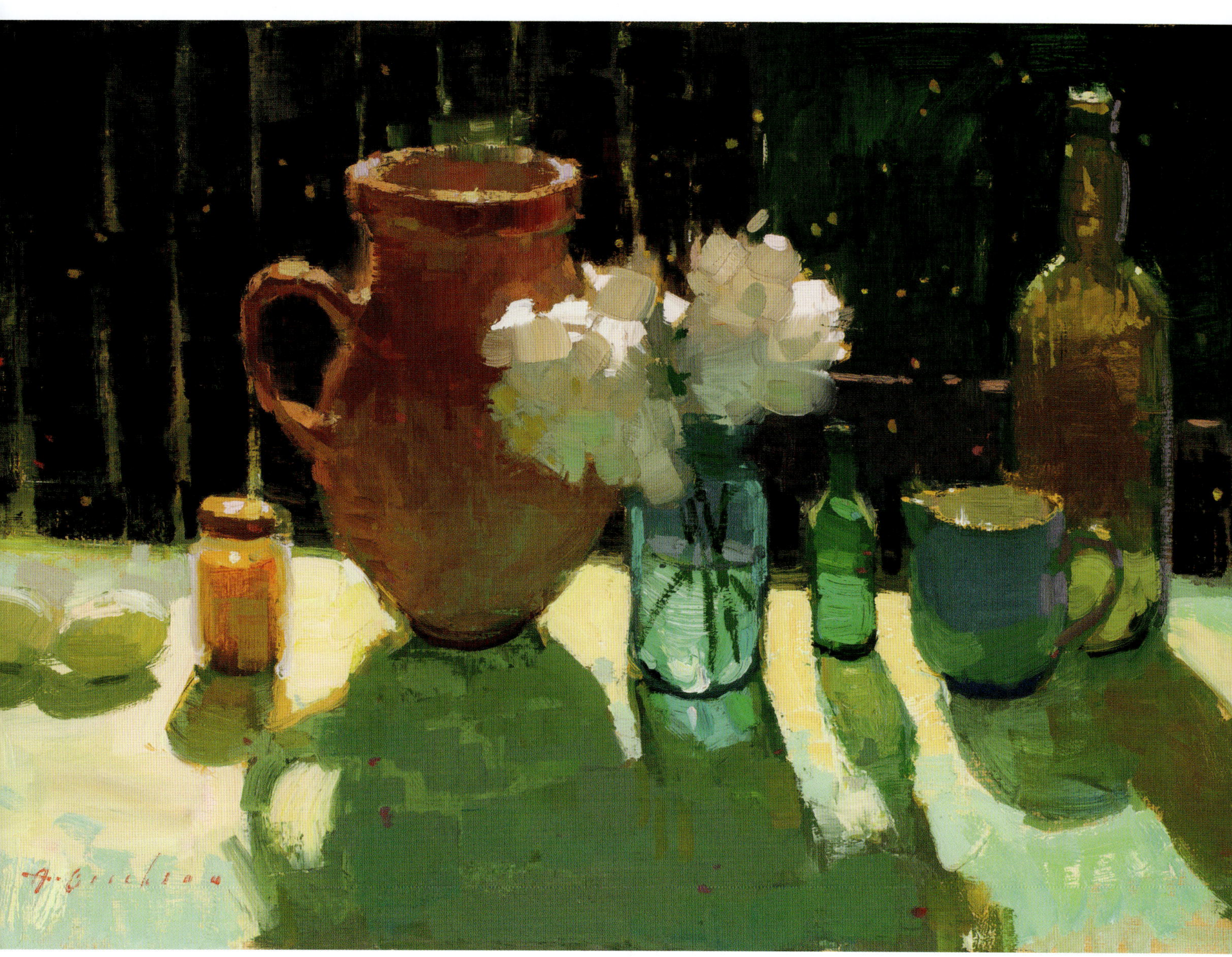

Aimee Erickson, *Peonies in the Sun*, oil on muslin panel, 17" × 24" | 43.2 × 61 cm

Explore the effects of sunlight at different times of day by setting up a still life outdoors. Backlighting creates dramatic foreground shadows and a beautiful glow through the glass in this plein air still life by Aimee Erickson.

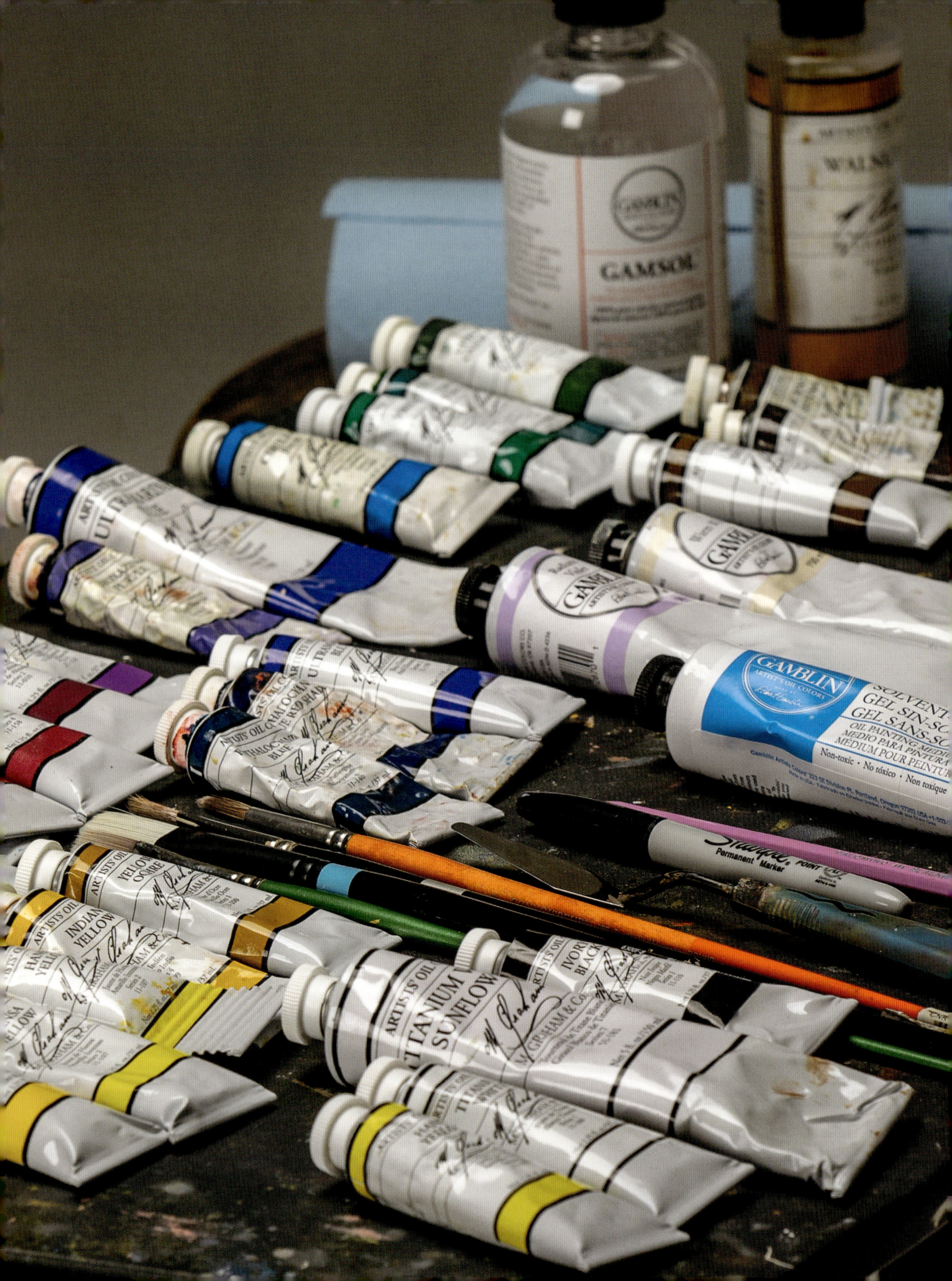

GAMSOL
GAMBLIN
ARTIST'S OIL COLORS
Non-toxic • No tóxico
ARTISTS' OIL
YELLOW OCHRE
INDIAN YELLOW
IVORY BLACK
Sharpie
Permanent Marker

STUDIO SETUP FOR STILL LIFE: THE BASICS

We'll go over *what to paint* later on—but first, the basic elements of your painting space. These include an easel, a surface upon which to place your palette (unless you hold it while painting), a spot for your still life setup, and a light source. Simple!

I recommend standing while painting. This helps get the entire body involved, so brushstrokes flow more freely, and also encourages you to get back from the canvas periodically to check your work. Of course, sometimes sitting is necessary, so it's great to have an easel that adjusts to allow for both. It should be movable—even if it doesn't fold up for storage—so that you have flexibility to change your view of the still life. I use a small but sturdy H frame easel in my studio and a tripod-based setup for travel, plein air, and workshops. I also recommend wooden French easels—they worked for the impressionists, and the design is still serving painters well!

Palettes can be made of wood, glass, plexiglass, enameled metal, plastic, or wax paper. The workhorses of my studio are disposable palette pads, which come in both white and

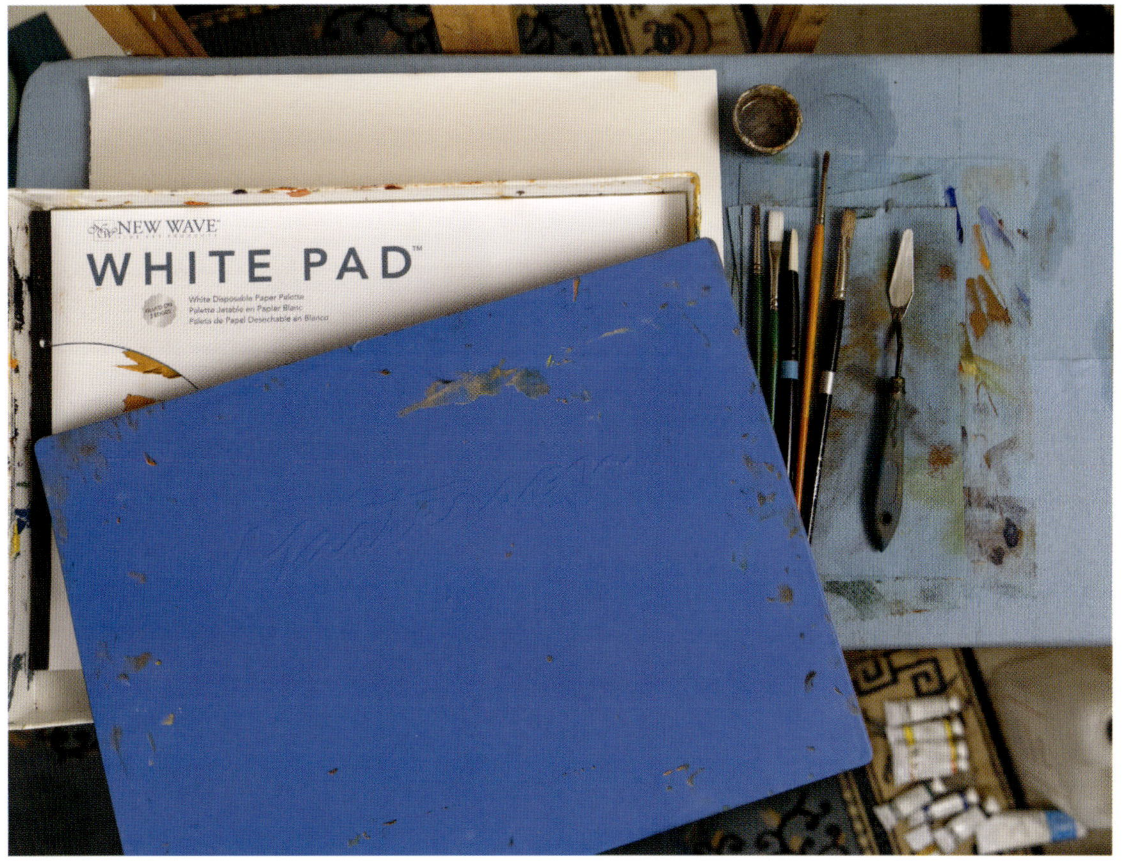

A plastic palette box keeps your paint fresh longer and is great for travel—and freezer storage, which will keep your oils wet and usable for weeks. Pictured here is the White Pad disposable palette by New Wave and the Sta-Wet palette box by Masterson.

gray. I always keep several on hand, in addition to my glass palettes. You can make your own glass palette simply with a piece of glass placed on top of a double layer of foam core, secured with masking tape around the edges. I recommend at least 12 by 16 inches (30.5 by 40.6 cm) for a palette, or larger if that's your preference. A plastic storage box like the Sta-Wet palette from Masterson fits a 12-by-16-inch (30.5 by 40.6 cm) palette perfectly for storage and paint saving. While working, I place my palette on a narrow, height-adjustable table between myself and my easel. This table also holds my solvent and various other tools and has the huge bonus of separating me from my canvas, keeping my nose out of the paint and my eye on the bigger picture.

Where you set up your still life will determine your vantage point. For a bird's-eye view, a low-height table works well. You can even place your subject on the floor! I use a box with a board on top—sometimes two boxes—placed a couple of feet away from me for my top-down viewpoint work. I also have a standard-height table against a wall, which I often place boxes on to raise my still life to eye level. Using a flat-bottomed chair as a still life stage also provides a place to clip your light—the chair back! Shadow boxes are an option when ambient light in the room prevents strong shadows. This can be as simple as cutting the flaps off a cardboard box and shining a light on the still life inside.

Whichever height you choose for your subject, you want to be close enough that you can see it clearly, and far enough away that you can squint and simplify your view. I like to place my still life on the opposite side of my painting arm, so I don't have anything between my eyes and my subject. Since I am right-handed, this means that my still life will be either in front of me, with my easel at a slight diagonal on the right side of my body, or the still life will be on my left. However you arrange yourself, your easel, your palette, and your still life, ideally you won't have to shift, move, or pivot to look from one to the next. A slight turn of your head should be all that's required.

A low-height still life stage positioned close to the easel is great for painting in small spaces—and for getting a bird's-eye view of your subject.

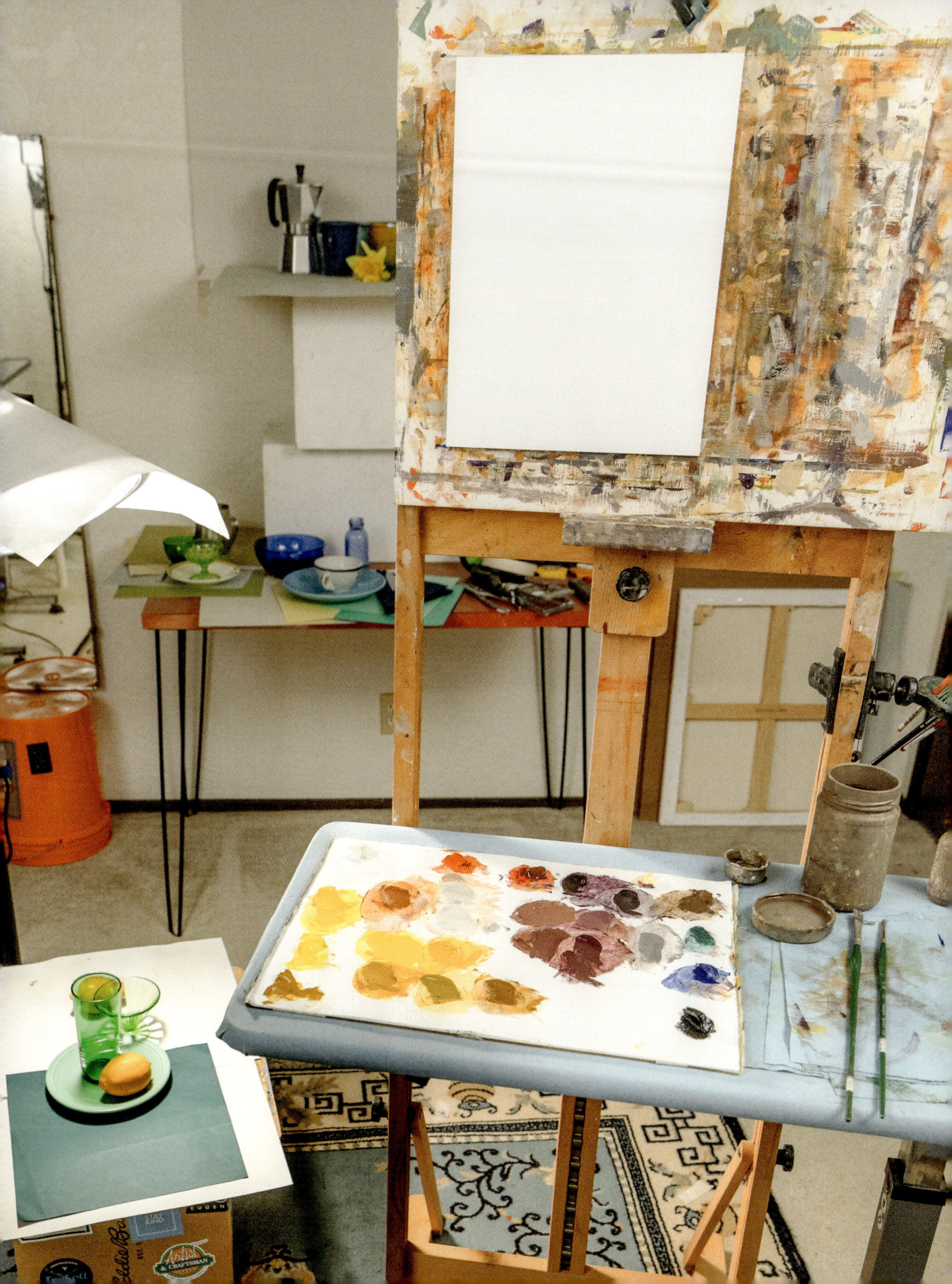
Artist
& CRAFTSMAN

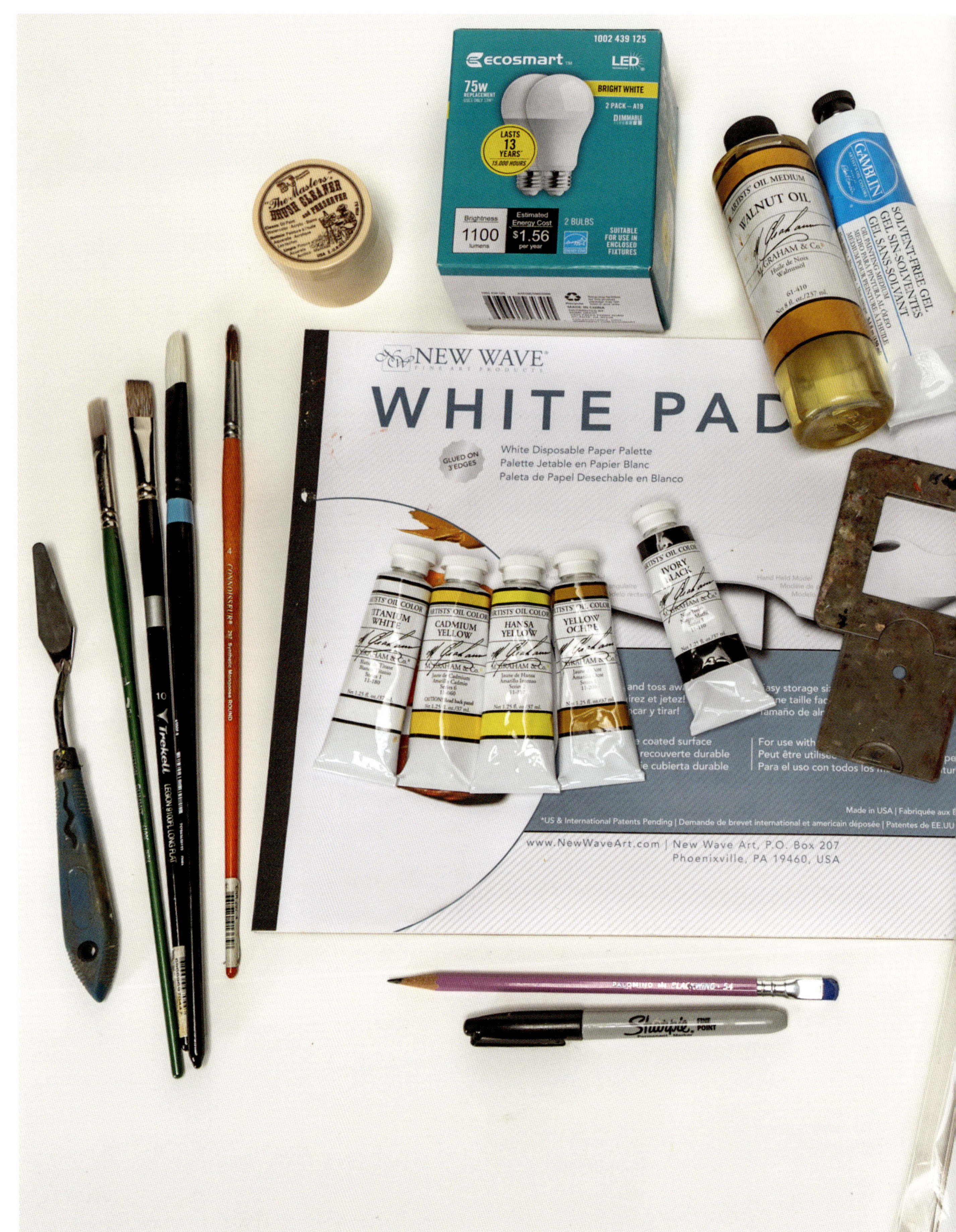
1002 439 125
ecosmart
LED
75w
BRIGHT WHITE
2 PACK – A19
LASTS 13 YEARS 15,000 HOURS
Brightness 1100 lumens
Estimated Energy Cost $1.56 per year
2 BULBS
SUITABLE FOR USE IN ENCLOSED FIXTURES
The Masters BRUSH CLEANER and PRESERVER
ARTISTS' OIL MEDIUM
WALNUT OIL
M. GRAHAM & Co.
Huile de Noix
Walnussöl
61-410
Net 8 fl. oz./237 ml.
GAMBLIN
SOLVENT-FREE GEL
GEL SIN-SOLVENTES
GEL SANS-SOLVANT
NEW WAVE
WHITE PAD
GLUED ON 3 EDGES
White Disposable Paper Palette
Palette Jetable en Papier Blanc
Paleta de Papel Desechable en Blanco
ARTISTS' OIL COLOR
TITANIUM WHITE
CADMIUM YELLOW
HANSA YELLOW
YELLOW OCHRE
IVORY BLACK
*US & International Patents Pending | Demande de brevet international et americain déposée | Patentes de EE.UU
www.NewWaveArt.com | New Wave Art, P.O. Box 207
Phoenixville, PA 19460, USA
CONNOISSEUR
Trekell
Sharpie
FINE POINT

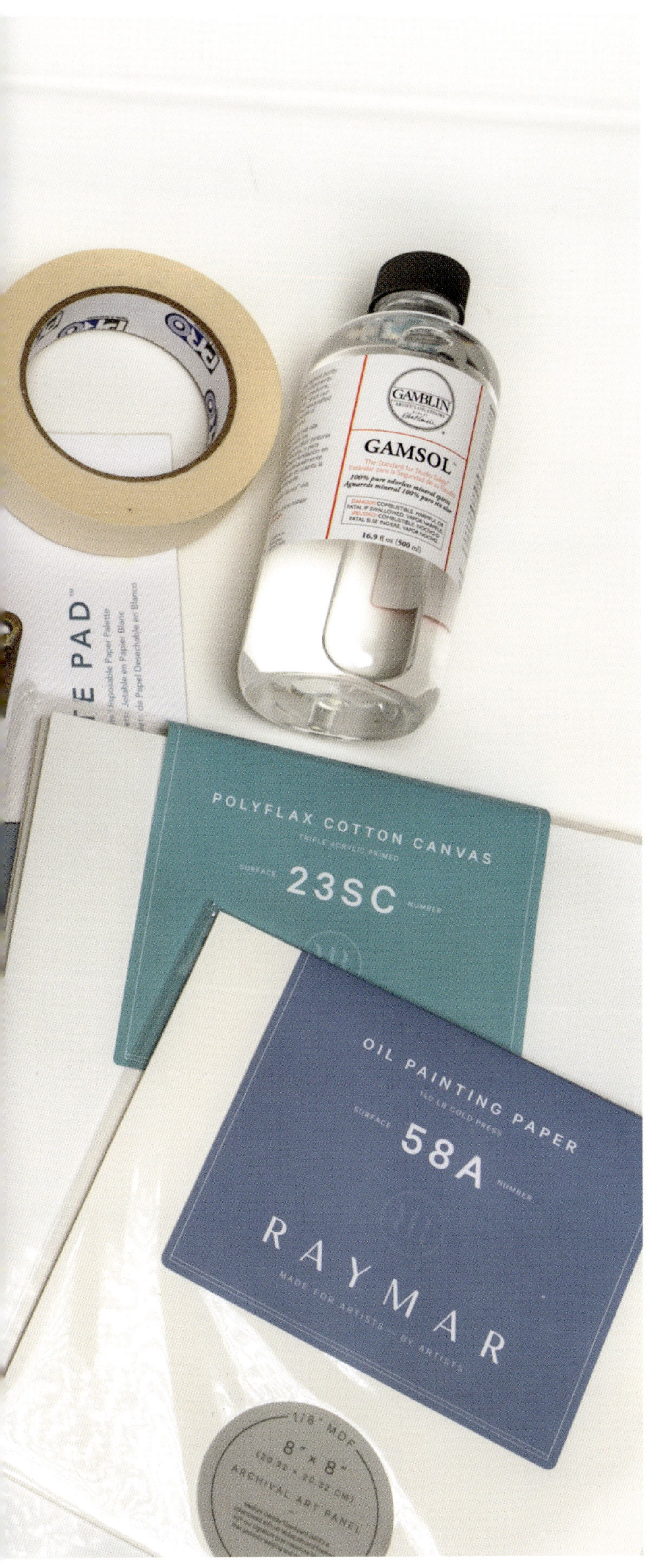

MATERIALS AND TOOLS: THE MUST-HAVE AND THE GOOD-TO-HAVE

Artists choose their materials for various reasons. Many of us simply carry on using the same colors, brushes, and surfaces that our teachers used. I still lay out my palette the way I was first instructed to do it in art school! When you find something that works for you, stick with it. The flip side of that advice is that you'll need to experiment with a variety of materials to find the ones that do work. Often, I see my students struggling with their work, thinking the problem is them, when really the materials are either subpar or not well suited to their painting style.

Some artists hesitate to try oil painting because there's a belief that the materials are complicated, smelly, toxic, expensive, and messy. These things *can* all be true, but they certainly don't have to be! While I don't maintain a solvent-free studio, the materials I use are nearly odorless. Although Gamsol, my preferred solvent, is expensive, it is reusable, because the paint sediment settles after a day or two and clean Gamsol can be poured off the top. Air filters or purifiers are a great option in painting spaces, but even a small amount of ventilation is enough unless you are quite sensitive to smells. The smell of oil paint was actually the first thing I fell in love with about it—and in those days, it was a much smellier prospect than it is now!

An array of my go-to painting supplies.

MUST-HAVE MATERIALS AND TOOLS

Following is a sample materials list for one of my workshops, and it neatly sums up my everyday studio needs:

- **Palette.** New Wave brand 11" × 16" (28 × 40.6 cm) White Pad disposable palette, or similar.
- **Palette knife.** Not a teeny one. You want to be able to scoop up a pile of paint with it. I like the RGM soft-grip no. 45 (blue handle).
- **Rags or paper towels.** Blue shop towels are the best!
- **Solvent.** Gamsol 16 oz (470 ml) or larger.
- **Medium.** Gamblin Solvent-Free Gel or M. Graham walnut oil.
- **Containers.** For solvent and medium.
- **Paint.** I use M. Graham brand. Here is my split-primary palette (substitutions okay!):
    - Titanium white
    - Alizarin crimson
    - Cadmium red (medium or light)
    - Ultramarine blue
    - Viridian or phthalo blue
    - Cadmium yellow (medium)
    - Hansa yellow
    - Optional colors: yellow ochre, ivory black, dioxazine purple
- **Viewfinder.** I use the ViewCatcher by The Color Wheel Company.
- **Brushes.** I use Princeton Summit Series 6100 white Taklon and Aspen brushes (a good starter kit is a #2 round and a #4 flat), Trekell Legion long flats (size 10), and Rosemary Ultimate bristles (flats or filberts, size 5 and up), but *please use what you're comfortable with.*
- **Painting surfaces.** Raymar 23SC canvas panels, stretched canvases, and Arches oil paper are my go-to surfaces.
- **Miscellaneous.** Pencil, sketchbook, black Sharpie, masking tape.

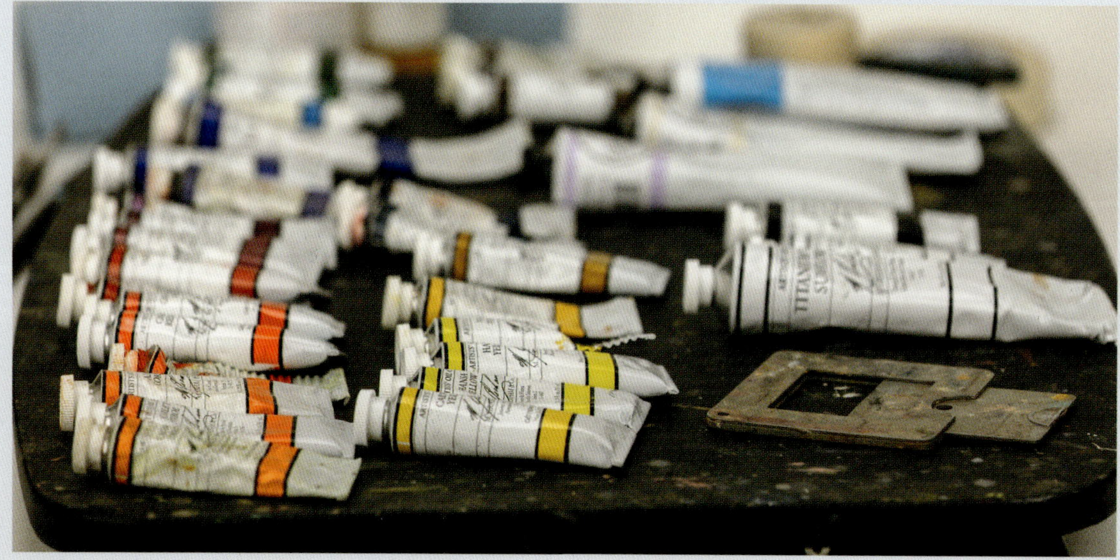

GOOD TO HAVES

In addition to the list on the previous page, there are many studio "good-to-haves"—things you don't need in order to paint, but they definitely make life easier! A sample of my studio "good-to-haves" includes a sturdy clip-on brush holder that attaches to the easel, a rubber scraper tool for adding or removing paint, a pair of pliers for stubborn paint caps, a metal tube wringer for getting every last drop of paint out of each tube, sandpaper, sponge brushes, an X-Acto knife and scissors, a ruler and measuring tape, and masking tape. I know I have masking tape on the list above, but it's worth mentioning again. I'm not sure I could be a painter without masking tape! Also plastic clamps in various sizes. And, of course, a sturdy side table—or three! One of my favorite studio "hacks" is a hospital bedside table, the kind that raises and lowers easily, with one leg on the side and four wheels. They are just narrow enough to fit in between me and my easel—the perfect palette table.

In the next chapters, we'll discuss sketching as a painting planning tool. There are so many great media options—ink, pencil, charcoal, even digital. My favorite sketching tool is a Blackwing balanced graphite pencil, and I love Sharpie markers! I often use a combination of ballpoint pen, Sharpie, and white Pitt pen—or white Uni-Ball Signo gel pen—on Strathmore Toned Tan paper to create preliminary sketches.

For more on materials, see the Resources list on page 153.

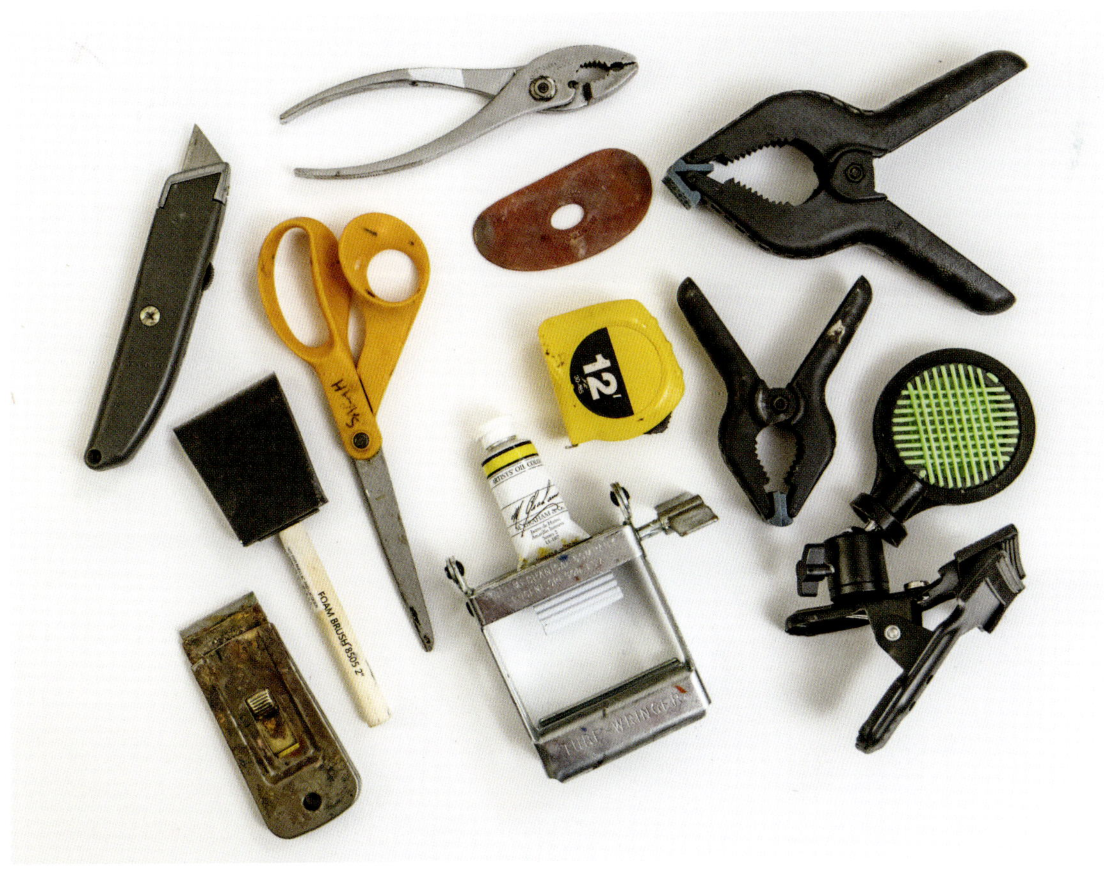

Some of my studio "good-to-haves." You could paint without them, but why?

PAINT CHOICES AND PALETTE LAYOUT

In the materials on page 26, you'll notice the words "substitutions okay!" next to the list of my paint colors. I often work with a split-primary palette—a warm and a cool version of the primaries red, yellow, and blue—plus white. But I don't always choose the same pigments. So, one day my reds might be cadmium and alizarin, and another they might be pyrrole and quinacridone magenta. Two reds of different temperatures, two different sets. No matter which pigments I choose, they remain in the spot on the palette designated for that hue. So, my yellows always occupy the left edge, my reds and violets the top, and my greens and blues on the right edge, with white in the upper left corner. This eliminates the extra thought-step of hunting for a color each time I go to the palette to load my brush. Color mixing is difficult enough without giving our brains extra work during the process!

The white palette is my preference—it's what I was trained on. Trying new things is important, experimenting with all kinds of brushes, surfaces, etc., is great—but when you find something that works for YOU, sticking to it is also great! When I was in art school, back in Painting 101, I was told to use a white palette. It worked for me, so that is what I prefer now. One thing I love about it is the stain you create while mixing on white—it helps you see the hue of your darkest mixtures, almost like creating a tint by adding a bit of white paint.

Many artists work on gray palettes—or wooden palettes—and they have learned to judge their colors and values against that surface as they're mixing. There is a strong argument that if you are going to paint on a mid-value toned canvas, you should mix on a toned palette. So, if the gray palettes appeal, give them a try!

My favorite painting mediums are Solvent-Free Gel by Gamblin and walnut oil. I usually have them both on hand as I'm painting, perhaps choosing the gel when I want to add a bit more body to my paint, and the oil when I want a spreadable yet rich and opaque consistency. If I had to choose one, I would choose the gel for travel (because it sits nicely on the palette, with no extra container required), and oil for the studio, because it's the time-tested, standard additive and has such luxurious working properties, though it can slow drying time. Some mediums, like Galkyd and Liquin, speed drying time and/or add gloss to your paint. There are lots of options to experiment with. Keep in mind that you don't actually need any medium—or any solvent, for that matter—in order to paint, so don't let this choice become overwhelming. The simplest way to begin is with Gamsol alone.

Brush choice is also largely a matter of preference—and training. Generally, long-handled brushes are meant for oils and acrylics, and short-handled brushes for watercolor and gouache. Softer brushes are more likely to be meant for acrylics, and stiffer, springier brushes for oils—but it's truly up to the artist's preference. Some artists swear by top-of-the-line brushes, and some artists buy theirs from the hardware store. In my studio, brushes are considered

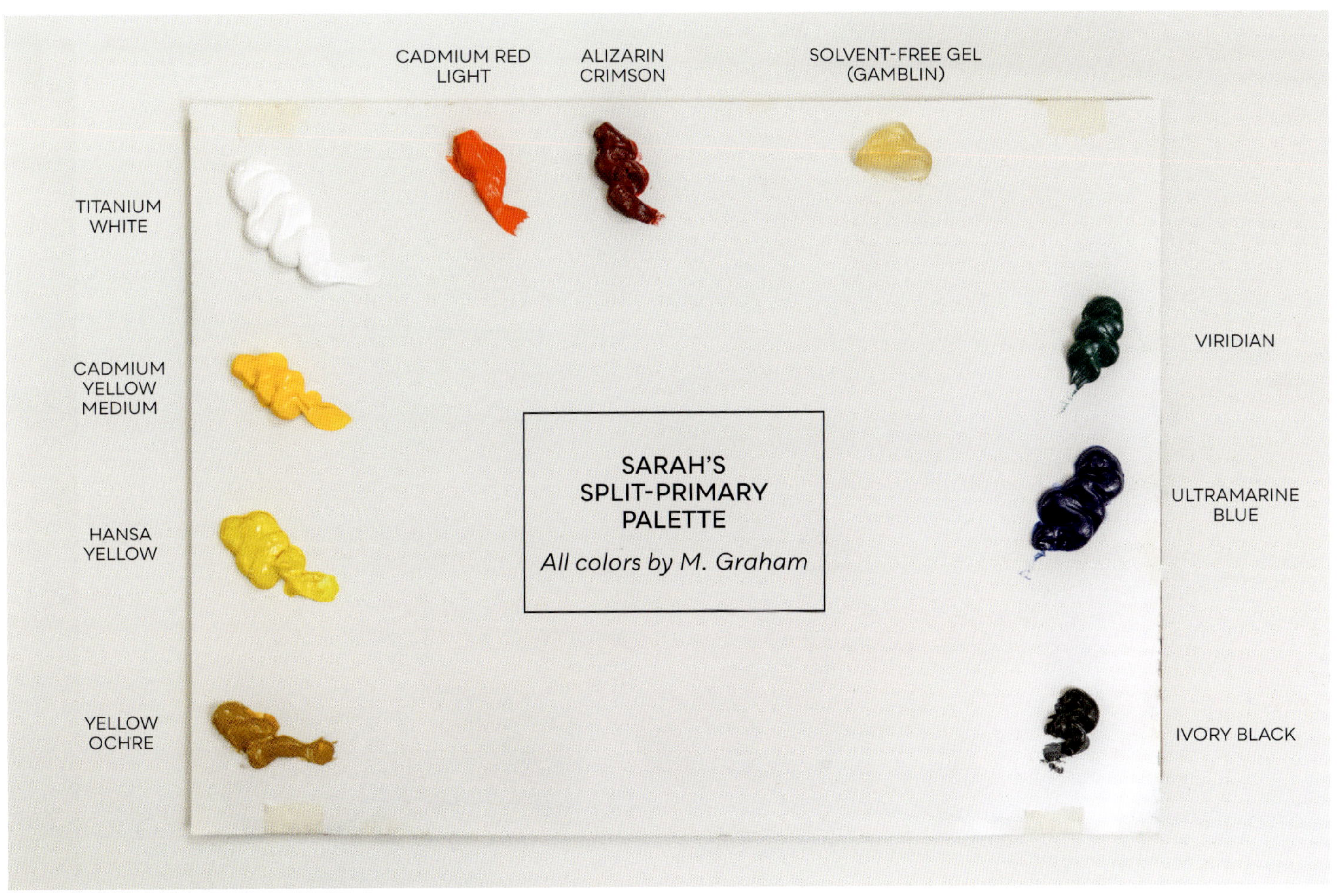

Layout of one of my favorite split-primary color palettes. No matter which specific pigments I choose, my reds, yellows, and blues always go in the same place, as do white and black.

disposable. It's not that I don't take care of them—I clean them after every painting session. But I know that they will wear out—the more I paint, the sooner—and I expect to replace them regularly. So, not for me the myth of the thirty-year-old lucky paintbrush, worn down to the ferrule, and still in service. I buy affordable brushes, often. The line at which a cheap brush becomes unacceptable is when it sheds hairs in your painting. If you're picking brush hairs off your painting, it's time to shop for a different brand.

Long story short: when it comes to materials, if you like it, use it! There are VERY few wrong ways to oil paint!

STUDIO LIGHTING

Studio lighting is a subject that everyone is interested in, and it can sometimes feel like a total mystery. How to get enough light on your canvas and palette that you can see to paint, but not so much that glare on your painting obstructs your view? How to light the room sufficiently and still create strong shadows on your still life setup? Which light bulbs to buy? All good questions! I will share what has worked for me.

I don't use natural light in my studio. If I do want to paint with window light as the light source on my still life, I probably still need to illuminate the room so that I can see my canvas. Small lights that clamp onto the easel and shine directly onto the canvas don't work for me. They are too bright and create too much glare on wet paint. Instead, I light my studio with LED panel lights on tripod stands, which I aim at the corners where the ceiling meets the wall so light bounces off the ceiling and fills the room evenly. In a smallish room, I use two of these, one on either side and slightly behind me. Both the intensity and the temperature of these lights can be adjusted, and they work well as light sources on a still life or a model too.

Now, for lighting the still life itself. You want something height adjustable, lightweight, and sturdy. I love the economy of metal clip lamps and the flexibility to choose any light bulbs I want to use in them. My preferred still life lighting is warm—2700 to 3000 K, or Kelvin. You can find this information on the side of the light bulb box. Clip your light to a height-adjustable tripod light stand and you're ready to create glorious cast shadows on a still life at any vantage point!

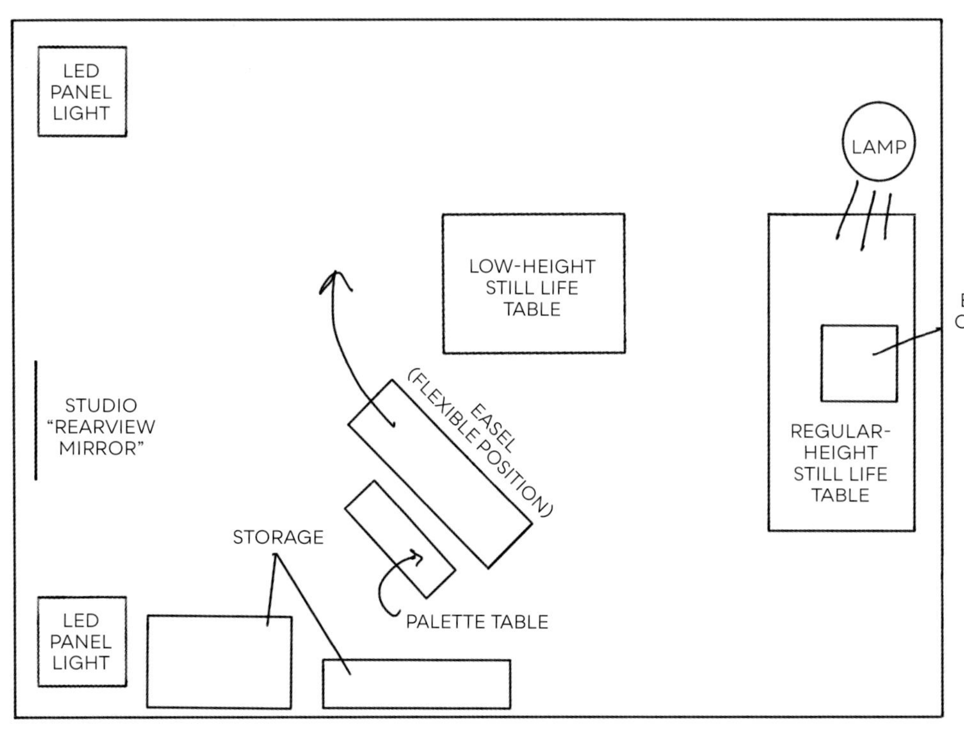

A bird's-eye view of my studio.

▶ LED panel lights illuminate my studio and are both color temperature and intensity adjustable. Bounce light off the walls and ceiling and use barn door attachments to cut the glare on your painting.

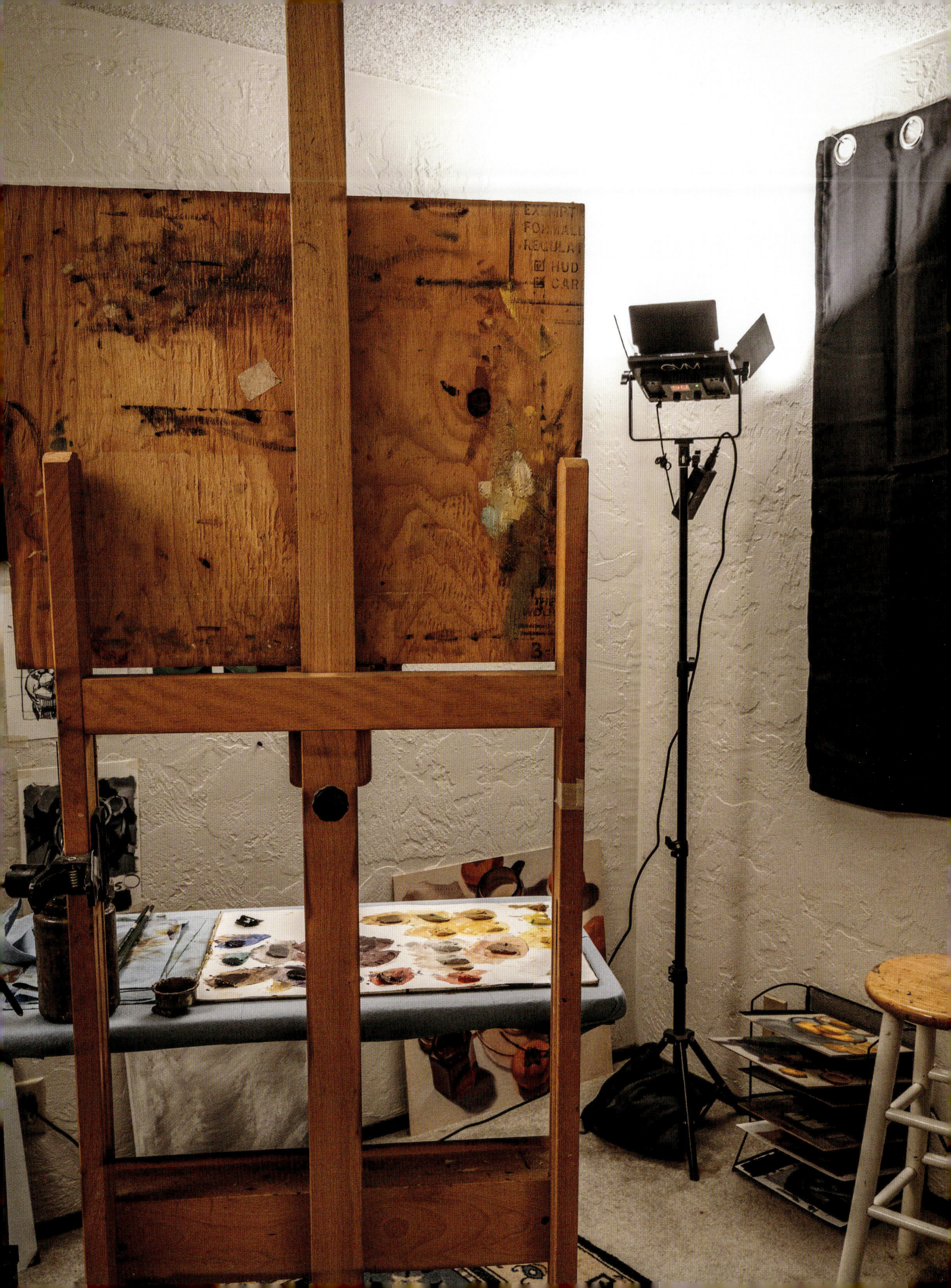

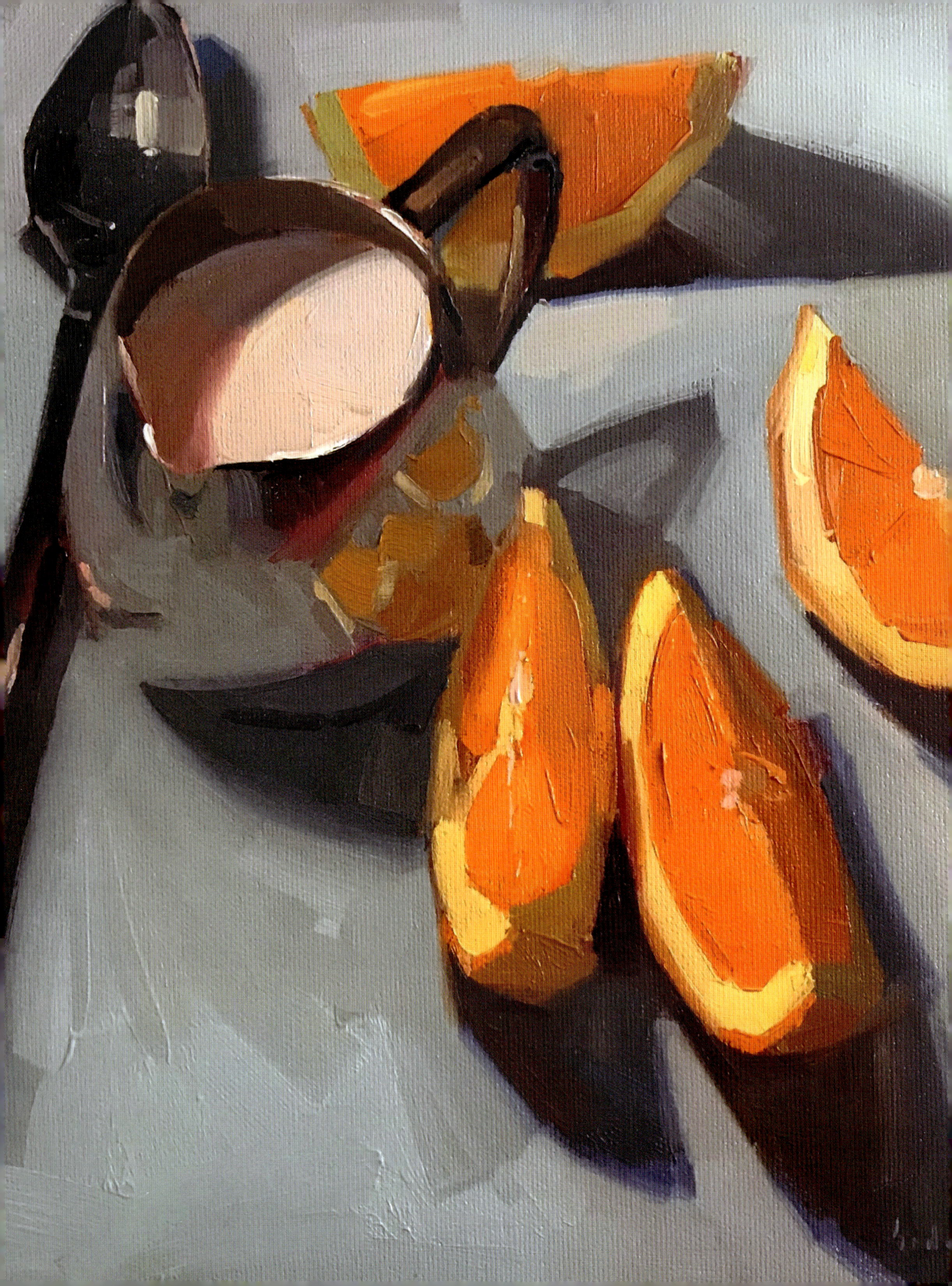

2

WHAT TO PAINT? SETTING UP A STILL LIFE THAT "CLICKS"

Inspiration is everywhere—from your social media feed to your kitchen counter, not to mention the garden and the farmers' market! Almost anything can become the subject for a still life painting, so how do we choose? Intuition and personal meaning nudge us toward certain subjects, but still life doesn't have to be "deep" or tell a story, though many wonderful ones do. Some of my paintings begin with color theory—incorporating analogous or complementary color schemes—and some are inspired by texture. Lighting can play a big role in elevating the ordinary into a dynamic still life.

◀ **Sarah Sedwick, *Orange and Cream* (detail), oil on canvas, 10" × 10" | 25.4 × 25.4 cm**

A simple complementary color scheme was the starting point for this still life arrangement.

DIVING INTO STILL LIFE

When what to paint feels like a conundrum, heading to a thrift store or antique mall, the grocery store or an Asian market, can spark creativity. I love the idea of "found object" still life—the jumbles of objects that randomly accumulate and can be discovered around the house. Your car keys? A houseplant in a window? If inspiration is still lacking, just paint something simple. The act of painting *anything* tends to lead to the next great thing!

Color mixing begins in the still life. The elements you choose to incorporate in your setup create the color scheme of your painting. I often begin with one object and choose the rest of my still life elements based on that first object's color. If I have some beautiful oranges in the kitchen, I might choose a blue plate for a complementary color scheme or combine them with yellows and reds for an analogous color scheme—one in which all the hues are next to one another on the color wheel. For backgrounds, the scrapbooking aisle at craft stores offers paper in a wide range of hues and sizes. Fabrics—old curtains, quilt scraps, cloth napkins, tea towels, or tablecloths—are another great prop to have on hand for crafting the color scheme of your painting.

If you like to work from photos, you can plan a series of paintings well in advance. Some artists like to spend a whole studio

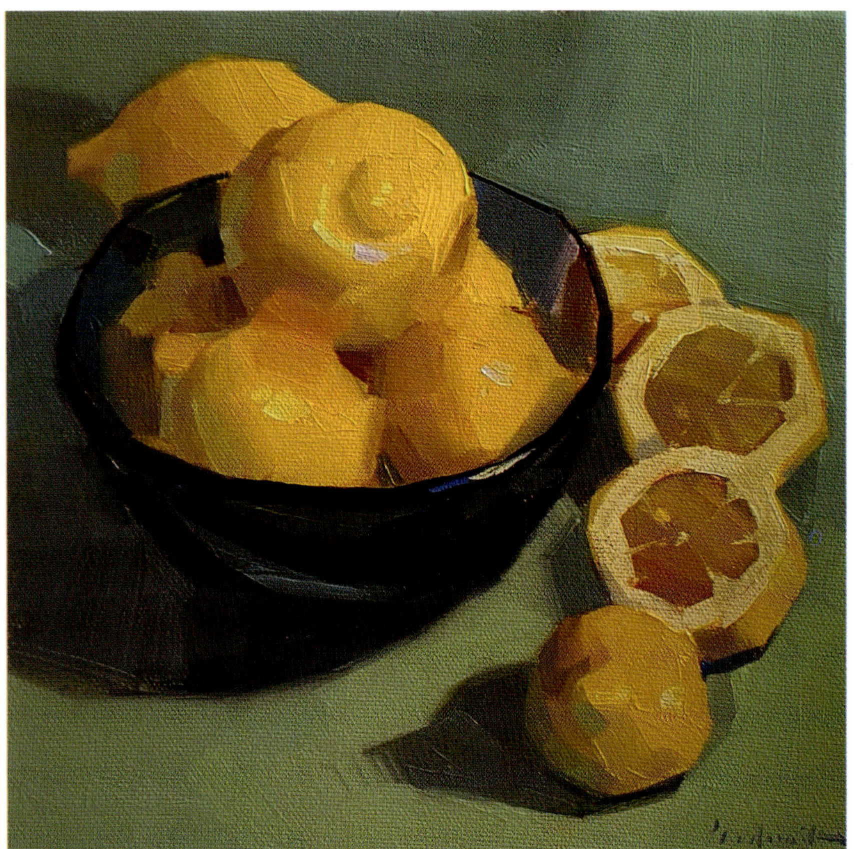

Sarah Sedwick,
Lemon Wheels,
oil on canvas,
8" × 8" | 20.3 × 20.3 cm

Once I chose lemons as my subject, adding a blue bowl and a green background created an analogous color scheme: yellow-green-blue, next-door neighbors on the color wheel.

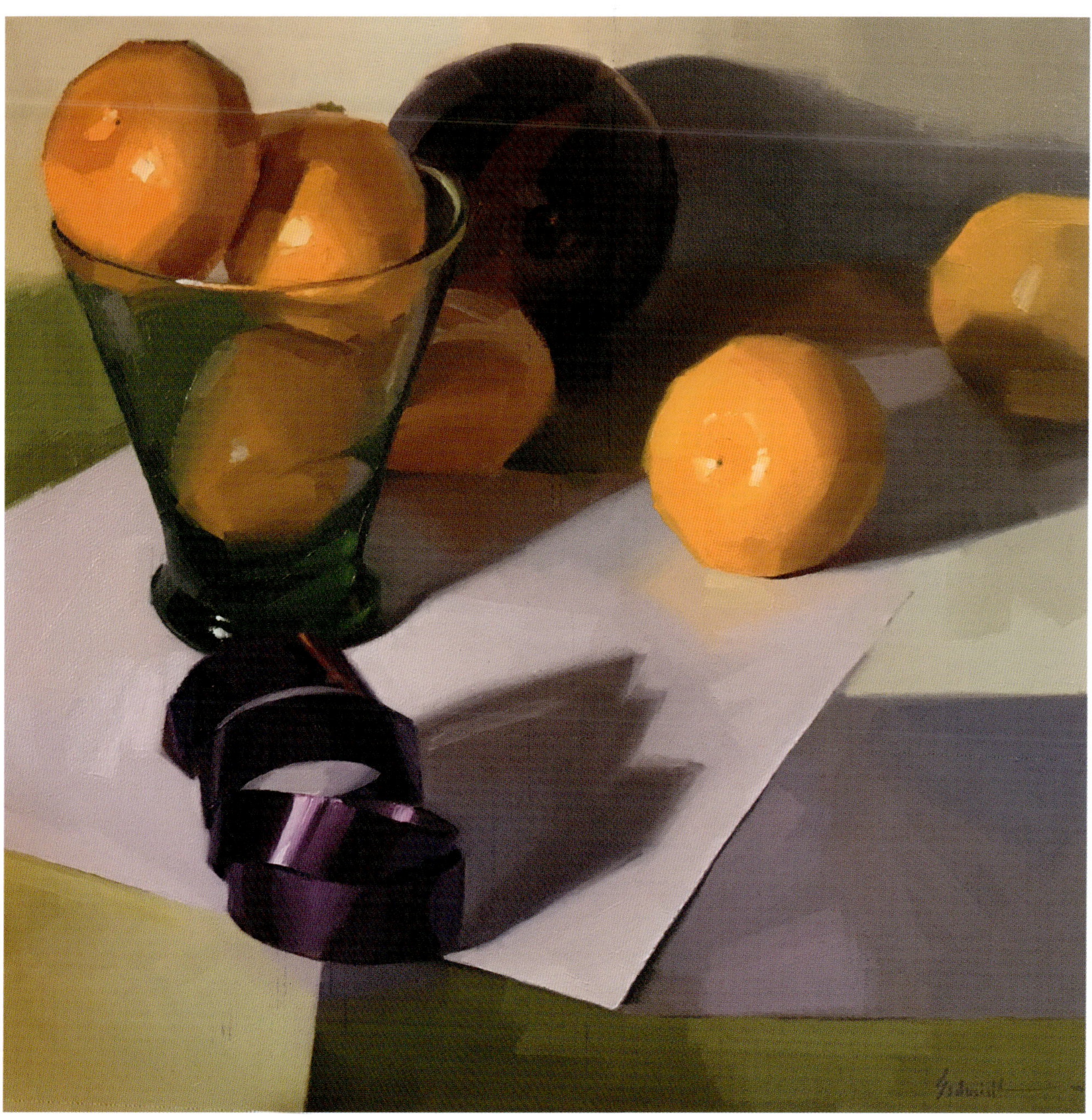

session on still life setup—creating a "photo shoot" with a set of objects, rearranging them and taking a series of pictures to use for later paintings. When working from life, taking a photo of your setup can also be helpful—in case flowers wilt or fruit goes brown before the painting is finished. (I try to paint perishable elements first. Vases, plates, and drapery will still look fresh tomorrow!)

Sarah Sedwick,
Purple Coil**,**
oil on canvas,
12" × 12" | 30.5 × 30.5 cm

The inspiration for this still life was a secondary color scheme: orange, green, and purple, or, as I like to call them, Mardi Gras colors!

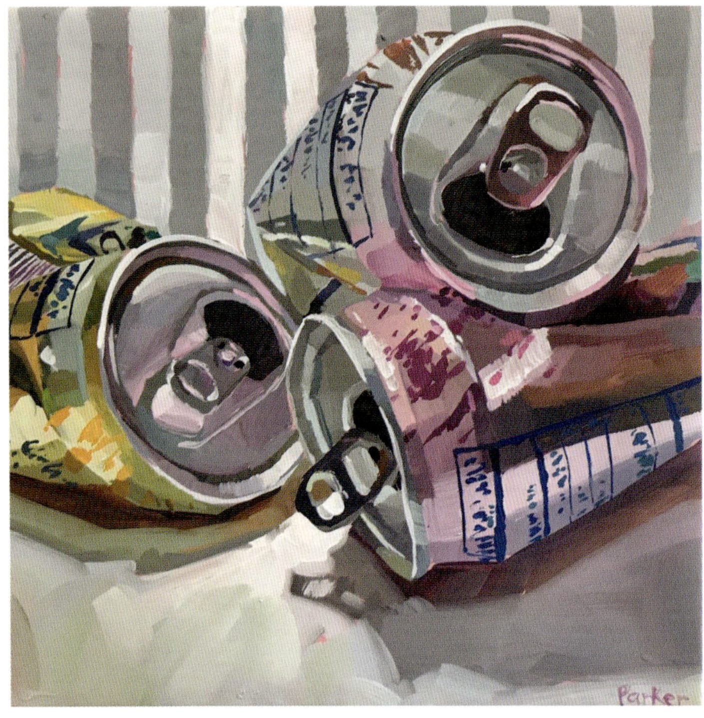

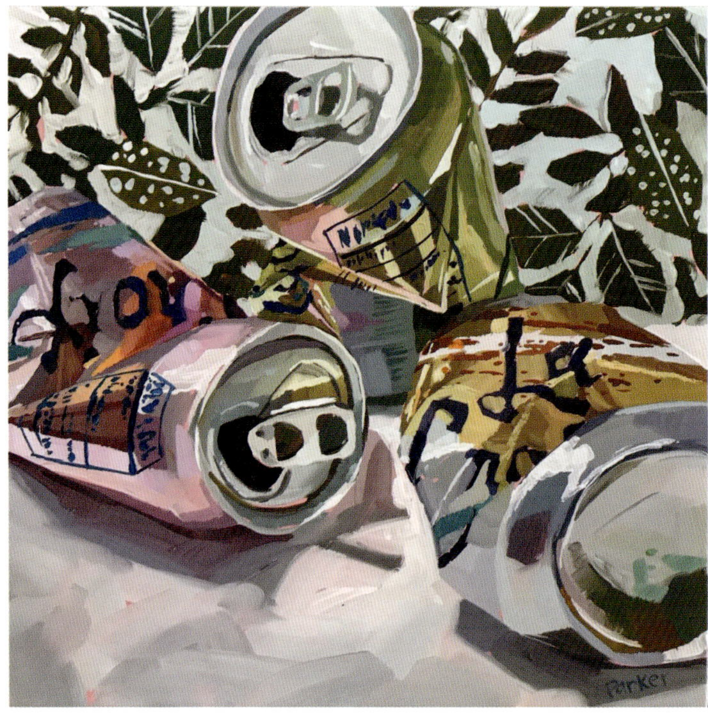

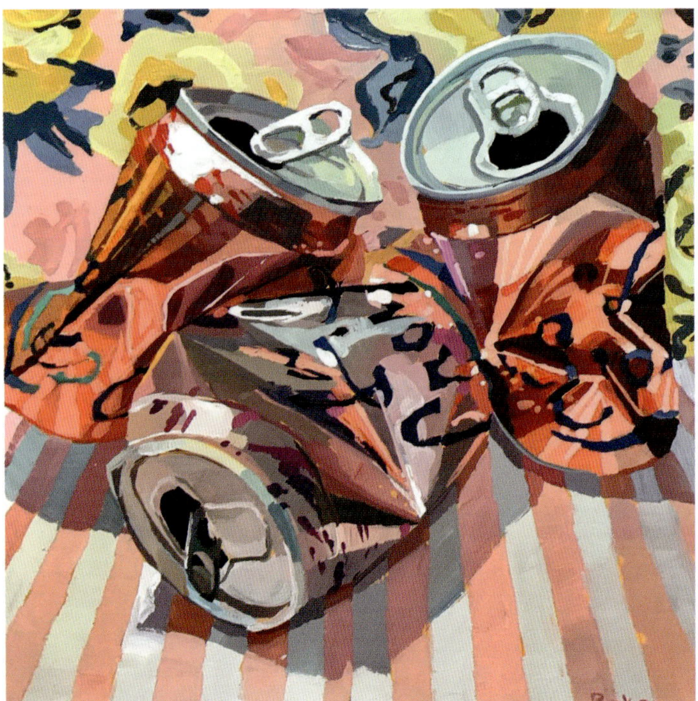

◤ Teddi Parker, *La Croix on Pink Pattern Love*, acrylic house paint on canvas, 14" × 14" | 35.6 × 35.6 cm

▲ Teddi Parker, *Pile On*, acrylic house paint on canvas, 12" × 12" | 30.5 × 30.5 cm

◀ Teddi Parker, *Your Trash Is My Treasure*, acrylic house paint on canvas, 14" × 14" | 35.6 × 35.6 cm

Three paintings from one "photo shoot"! This is a great way to create a bank of images to use for future paintings or plan a series of related pieces.

▶ Julie Beck, *The Birds and the Bees*, oil on canvas panel, 17" × 28" | 43.2 × 71.1 cm

Although there are many objects in this painting, the color scheme has been kept simple and harmonious, using the complements red-orange and blue-green against a dark-neutral background.

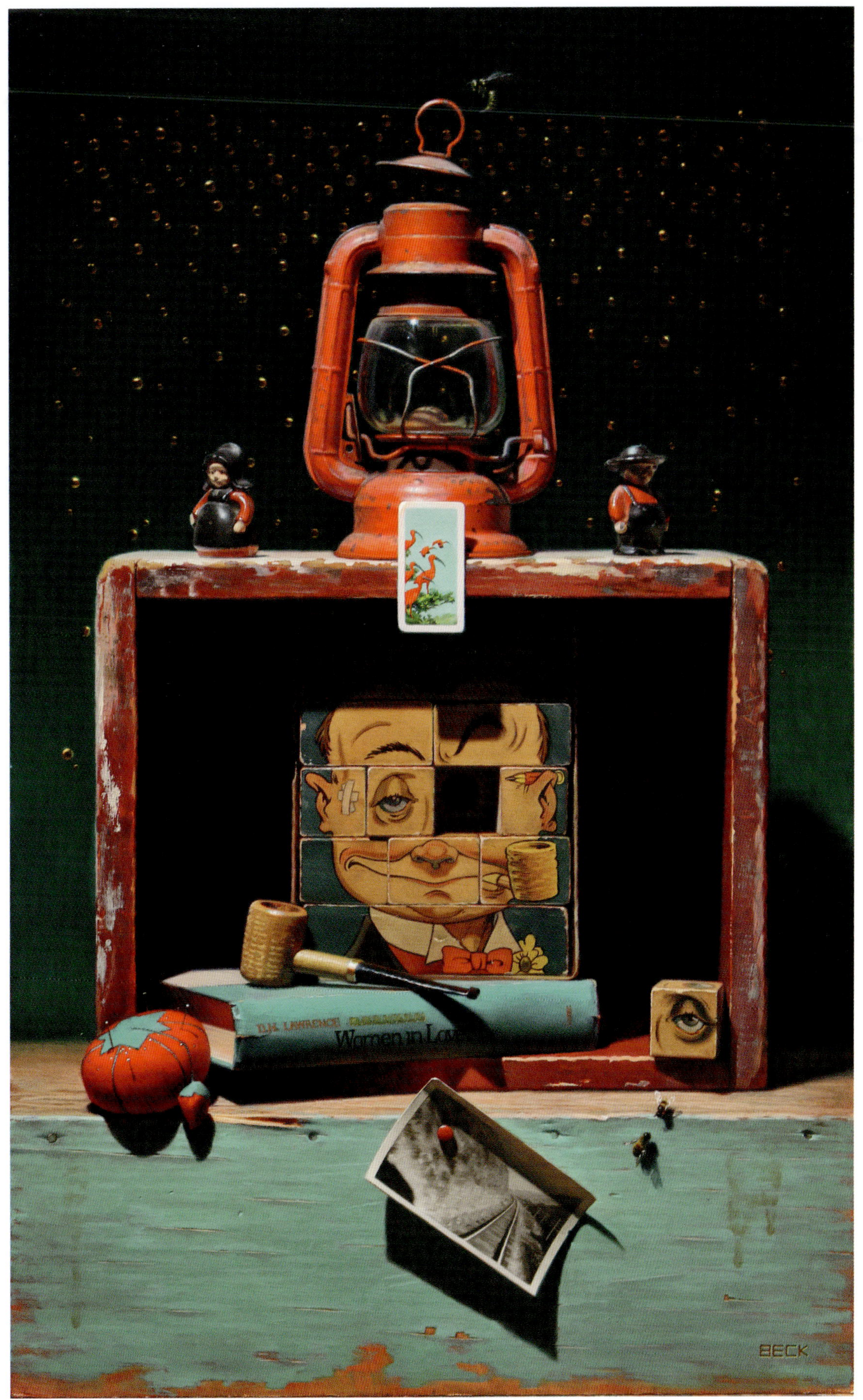
D.H. LAWRENCE
BECK

Still life setup can be the most frustrating part of being a still life artist. Small changes to the setup feel like they can go on endlessly, and the almost limitless options for subjects and color schemes can get overwhelming really fast! A wonderful rule of thumb when things aren't going smoothly is to *take something out*. Adding more elements is almost never the solution to a still life that doesn't "click." And often, the problem can be solved by changing things outside the setup—the angle of the light source or our vantage point. With a little practice, and a lot of listening to our artistic intuition, we begin to hear the "click" when a still life is just right!

What should our considerations be when setting up a still life? Let's dive into the nuts and bolts!

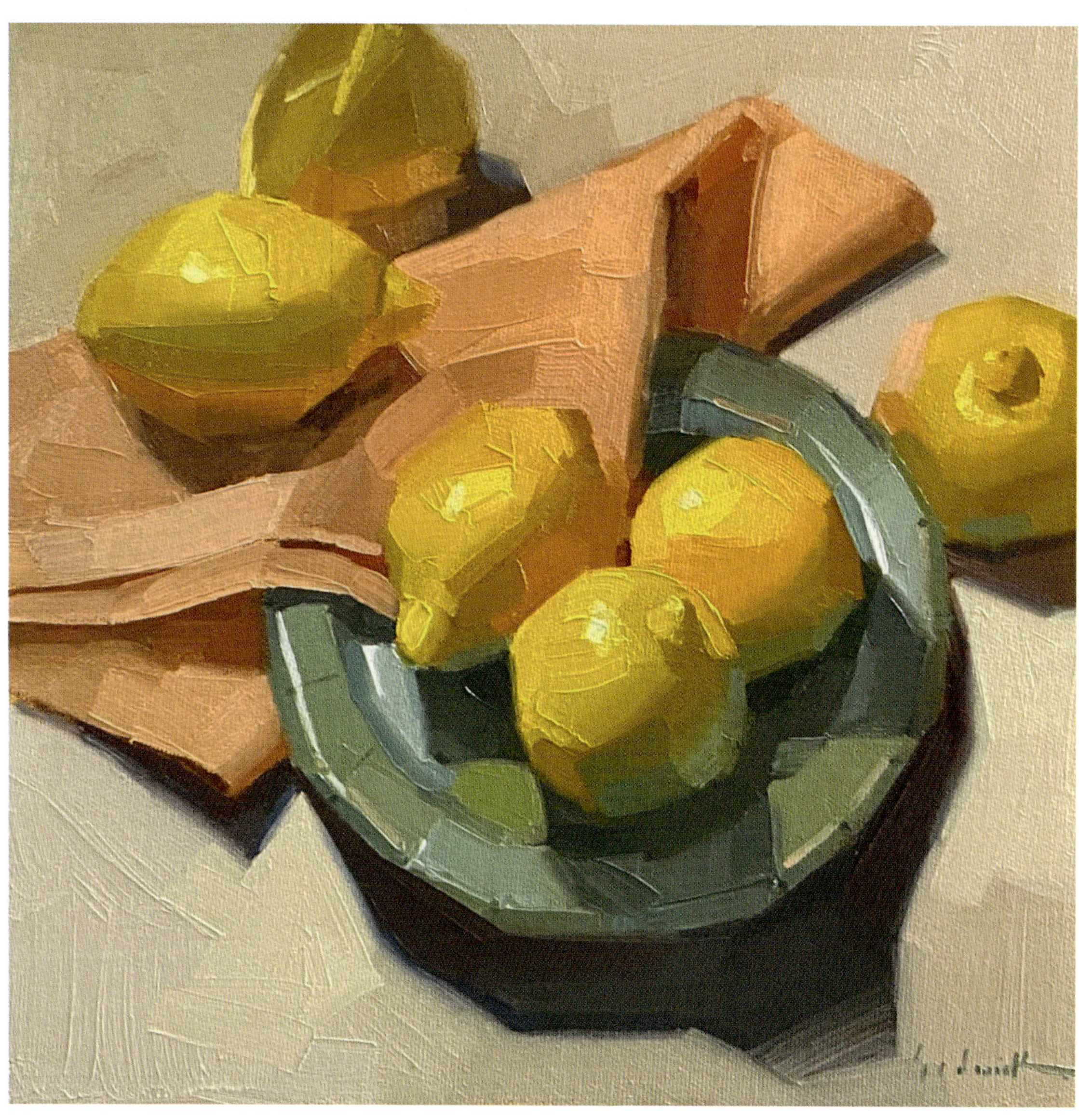

Sarah Sedwick, *Lemons on a Blue Paper Plate*, oil on canvas, 10" × 10" | 25.4 × 25.4 cm

Very ordinary objects can look great in a painting. In this piece, a cloth napkin from the thrift store and a paper plate set the scene.

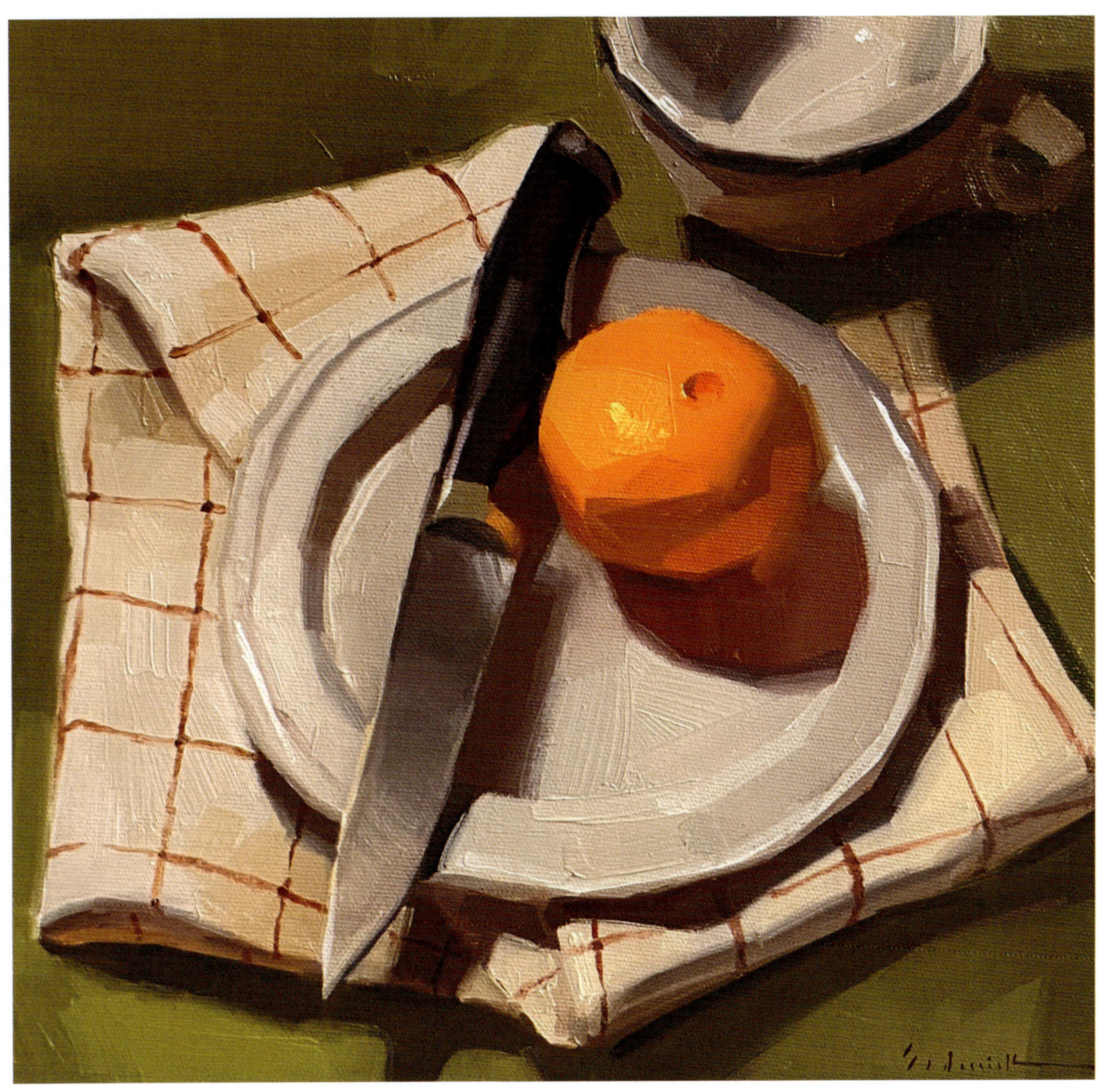

Sarah Sedwick, *Red Stripes*,
oil on canvas, 10" × 10" | 25.4 × 25.4 cm

Fabric, metal, ceramic, and the skin of the orange combine to create texture contrast.

STILL LIFE SETUP: THE THREE VS

We make many decisions before we even pick up a paintbrush that affect the outcome of our painting. I like to start from a place of intuition—choosing an object I'm drawn to and then asking myself what colors or textures could work with it—and what the mood or feeling of the resulting painting would be.

My studio usually resembles a rummage sale, with various groupings of objects and colored papers everywhere. This is the "marination" phase of still life setup—experimenting with combinations of objects, colors, and textures. As I'm passing by the studio or working on another painting, I'll pause to rearrange the elements—or just spend a few moments gazing at them. We artists are visual thinkers, so having an actual arrangement to examine and experiment with can be easier than imagining a still life first and then attempting to put it together.

As I'm choosing my objects and colors and experimenting with arrangement and lighting, I consider what I've come to think of as the "Three Vs": variety, value, and vantage point.

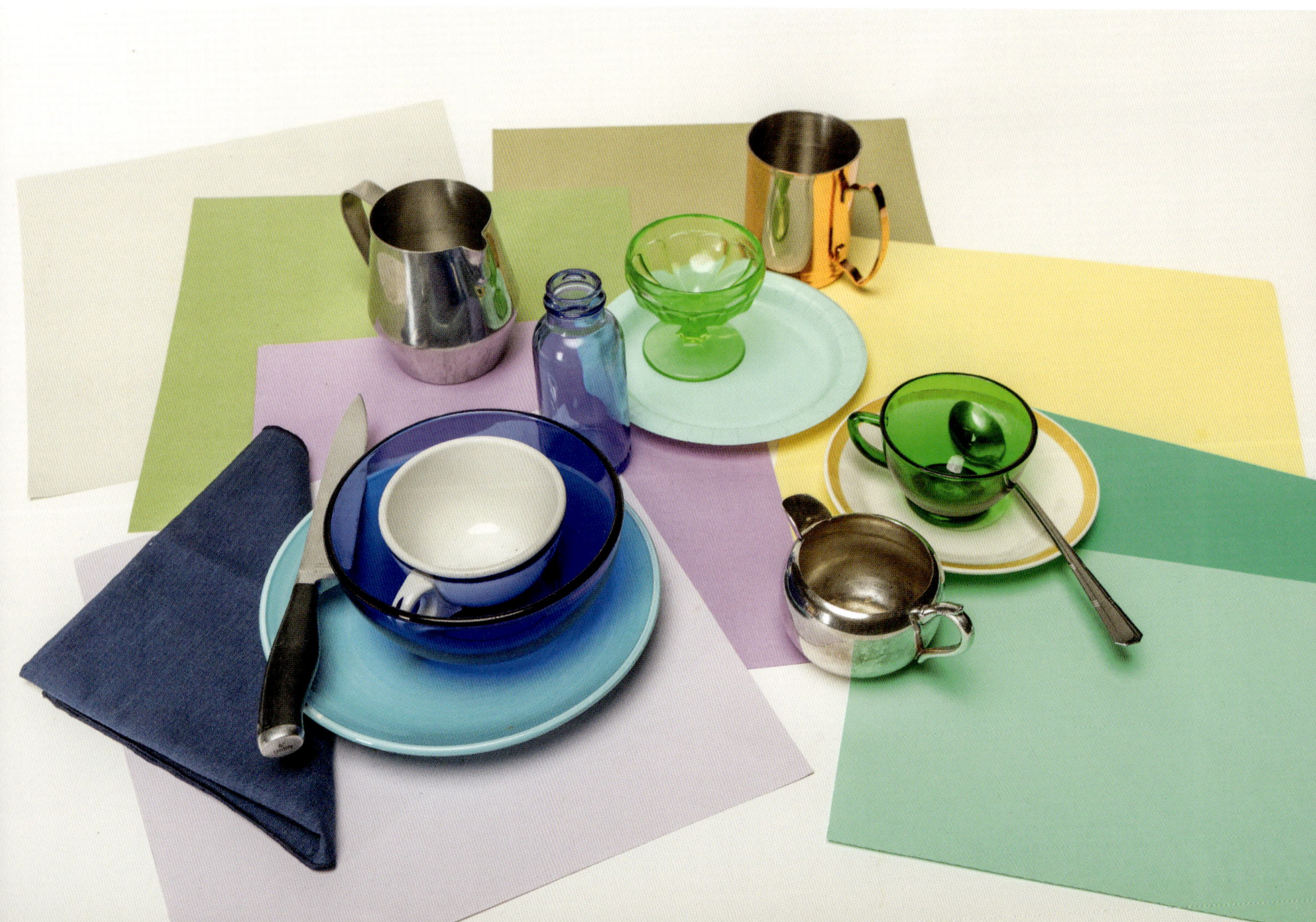

VARIETY

Variety is the spice of life—and it's the key to successful paintings. We don't want our still life elements to feel disjointed, random, or unrelated, but we *do* want to keep things interesting. So we need not only *variety*—we need *repetition with variety*.

Beginning with objects in a variety of colors, sizes, and textures, ask yourself: Is there repetition, a pattern, a theme? Are there two kinds of yellow in the grouping? Is there blue repeated in a bowl and a piece of fabric? Are there two different objects made of shiny metal? Is there a color in the negative space that is repeated in one of the objects?

Vary the heights and sizes of your objects. Visual overlap can create opportunities for lost edges. A grouping or bunch of objects that are all the same—a bowl of oranges, a clump of radishes, a bunch of grapes—can be painted first as a "big lumpy shape," and then separated out, choosing one or two of the elements for a higher degree of detail and letting the rest become supporting characters.

When considering composition, variety also comes into play. If, for example, the shapes in your negative space are all of similar size—or if your objects are spaced evenly between the edges of the picture plane—your composition can be made more dynamic by moving things slightly off-center, and by thinking of "large—medium—small" negative shapes. As I'm evaluating a still life, looking at it through my viewfinder to find the painting within the setup I've created, I ask myself: If I were to fill up each shape in the negative space with sand, would I need a different amount of sand for each one? That lets me know that I have variety there too.

My collections of still life objects, colored paper, and fabric are the beginning ingredients for still life "marination."

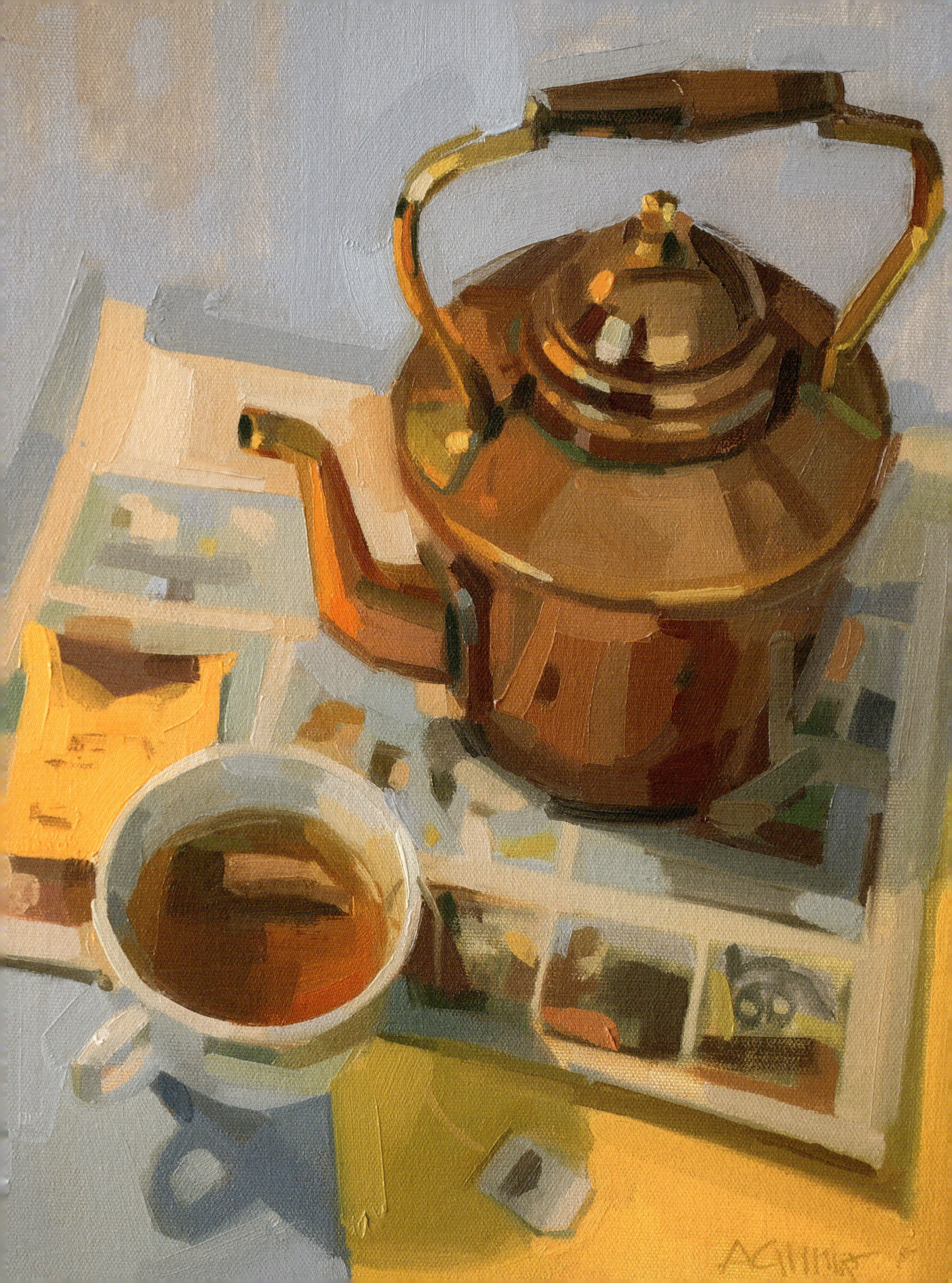

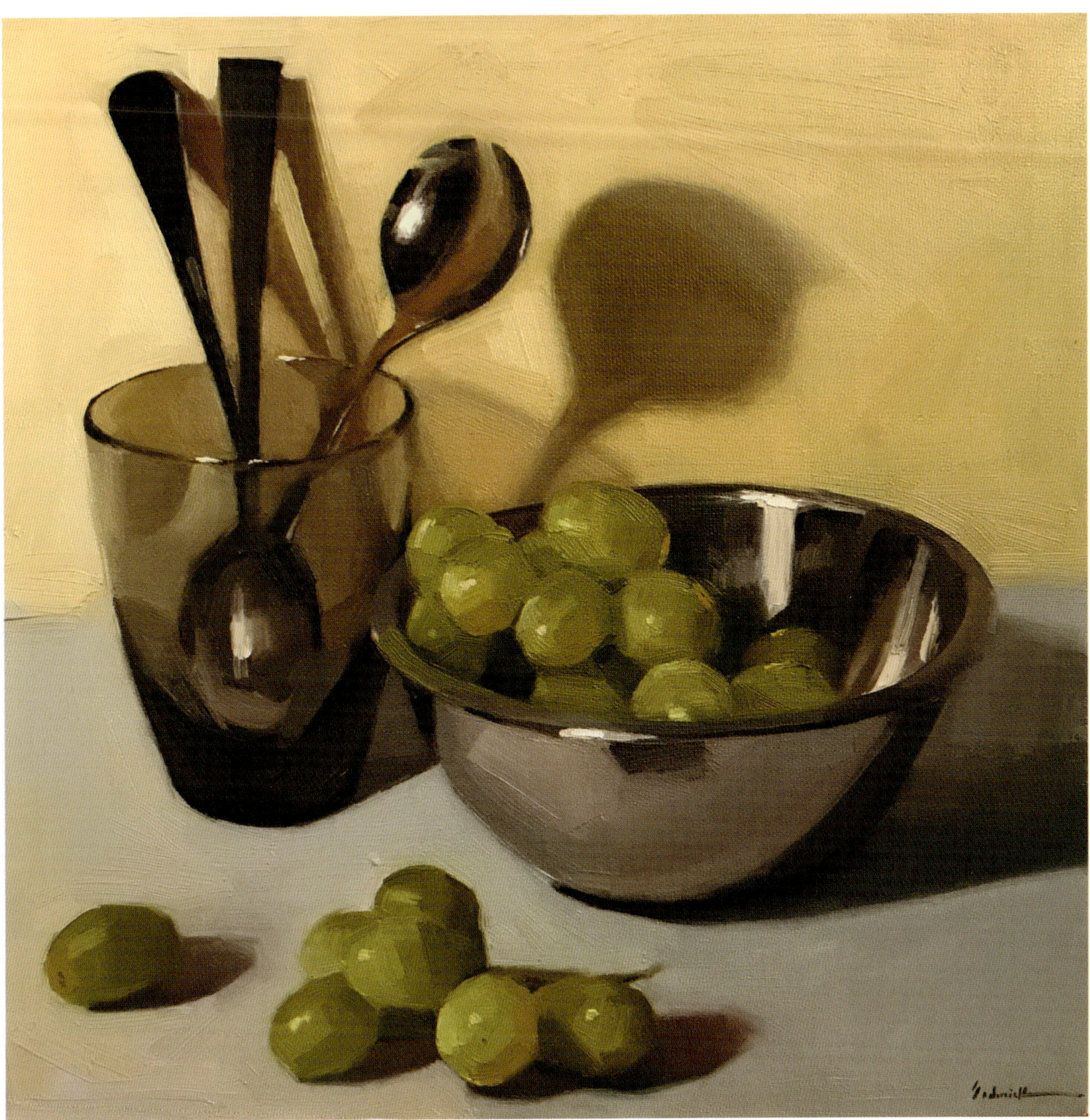

◀ Sarah Calandro, *Sunday Peanuts*, oil on canvas, 12" × 16" | 30.5 × 40.6 cm

Repetition with variety! Deep orange colors repeat in the copper and the tea, and bright yellows repeat in the background paper and the tea packet. A variety of textures—and of shapes in the negative space—bring interest to this painting by Sarah Calandro.

▲ Sarah Sedwick, *Shadow of a Spoon*, oil on canvas, 12" × 12" | 30.5 × 30.5 cm

Capturing the "big lumpy shape" of a bunch of grapes before getting into describing the detail of each not only helps maintain the overall gesture of the bunch but allows you to pick and choose which grapes will be your star players. In this piece, I chose to emphasize the grapes in the bowl, letting the ones on the ground be supporting characters.

VALUE

Consider the overall value of your setup. We require contrast in order to see *anything*, so make sure you create some! Your still life objects may be high key (mostly light values) or low key (mostly darks), but ask yourself, "Do I have at least a tiny bit of the rest of the value scale represented?" A pop of darkest dark in a high-key painting will really help it jump off the wall.

The key of a painting also determines its mood. A flower painting with a brilliant white background might suggest springtime and sunshine, while the same bouquet emerging from a velvety darkness might imply mystery, or even mourning.

Color has value. As you're evaluating your still life, use your eyes like a black-and-white camera—or take a black-and-white photo—to find the dominant value. If everything in a setup is very colorful, it can be hard to see it in terms of value, since bright, saturated colors often feel light to our eye, when they are really dark or midtone. This is a good time to locate your lightest light, your darkest dark, and the area of strongest contrast in the still life you're creating.

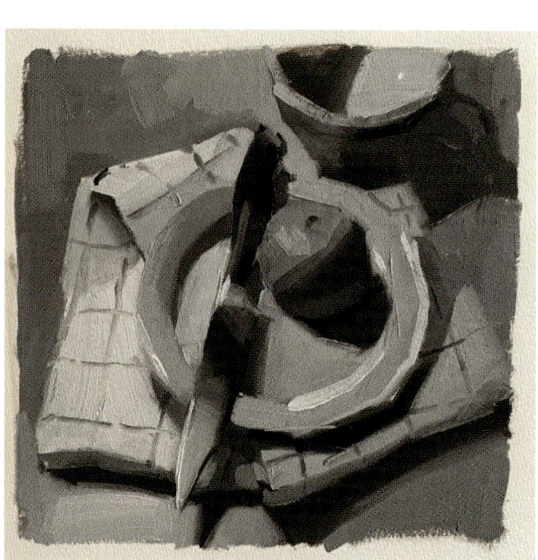

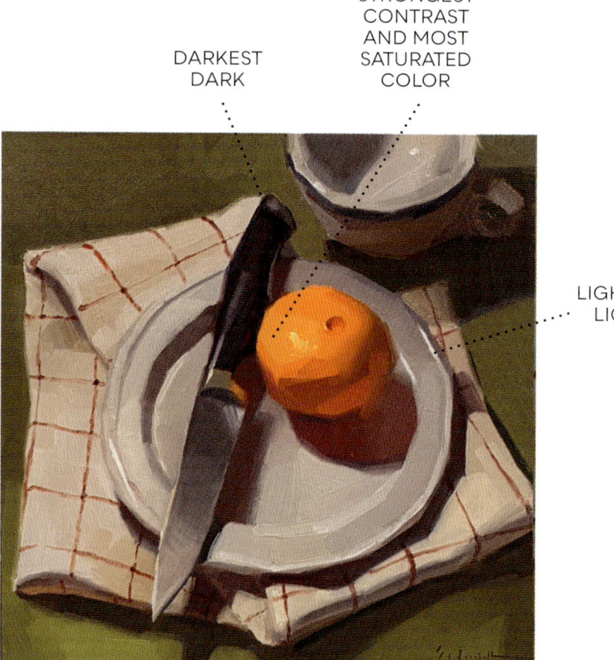

When beginning any painting, I ask myself, "What's the lightest light, the darkest dark, and the most saturated color I see in this still life?" The most saturated color may *feel* like the lightest thing I can see, when it is actually more of a midtone.

▶ Julie Beck, *Jeez Louise*, oil on canvas, 12" × 17" | 30.5 × 43.2 cm

Although all the objects appear to be the same color—and the same value—even the smallest, lightest light accents help this amazing trompe l'oeil painting by Julie Beck jump off the wall.

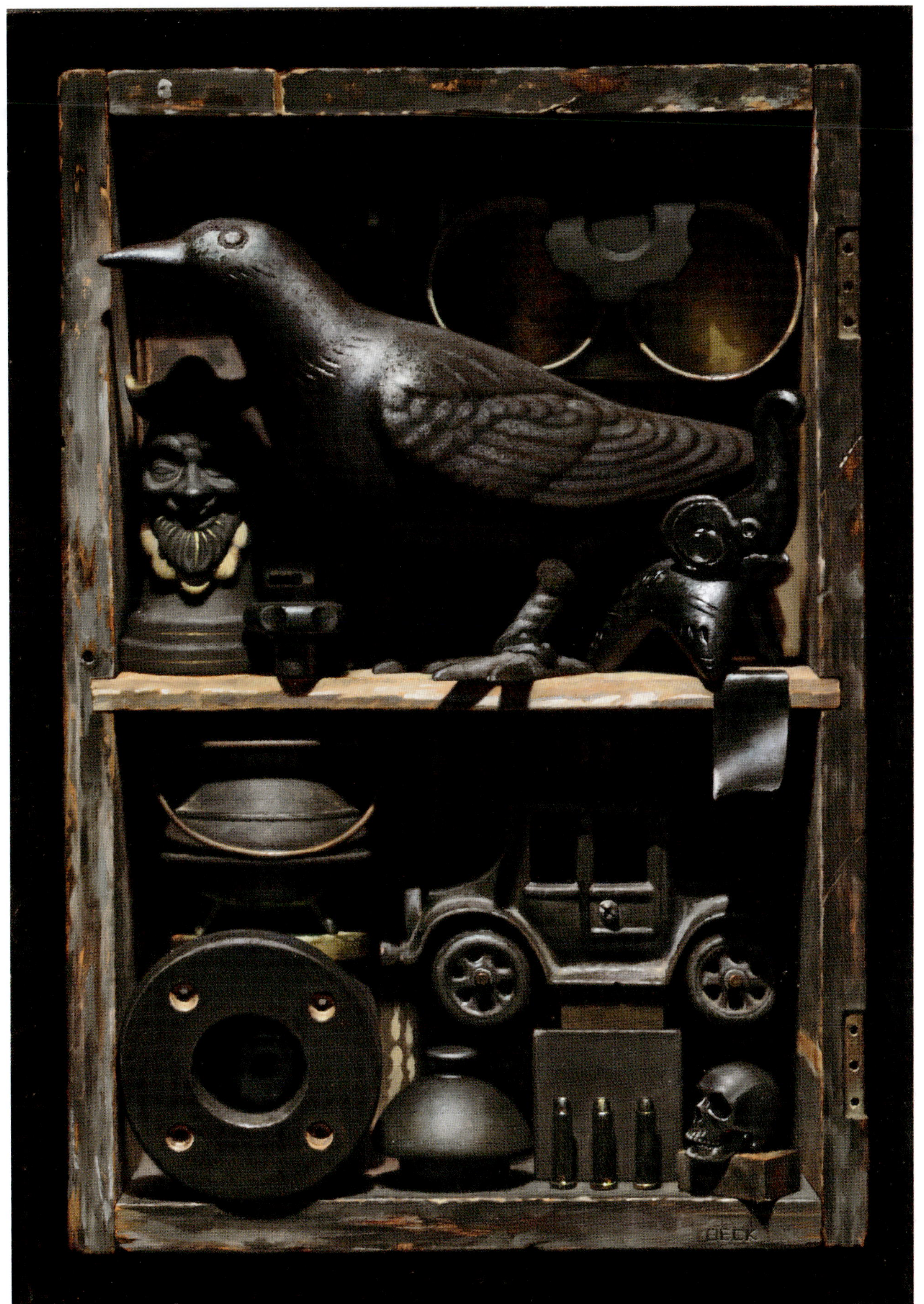
BECK

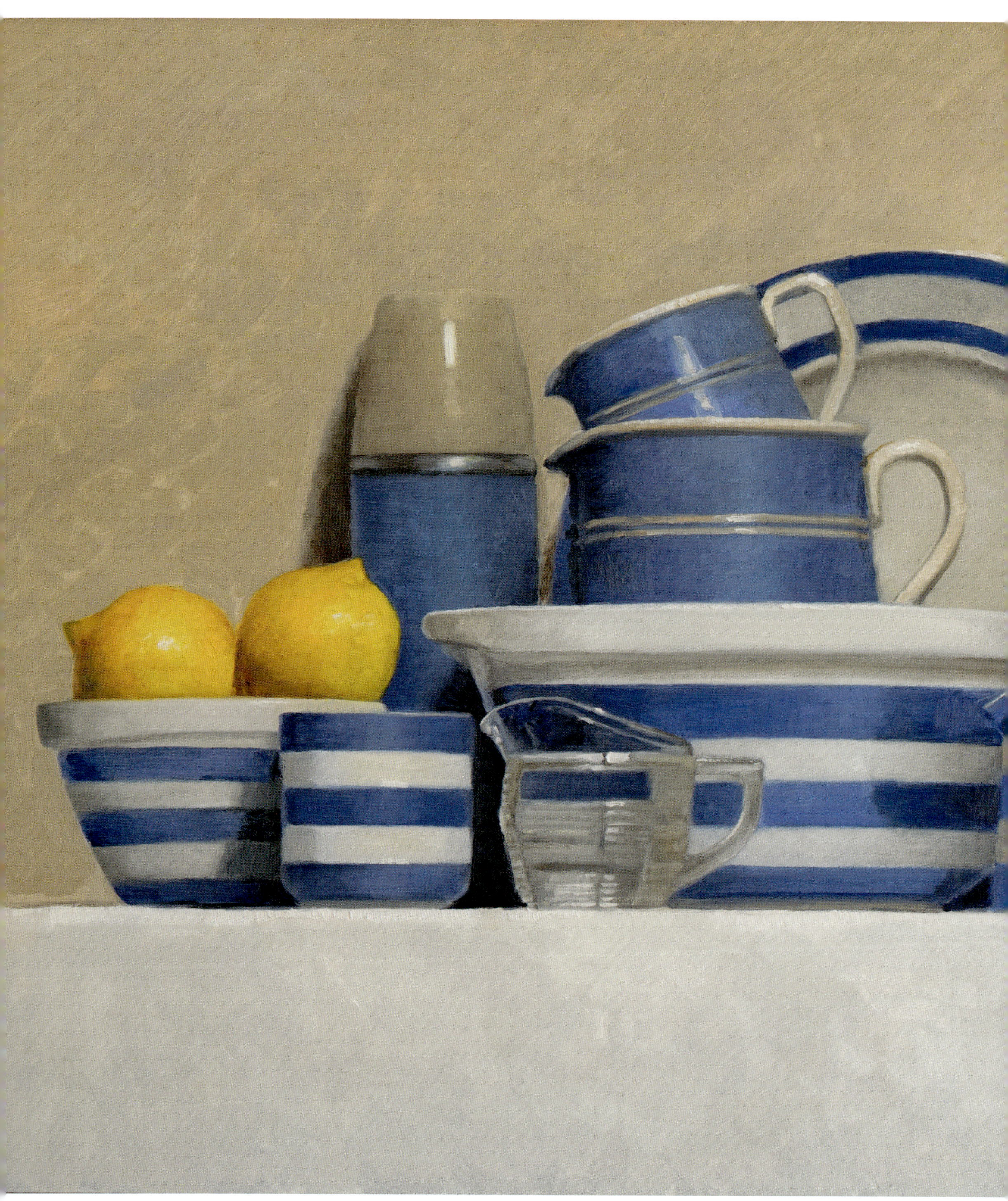

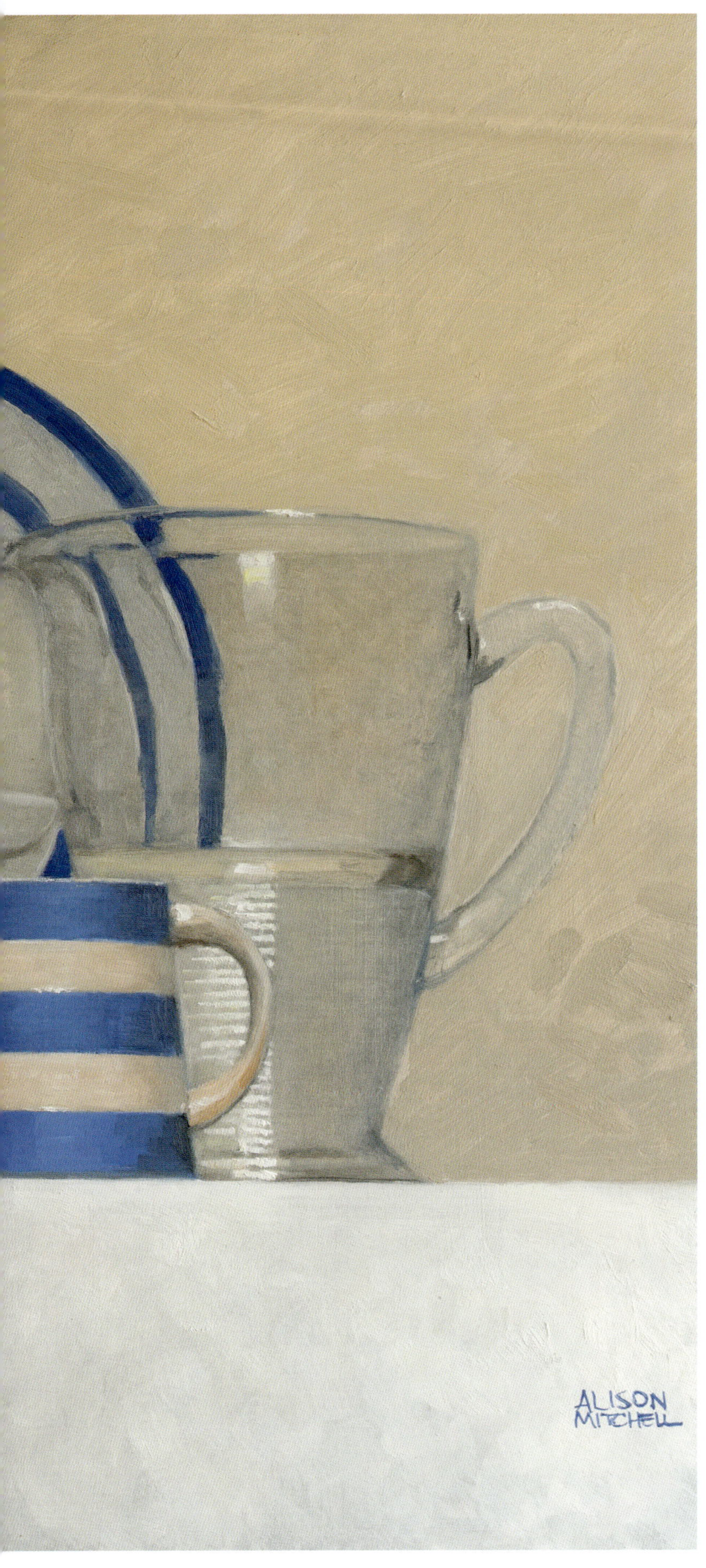

VANTAGE POINT

Vantage point can have a major impact on the mood and message of your painting. Where are you in relation to your subject? I like a bird's-eye view because it lets me use dramatic cast shadows as significant compositional elements. To achieve this effect, I set my still life up at a low height—a coffee table or small end table works well. I use a box with a drawing board on top, generally about knee height, though I sometimes add another box to raise my view slightly.

Alison Mitchell, *Cornish Ware*, oil on board, 24" × 36" | 60 × 90 cm

Arranging a still life at eye level creates a dramatic vantage point—and is also a great option for artists who struggle with ellipses! Rings around bowls and pitchers become straight lines in this painting by Australian artist Alison Mitchell.

Arranging your subjects at eye level or higher brings opportunities for interesting overlap, creates cast shadows on a rear wall, and literally "elevates" them with a sense of importance. Viewing your still life at table-top height can give it a comfortable sense of the everyday. Both of these vantage points allow for the front edge of the platform to be included in your painting, and for drapery cascading over it too. In my studio, in addition to my very flexible low-height still life stage, I have a table against one wall that I stack boxes upon to raise my still life to any height I want.

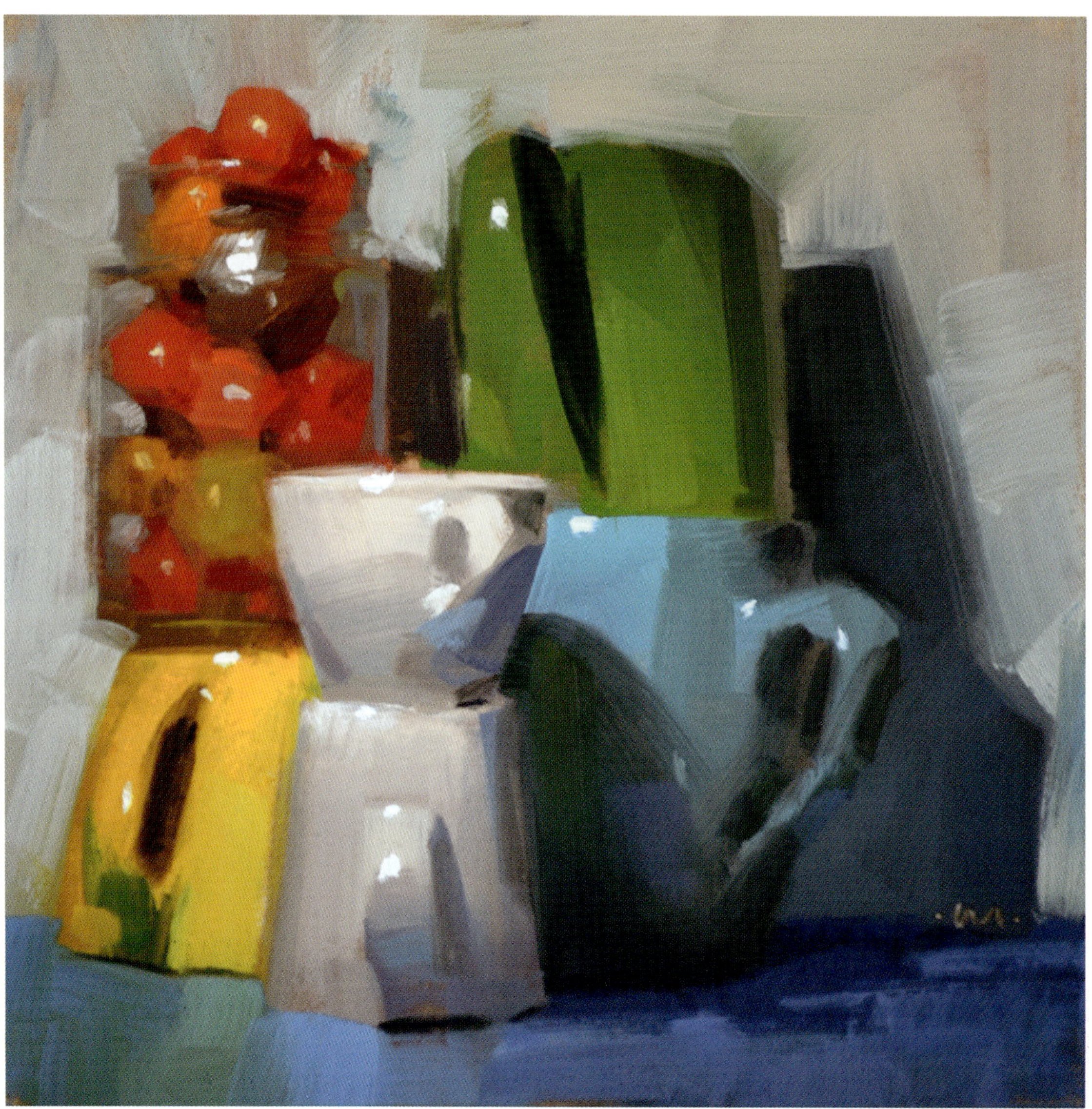

Carol Marine, *Up to No Good*, oil on panel, 6" × 6" | 15.2 × 15.2 cm

A table-height still life creates dramatic shadows on both the "wall" and "floor" planes in this masterful arrangement by Carol Marine. Give stacked and nested teacups a try for a real drawing challenge!

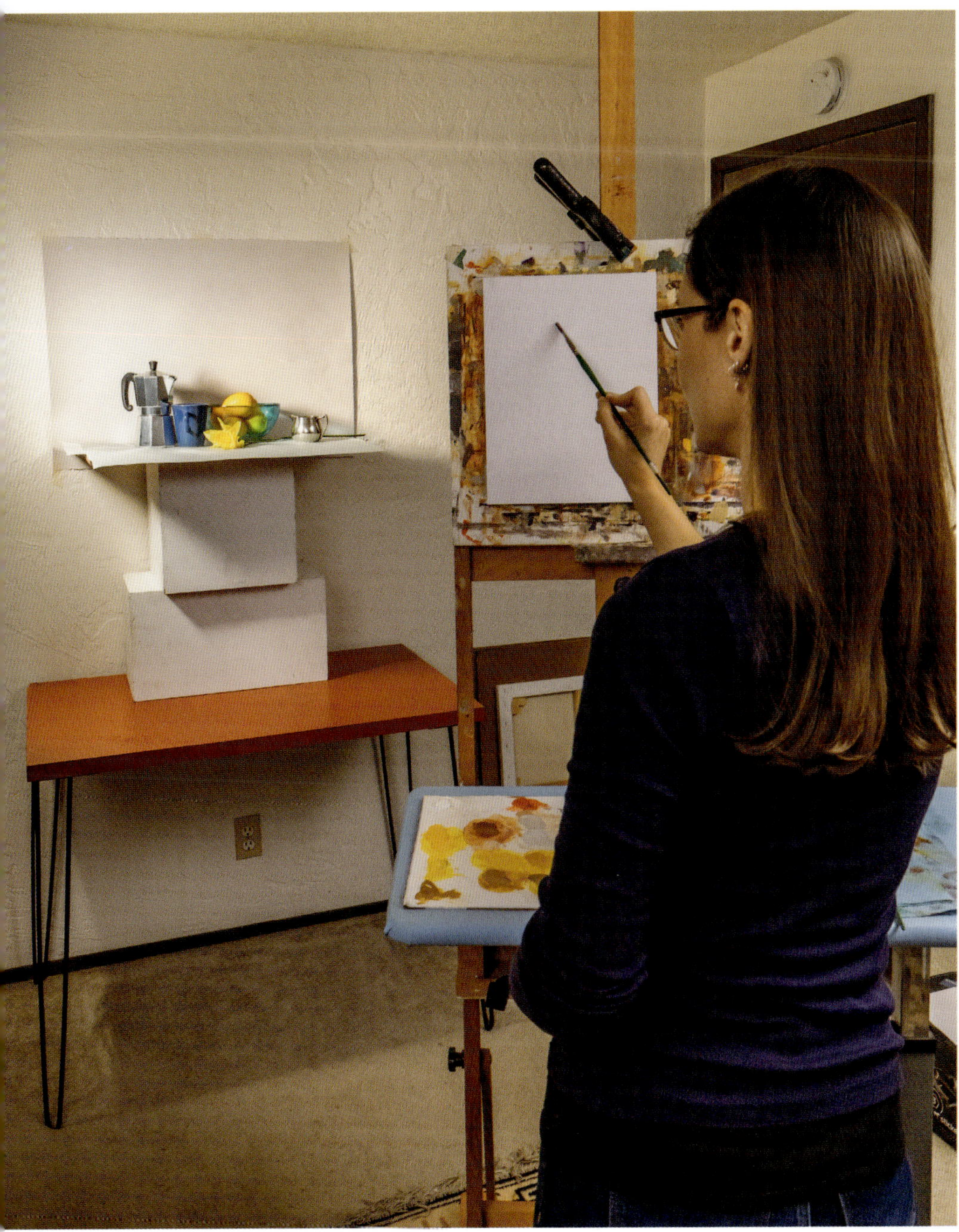

Standing while painting has many advantages. It encourages us to move more, backing away from our work more often, and it gets the whole body involved, not just the wrist and fingers, for freer, more expressive brushwork.

When I'm working from a low-height setup, my still life is pretty close to me—the box itself is only a couple of feet from my easel. Standing up to paint, that puts the still life about 5 feet (1.5 m) from my eyes. When my still life is on a higher table, the larger the still life, the farther away I stand. I am generally about 6 to 7 feet (1.8 to 2.1 m) from what I am painting at this vantage point.

Place a comfortable distance between yourself and your subject so that you can see it clearly and also easily see the entire thing. Remember that you can move yourself around the still life when things aren't quite clicking, for a new view. You can also stand up or sit down to change your vantage point, instead of adjusting the height of the still life itself.

LIGHTING YOUR STILL LIFE

When a still life is not "clicking," my first question is, "What can I take out?" And my second is, "How can I change the lighting?" The angle at which a still life is lit has a huge effect not only on the overall key of the finished painting but also on its mood—and more fundamentally, on the value structure of the resulting composition. The "big dark shape" that I'll be looking for in my thumbnail sketches in the next chapter changes a lot depending on the angle and strength of my light source.

It's ideal to have a light that's not only portable but also height adjustable. A low-angle light source can create long shadows in a bird's-eye view, or a dramatic "Halloween" effect on a still life with a higher vantage point. The higher the light is in relation to the still life, the tighter the cast shadow will be to the form, and the smaller the "big dark shape" in your composition becomes.

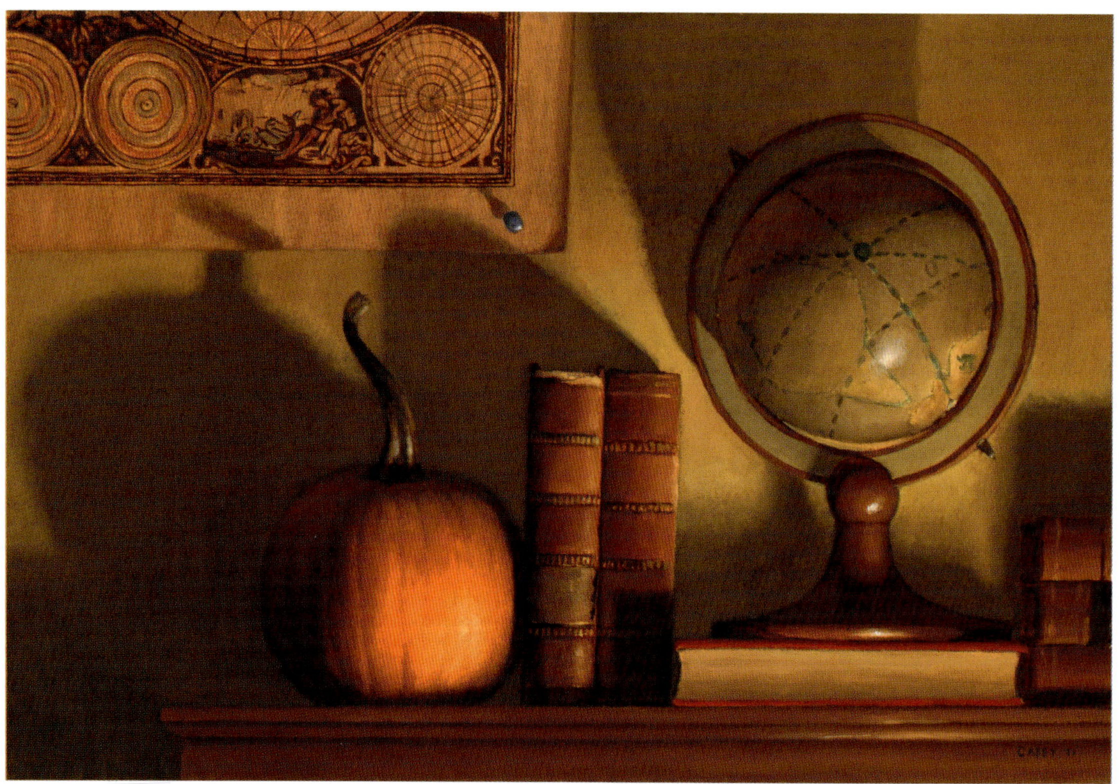

Todd M. Casey, *Globe with Pumpkin*, oil on linen, 11" × 16" | 28 × 40.6 cm

Lit from below, a still life takes on what Todd M. Casey calls a "creature-double-feature" feel. This is also a great way to light a portrait!

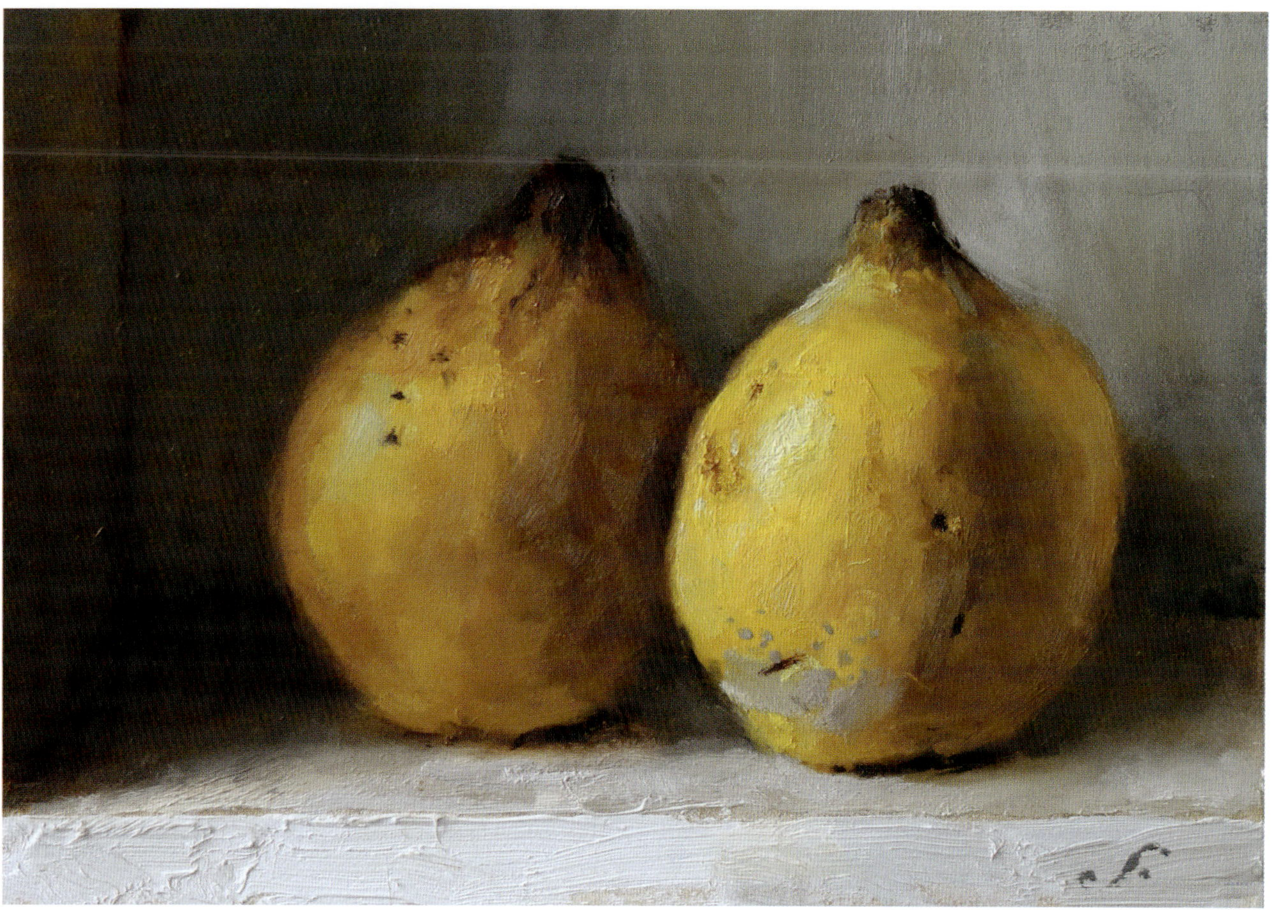

Paul Foxton, *Two Quinces*, oil on panel, 5" × 7" | 12.7 × 17.8 cm

Arranging your still life in a shadow box offers dramatic possibilities. Here, Paul Foxton creates a "shadow wall" by shining a light into the box from the left and adds a third spatial plane by including the back corner in his composition.

Shadow boxes are a great option for controlling light, especially when there's a lot of ambient light in the room, and can be created by simply cutting the flaps off of a cardboard box of the desired size. Shadow boxes can be lined with colored paper or fabric, and the light can shine in through a hole in the top or directly into the front of the box. Add a dramatic element to your painting by including a cast shadow from one of the walls of the box.

Although one of the things that I love about still life is that it's done indoors—perfect for all seasons—if you're an outdoorsy painter, try setting up a still life en plein air! The way sunlight bounces color around a still life outdoors is a wonderful thing to explore. My recommendation: find a spot where your still life can be in full sun—and you can be in full shade! Try painting the same still life at different times of day, or painting in dappled light beneath a tree, for a lovely effect.

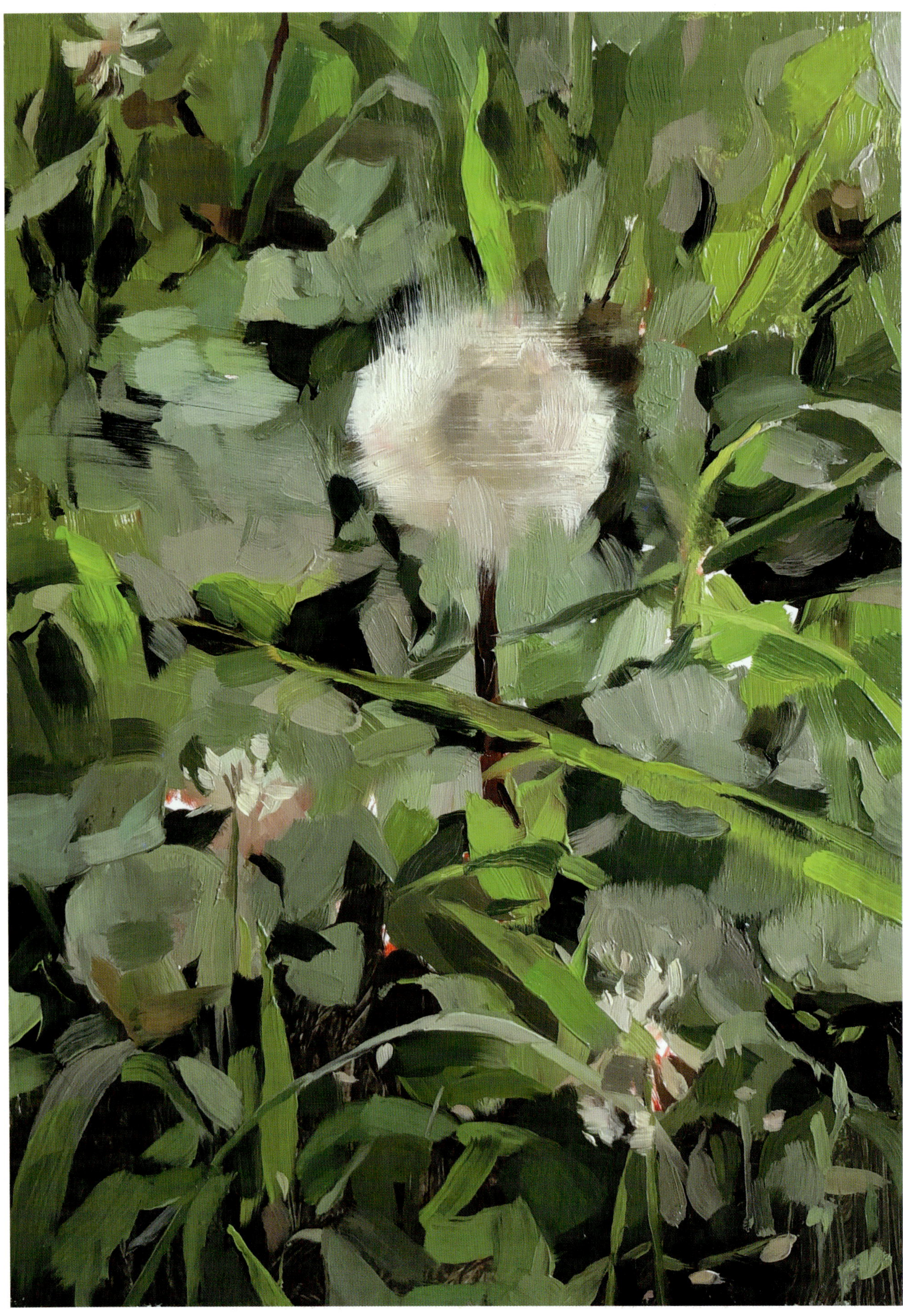

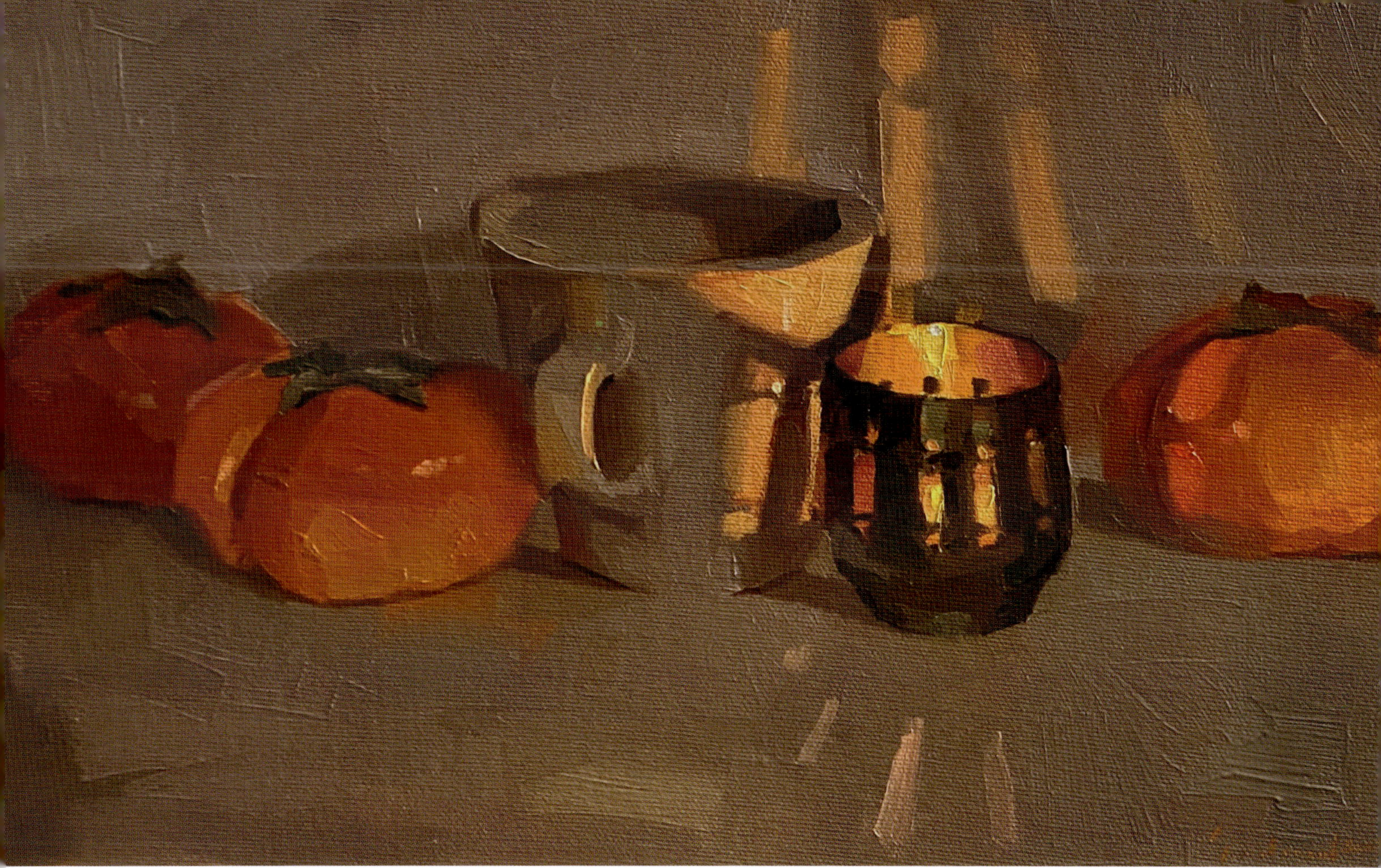

▲ Sarah Sedwick, *Glowing*, oil on canvas, 8" × 13" | 20.3 × 33 cm

Use a candle to illuminate your still life from within—and literally add warmth to your work! While painting this piece, I kept the lights in my studio just bright enough to see my canvas. When attempting to capture a glow, start with the brightest spot—in this case, the flame and reflections inside the candleholder—and then keep everything else in the painting *much* darker than that.

◀ Christina Weaver, *Blowflower*, oil on panel, 7" × 5" | 17.8 × 12.7 cm

You don't need to pick flowers in order to paint them. Christina Weaver creates the perfect marriage of still life and landscape in this plein air painting.

You can have fun with indoor lighting too! We all have preconceived notions about what color something is—eggs are white, tree trunks are brown—but the color of the light source, and the other colors that surround an object, have a strong effect on the actual hue we perceive. Teaching our minds to set aside our fixed ideas about color is a huge part of learning to see like an artist. Using a colored light source on your still life—or including strong color elements in your backgrounds to bounce the light off of—can turn an ordinary still life into an amazing workout for your eye-mind connection, and result in a truly arresting image. You can even make the light source part of the still life itself using a candle or lamp!

Remember—there's no wrong way to light a still life, but forgetting to experiment with different ways of lighting is always a missed opportunity!

SUBJECT MATTER: THINKING OUTSIDE THE BOX

Dynamic still life is not just about experimental vantage points, contemporary colors, and interesting lighting. Nontraditional subject matter brings still life into the modern era. Toys, candy, shoes—even hot dogs—make playful painting subjects! When my typical array of apples and lemons gets boring, I start cutting things up! Slices and halves create tons of fresh possibilities. I love painting seasonally. What holiday is coming up? What's blooming in the garden right now? A "found object" still life can be discovered amid the bustle of family life. An entire story can be told through an arrangement of significant objects. Place books or photographs in a still life to literally tell a story.

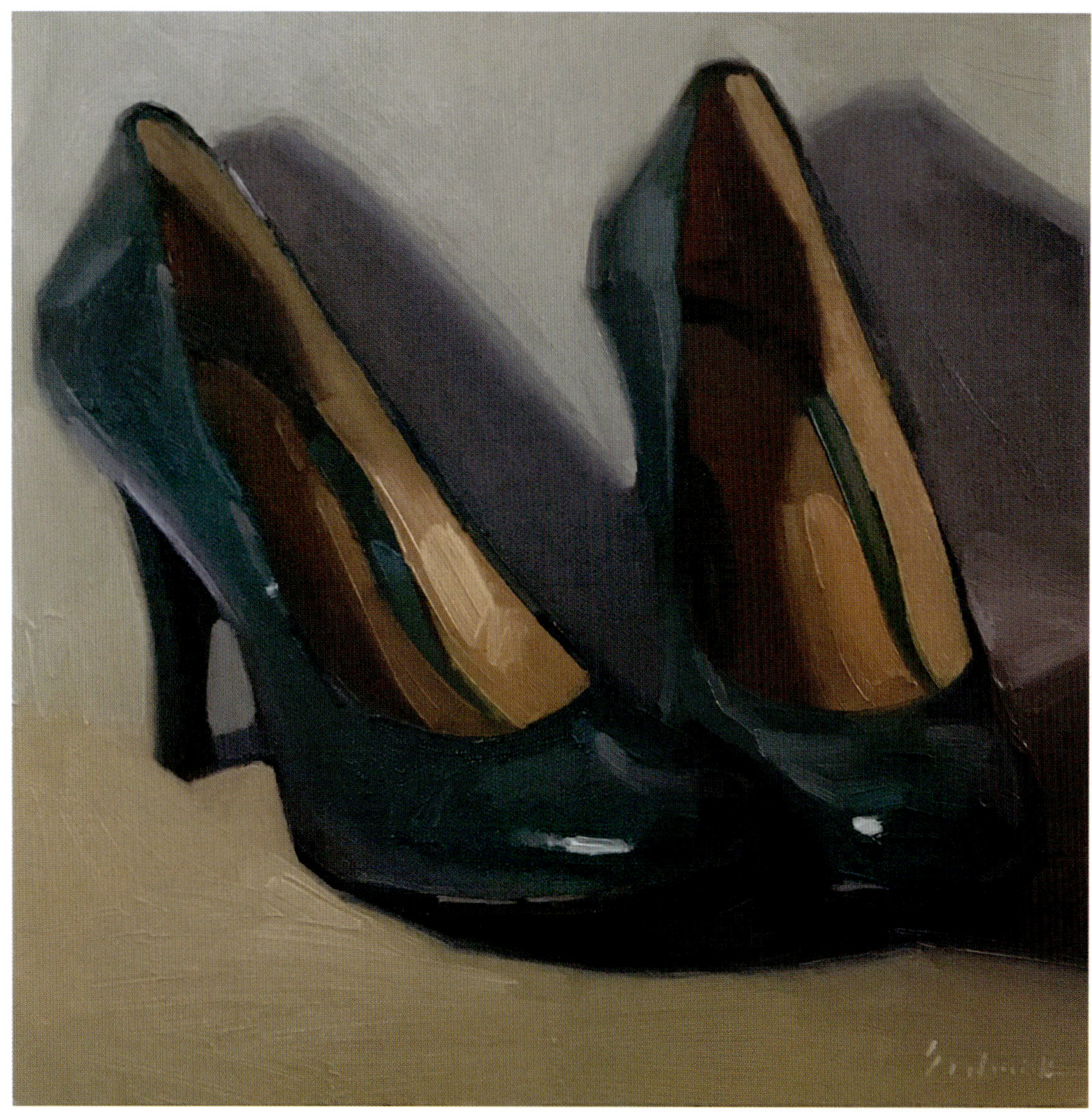

Sarah Sedwick, *Teal Toes*, oil on canvas, 10" × 10" | 25.4 × 25.4 cm

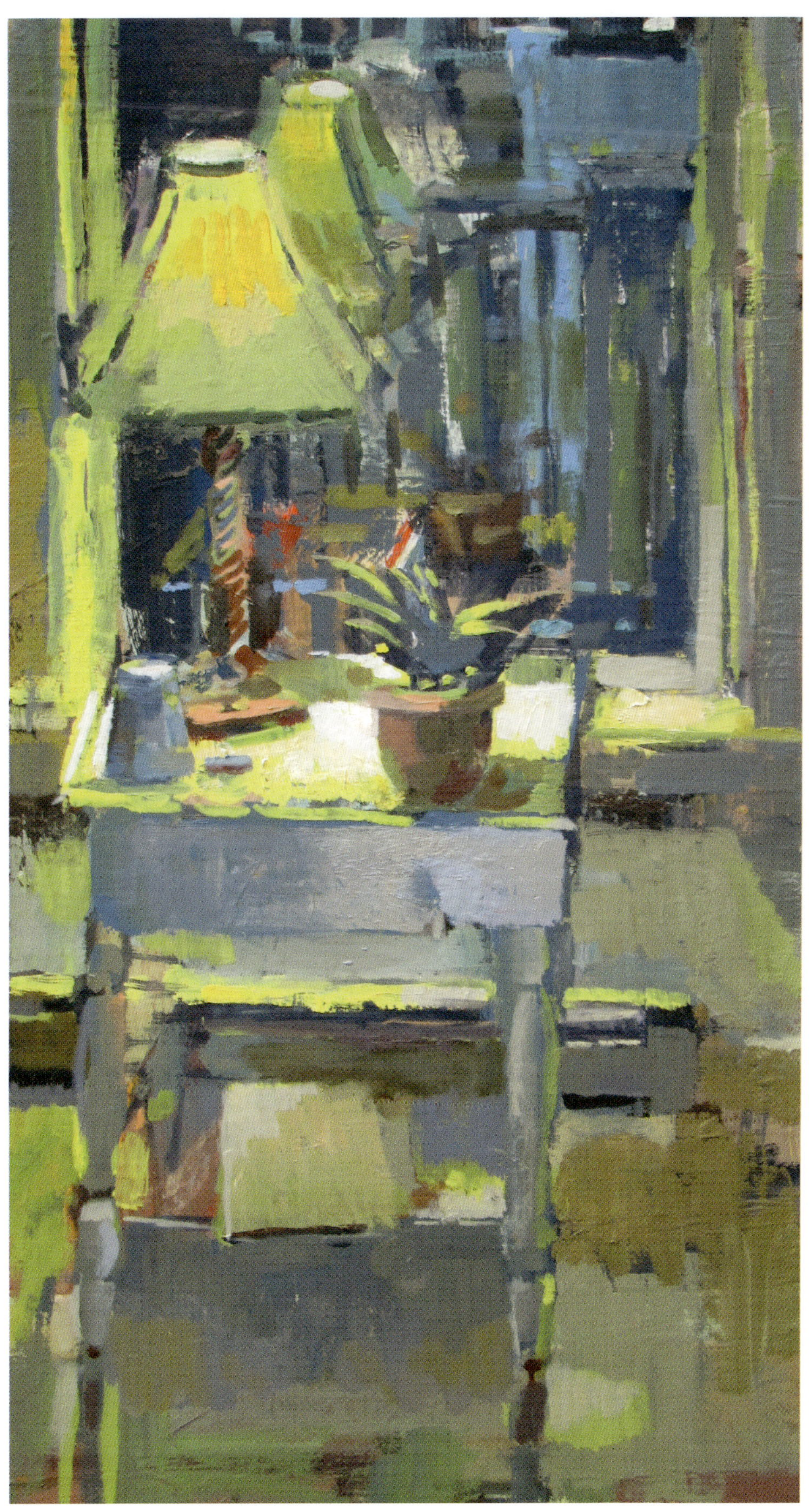

Carole Rabe, *Lamp Reflected in Window*, oil on canvas, 30" × 16" | 76.2 × 40.6 cm

In this beautiful example of an interior containing a window—but in which the light source is not the window—Carole Rabe has carefully maintained the hierarchy of values in this piece, keeping the lamp and the surfaces it is directly illuminating as the lightest lights.

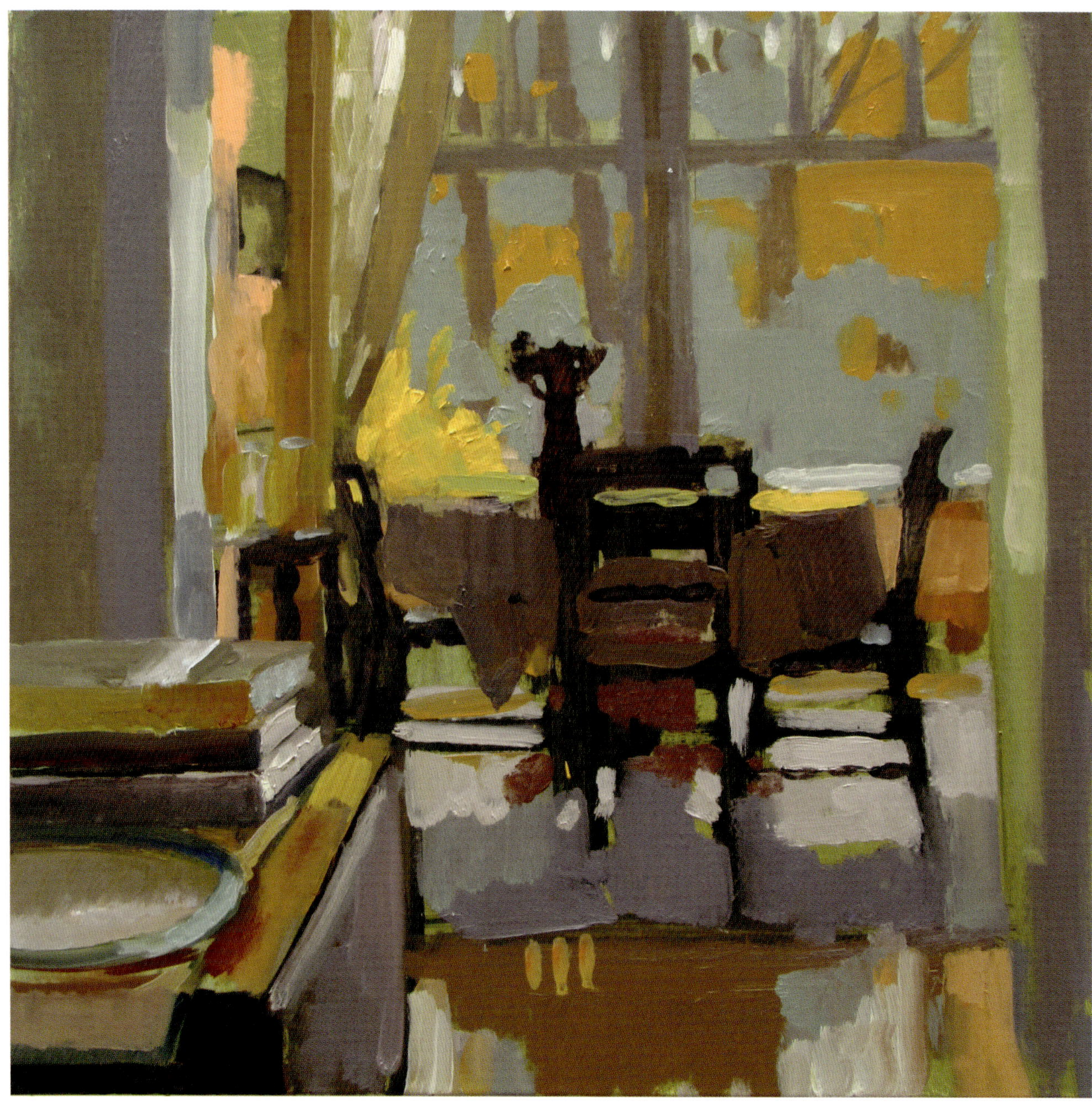

Carole Rabe, *Cloudy Day, Autumn*, oil on canvas, 20" × 20" | 50.8 × 50.8 cm

Interiors—depictions of indoor spaces—are the perfect marriage of still life and plein air landscape. Often including sunlight from a window, many interiors also feature an array of objects in a living space. And they usually involve simplifying and condensing a large, complex scene down to the essentials, just as you would need to if the subject were a vast landscape. Think of painting the jumble on your studio table or desk just as it is. Include the whole desk, the wall, and the nearby window, and you've got an interior.

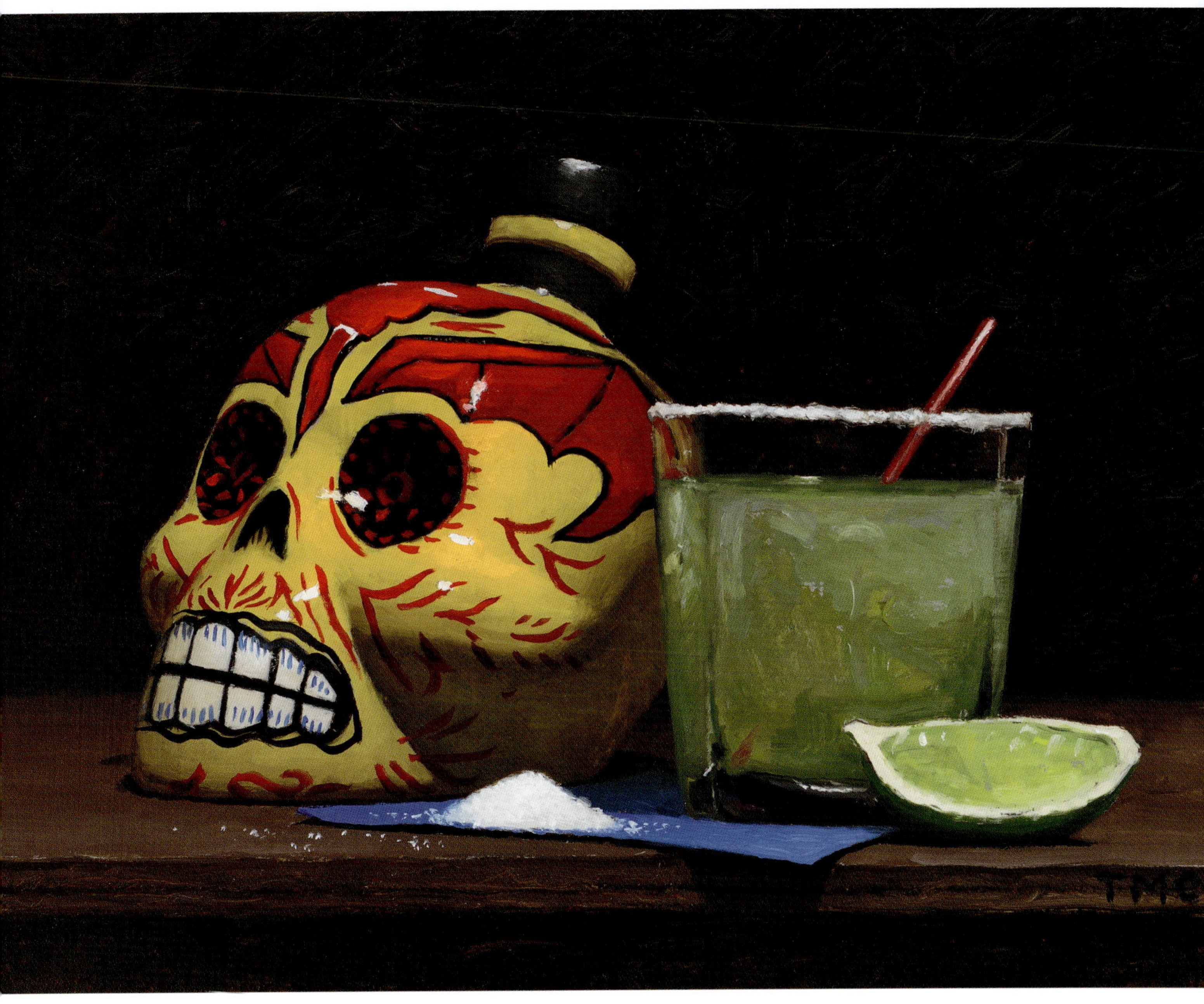

Todd M. Casey, *El Día de los Muertos*, oil on panel, 8" × 10" | 20.3 × 25.4 cm

Holidays, festivities, and seasons can be great themes for still life. The Mexican Day of the Dead and the margaritas of Cinco de Mayo were the inspiration for this piece by Todd M. Casey.

I've been making paintings of Christmas ornaments for many years. I've even been known to do it in the summertime! It's a no-brainer for me because metal is a texture I love to explore, and because the color combinations are endless with ornaments, so I'm thoughtfully crafting the color scheme of my painting as I'm choosing my elements.

Christmas is not the only holiday to inspire our paintings, though. How about candy hearts for Valentine's Day; a red, white, and blue still life for the Fourth of July; or a margarita for Cinco de Mayo?

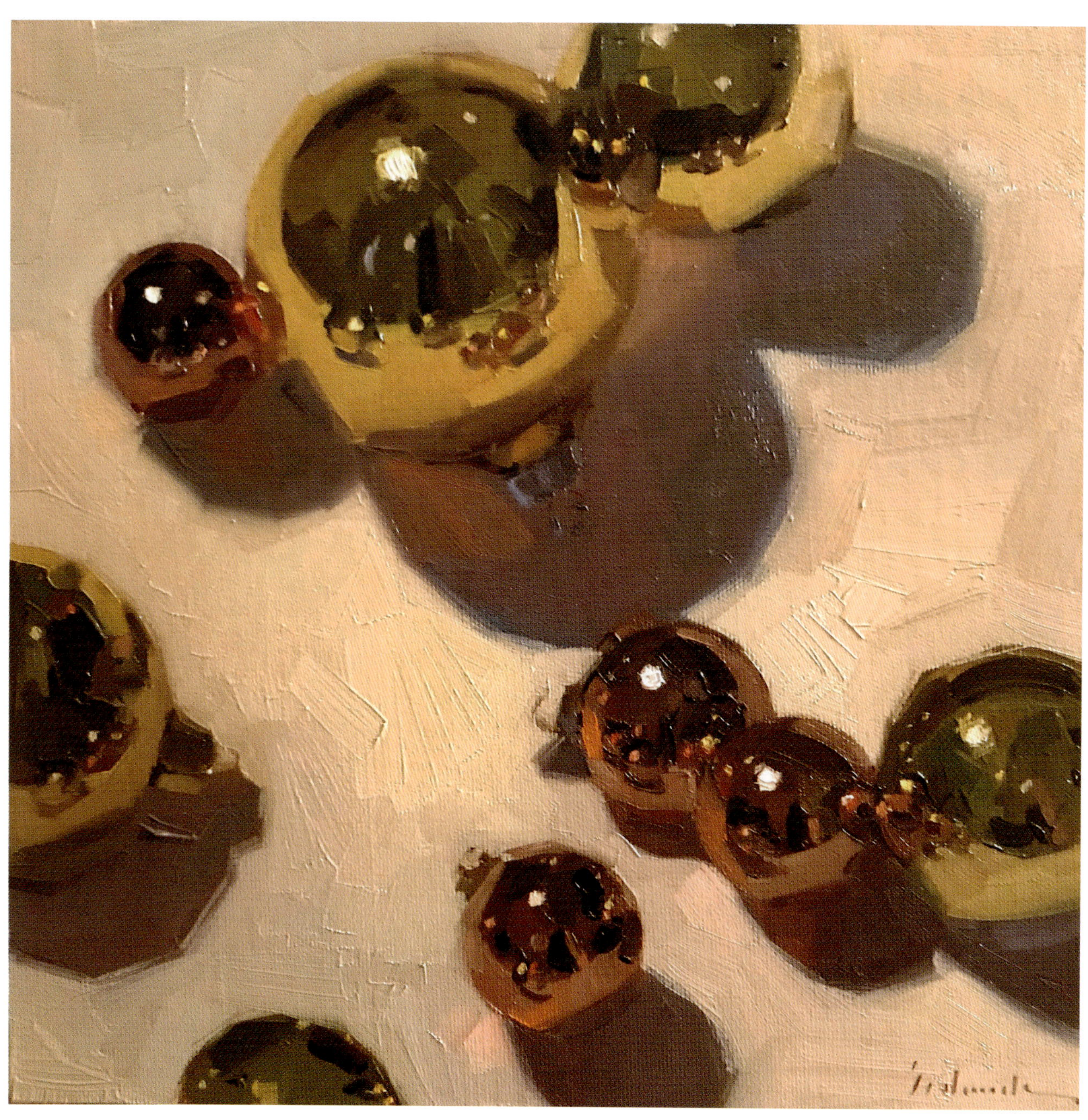

Sarah Sedwick, *Ready, Set, Gold!*,
oil on canvas, 10" × 10" | 25.4 × 25.4 cm

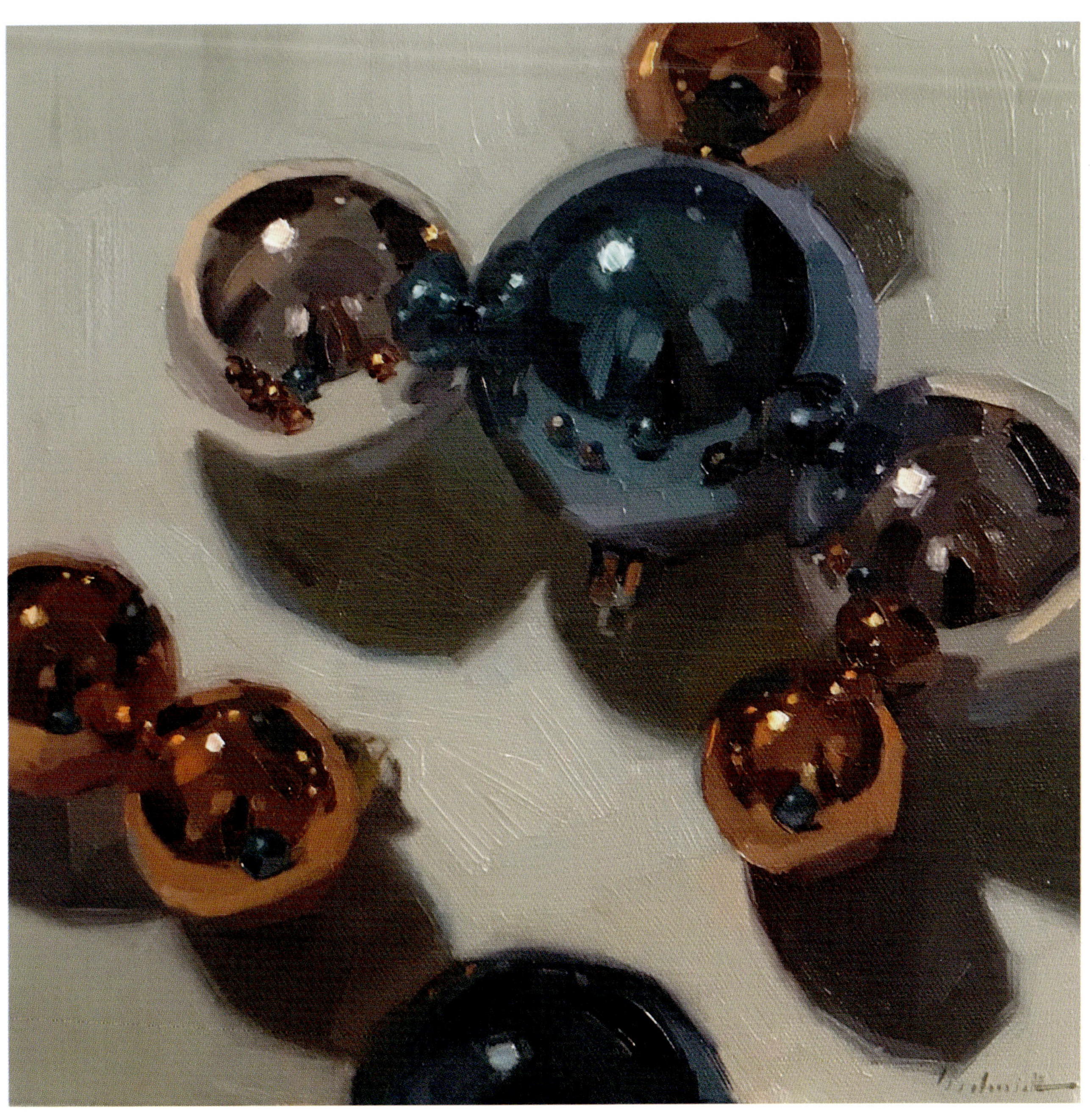

Sarah Sedwick, *Frosty Kisses*,
oil on canvas, 10" × 10" | 25.4 × 25.4 cm

BORROWING INSPIRATION

When I began my daily painting practice back in 2008, I looked at what the painters I loved were doing, and if it looked like fun, I tried it. Subjects that I thought would be terribly difficult turned out to be easy (onions, for example), and things I thought would be simple were agonizing (like tomatoes!). In the years since, I've made peace with the dreaded tomato, but my mind-set was changed by the experience. "Easy" and "hard" are just ideas. There's no way to know how fun and rewarding a subject can be until you give it a try!

As innovative as contemporary still life is, there's not much new under the sun. Artists have been "borrowing" from each other for centuries, putting their own spin on time-honored themes. When I'm lacking inspiration, I still look to the art I love as a springboard, whether it's for a subject to try or a color combination. Adopting the color scheme of a favorite painting is a wonderful way to choose your still life elements, no matter what the subject of the original painting is. And if you truly admire an artist's style, there's no better way to study it than to actually make a master copy of their work.

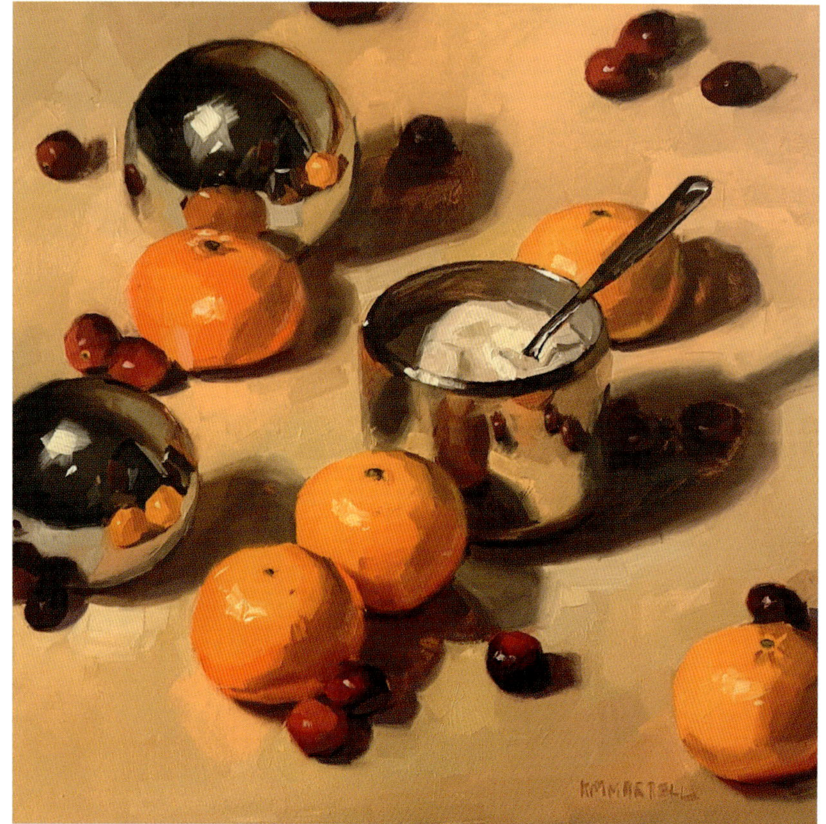

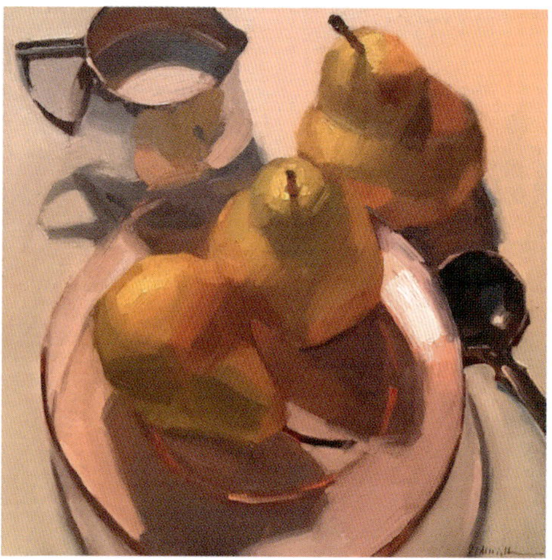

◀ **Kayla Martell, *It's Sugar, Baby*, oil on canvas, 12" × 12" | 30.5 × 30.5 cm**

See something in another artist's work that looks like fun? Give it a try! Artist Kayla Martell was inspired by my silver creamer collection (above) to create her own stunning metallic still life.

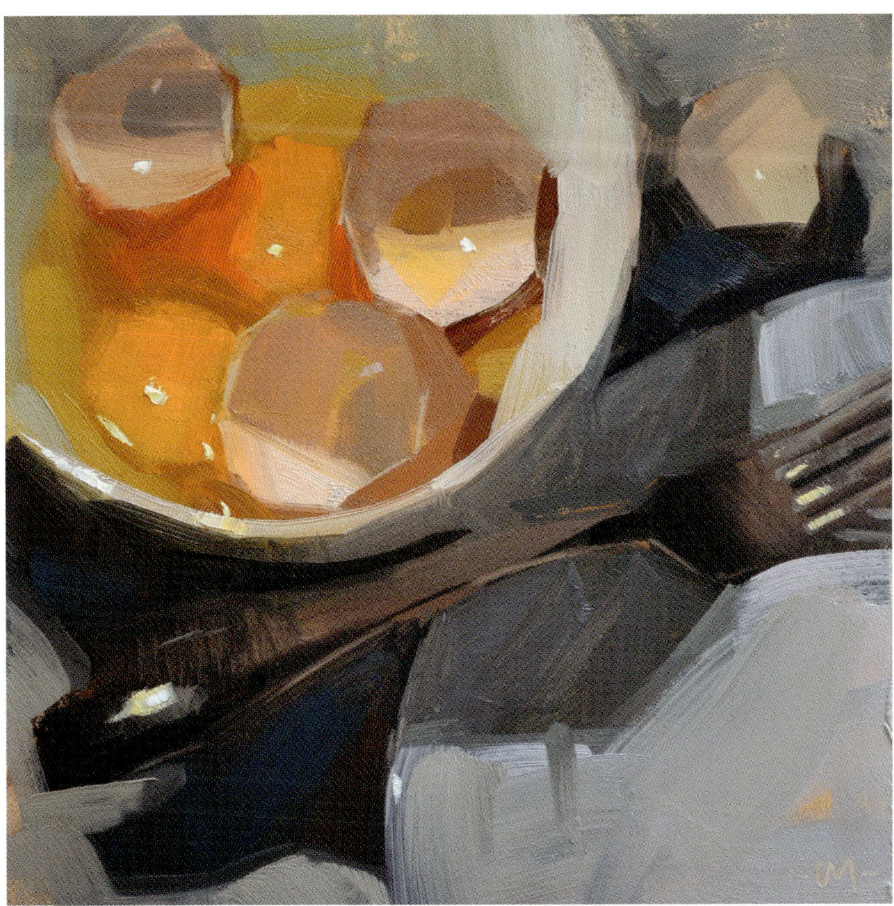

Carol Marine, *Eggtastic*,
oil on panel,
6" × 6" | 15.2 × 15.2 cm

Carol Marine has been a huge influence on me from the beginning. Her loose, exuberant brushwork is an inspiration, and her fun and funky subject matter is a fantastic example of "out of the box" thinking!

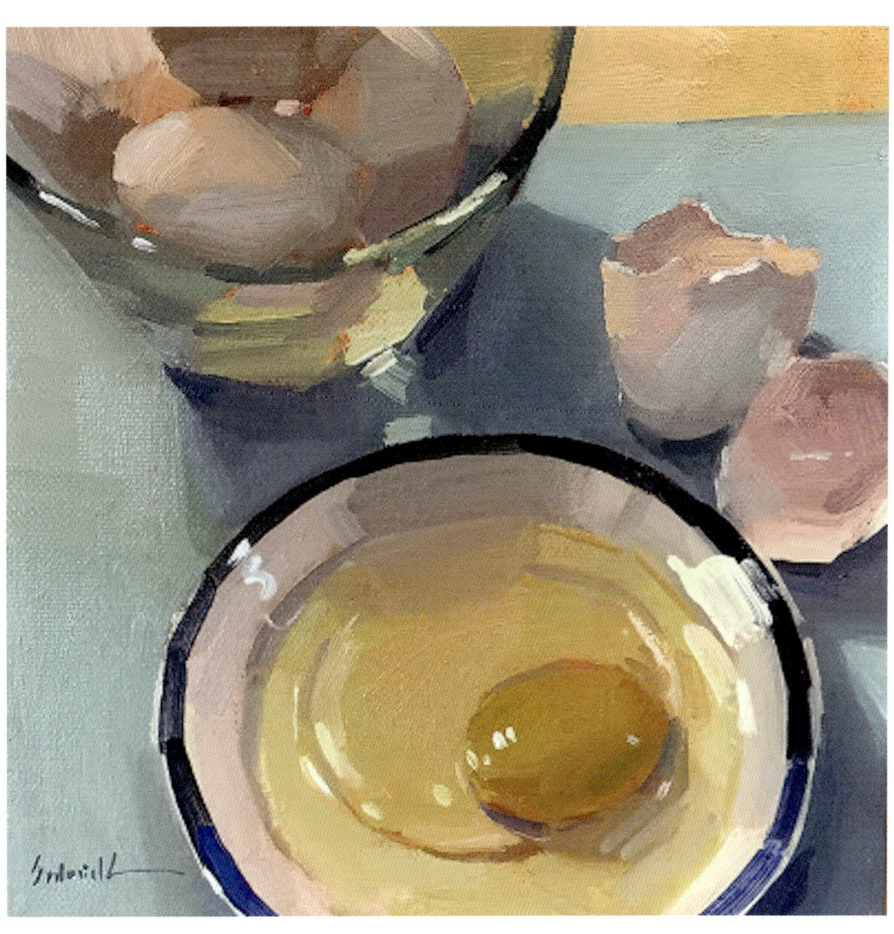

Sarah Sedwick, *Ochre Yolk*,
oil on canvas,
8" × 8" | 20.3 × 20.3 cm

EXERCISE:
EXPERIMENTING WITH STILL LIFE SETUP AND LIGHTING

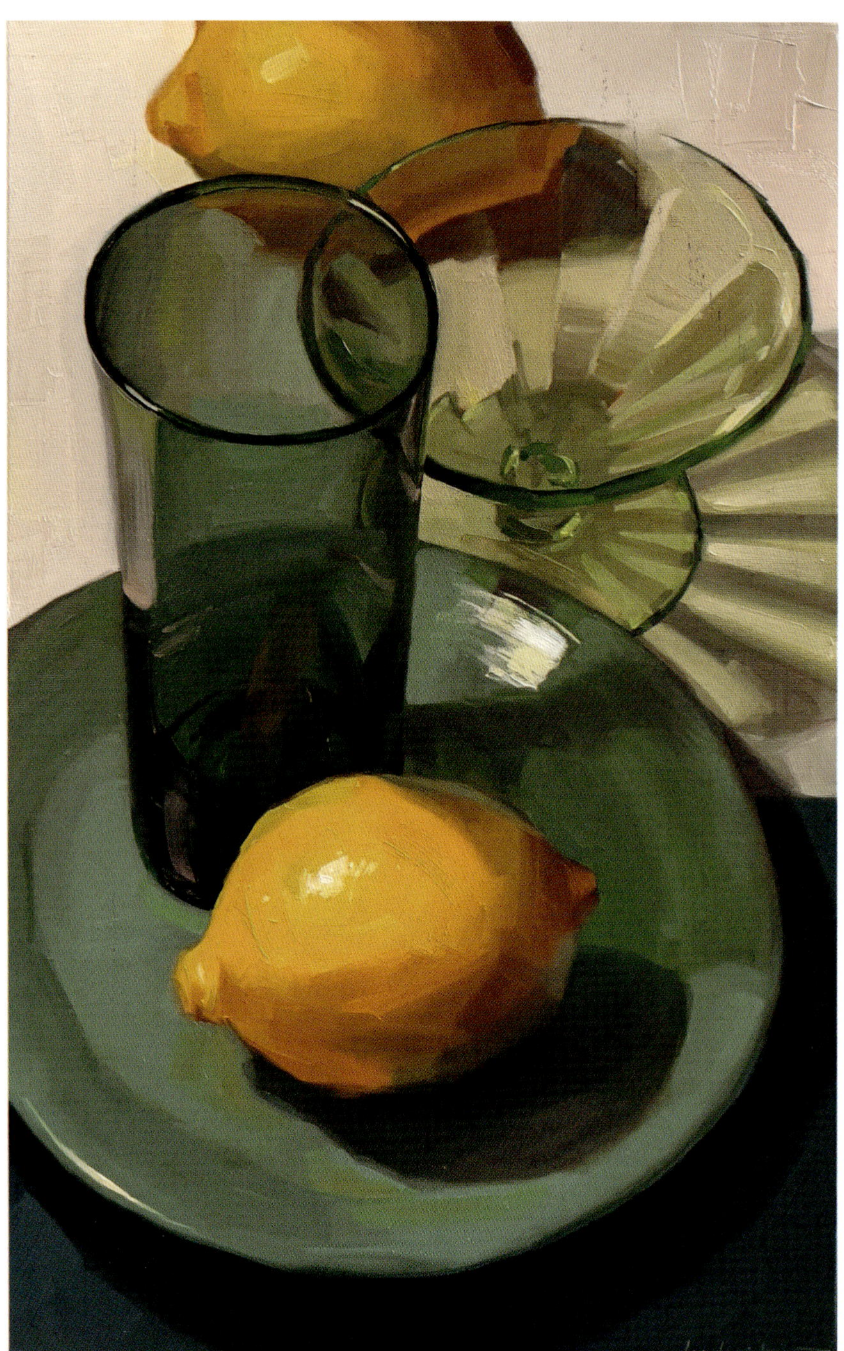

GOAL: Create a simple still life using a set of three to five objects and one or two background colors—paper or fabric. Think about *repetition with variety* in the colors, textures, sizes, and heights of the elements you choose.

Next, experiment with lighting—from the left, from the right, or from behind to cast long shadows forward—or raise and lower the light source to observe the effect. Squint to see the "big dark shape" you're creating and how it's affected by changing the light source.

Keep your favorite arrangement—or snap a series of photos—to bring with you into the next section!

Sarah Sedwick, *Lemons and Green Glass*, oil on canvas, 15" × 24" | 38 × 61 cm

Repetition with variety! Here, I have green in both glasses, but one is yellow-green and the other is a bluer green. Blues also repeat, with variety, in the background paper and the plate. Lemons repeat on and off the plate. Cut a lemon up for even more variety.

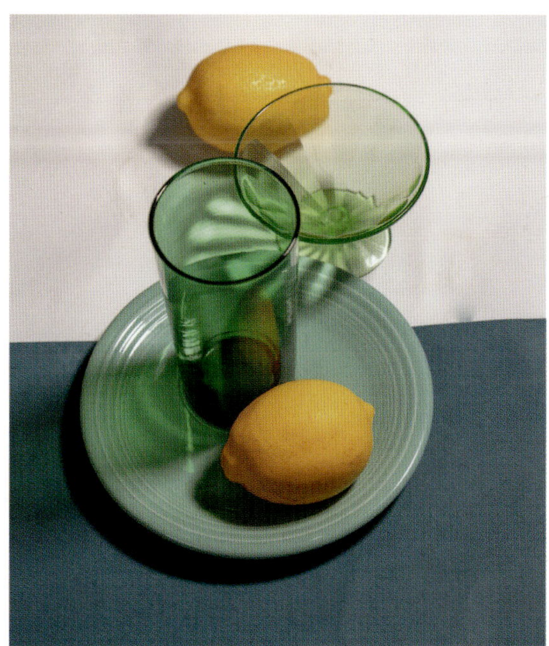

In this photo, my still life is lit from the right. I love the effect of the striped shadow seen through the dark green glass and the light shapes created on the plate by the lemon's cast shadow.

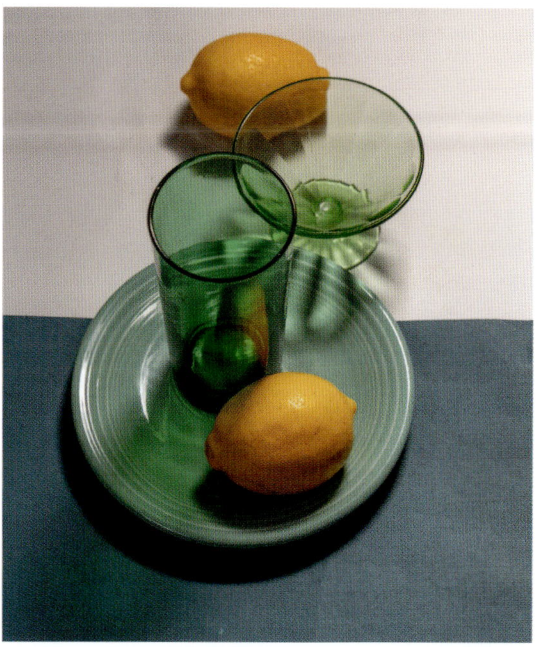

Backlighting casts long, dramatic shadows toward the viewer. In this photo, I am drawn to the green shadow being cast over the lemon on the plate.

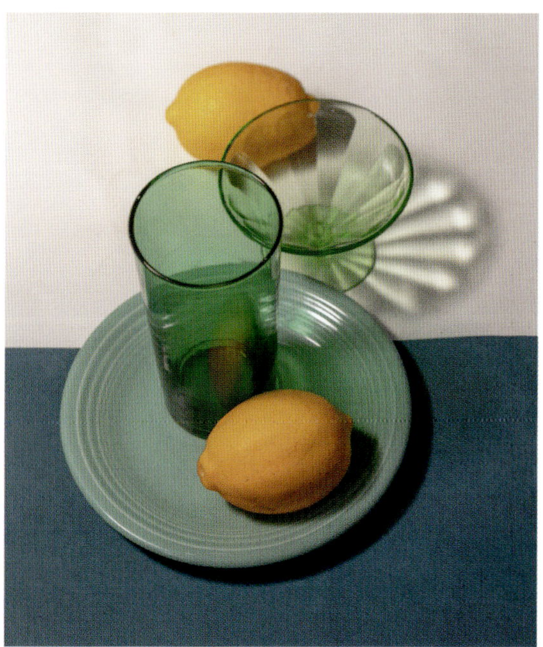

Here, lighting from the left creates a beautiful highlight on the plate and a radiating shadow on the right. I chose this lighting situation for my painting (see previous page), cropping in more tightly on the scene.

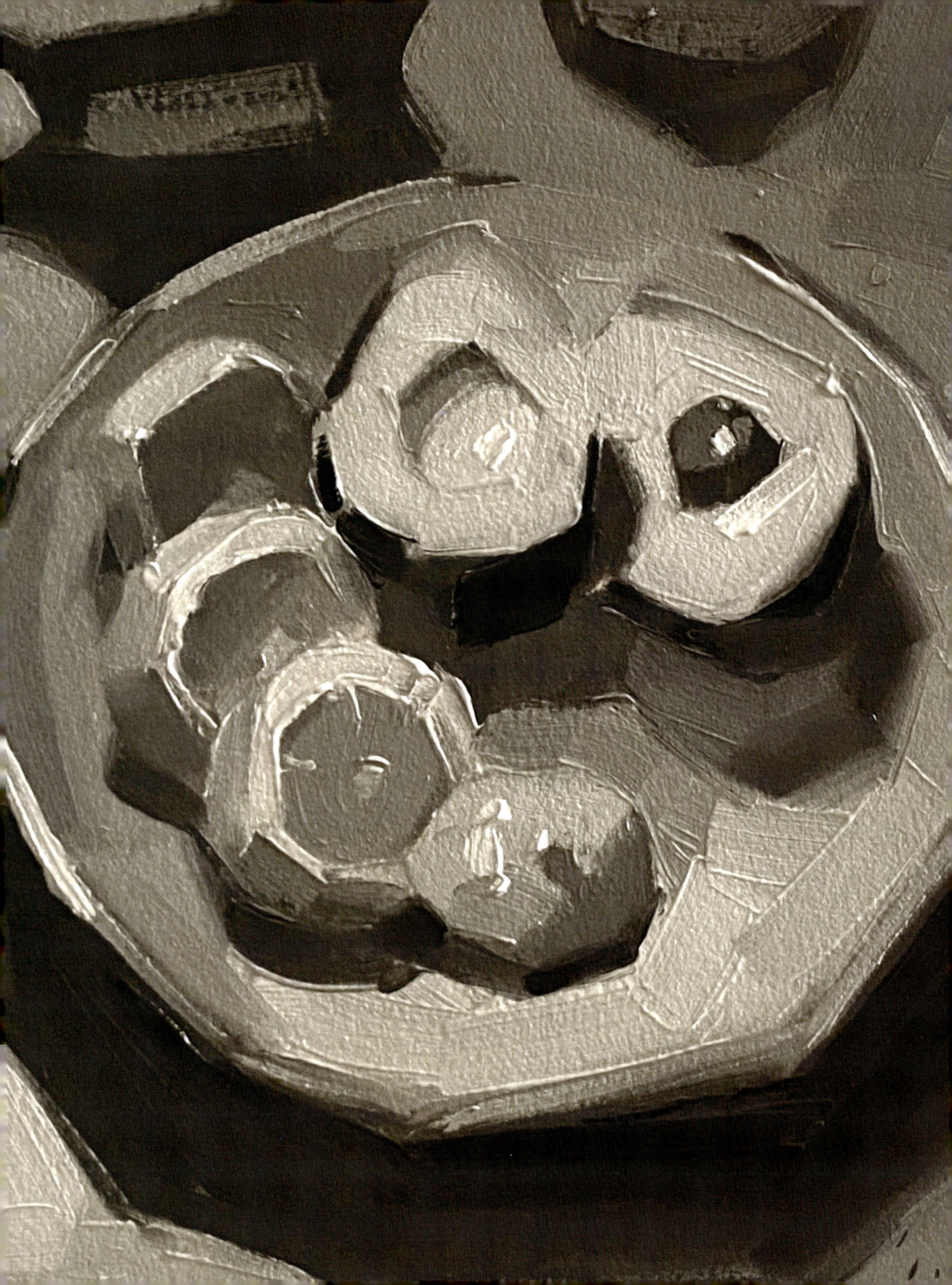

3

PLANNING YOUR DYNAMIC STILL LIFE: COMPOSITION AND VALUE STUDIES

Imagine walking into a gallery and seeing a painting on the wall thirty feet away. Before you can even tell what the subject is, you know you want to take a closer look, but why? The basic building blocks of the painting—the value structure, and the composition it creates—are appealing to your eye. The artist has achieved their goal: to create an arresting image—to grab your attention, and keep it as long as possible.

At its most basic, composition is the design and layout of a painting—the placement of objects within the picture plane and any cropping that occurs at the edges. These things create shapes in the negative space, which can be just as interesting and beautiful as the subjects of the painting. And all of this serves to lure the viewer in, capturing them with a strong focal point, and moving their eye around the painting in a pleasing way, rewarding them for long looking.

◀ Sarah Sedwick, *Lemony Avocado* study (detail), oil on Arches Oil Paper, 8" × 8" | 20.3 × 20.3 cm

PREPARATION PAYS OFF

Too often, we shortchange ourselves on the planning stages of a piece because we are excited to dive in and get painting! However, spending just a few minutes looking and thinking before picking up a brush usually results in a more successful outcome—in a piece that says what you intended—and a higher number of successful paintings overall.

How you design your painting is directly related to what you want the viewer to focus on, experience, and feel. That design is the essence of composition. And it's not just about the viewer! What do YOU feel when you look at your subject? As you examine your still life, visualizing it as a painting, which element is attracting you most strongly? It could be an interesting shadow shape, a brilliant pop of color, the overlap of two objects that creates a lost edge, a beautiful highlight...

Often what you are most drawn to will become your focal point, as you lavish more care and attention on it than the other elements in the piece. So, looking for that spark of attraction is a big part of creating any preliminary study for a painting, and knowing a few basic compositional dos and don'ts can really help you share that vision with your viewer.

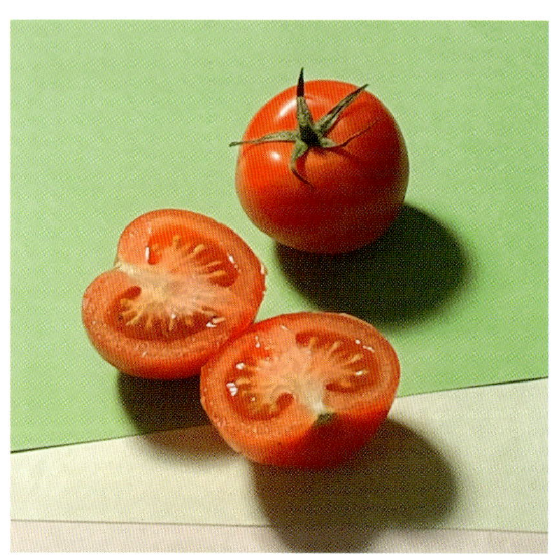

This still life setup has repetition, variety, and a fun complementary color scheme. But what shape canvas will capture it best?

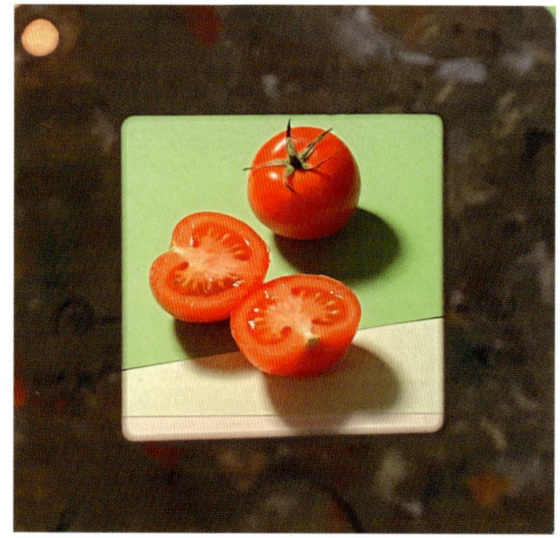

Using a viewfinder helps visualize the setup as a painting. "Zoom" in and out to experiment with cropping, and try looking at the still life in both a square and a rectangular frame.

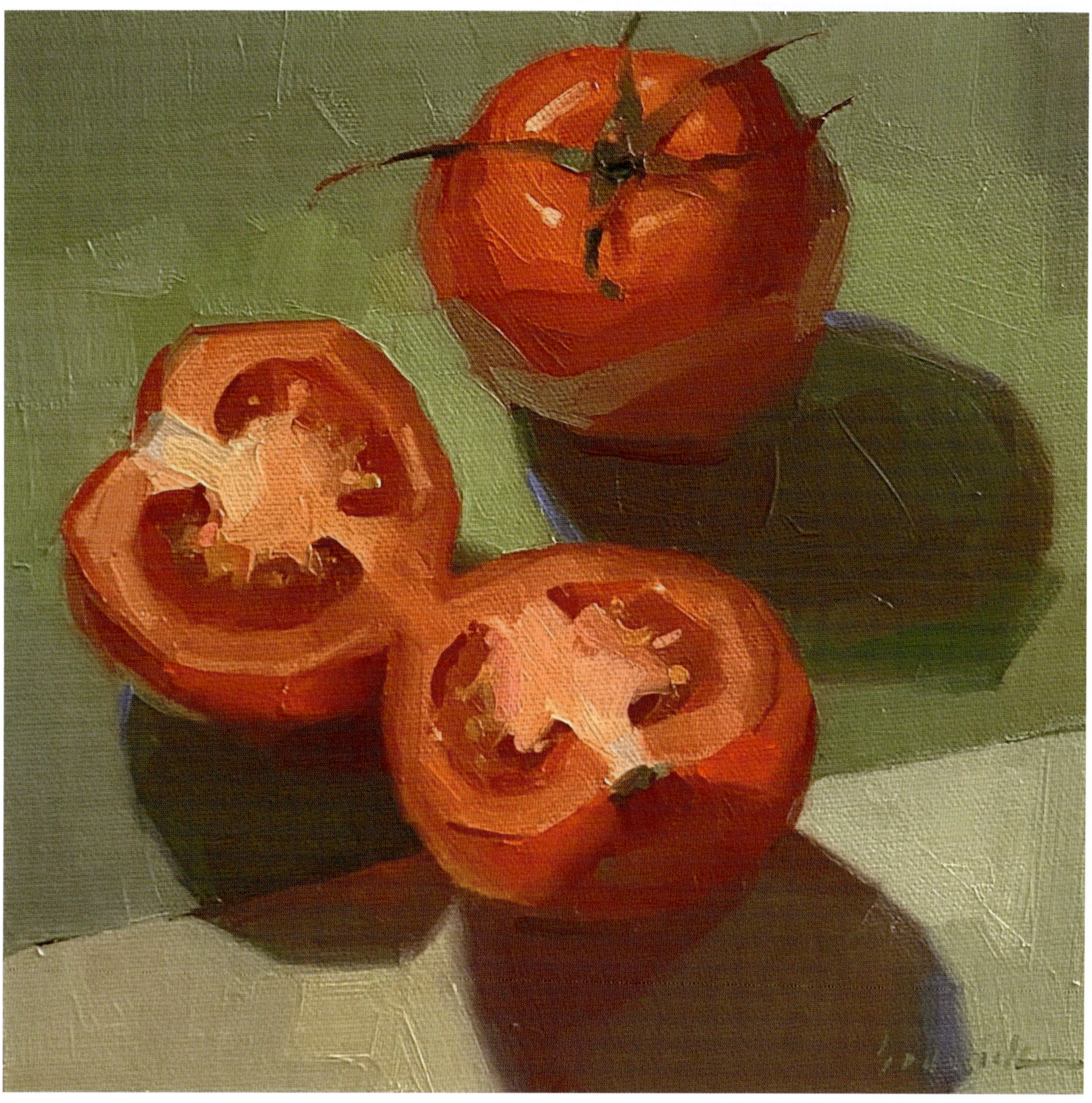

Sarah Sedwick, *Tomato in Two*, oil on canvas, 8" × 8" | 20.3 × 20.3 cm

The viewfinder helped place the focal point and determine the cropping that creates interesting and varied shapes in the negative space.

COMPOSITION: WHAT IS IT AND WHY DOES IT MATTER?

Composition is the "where," once you've figured out the "what" of a still life setup. Where does that lemon live on the canvas? Is anything cut off—or cropped—at an edge of the picture plane? Will you choose a square or horizontal or vertical format? Approaching a still life setup with a format already in mind (e.g., "I'm going to set up the perfect still life for my square canvas!") can make the setting-up process more challenging—trust me. It is far easier to set up a still life that "clicks," and then decide whether it belongs in a square, horizontal, or vertical frame than to go the opposite way.

Even if a setup looks like it naturally belongs on a certain shape of canvas, experimenting with other formats by looking through a viewfinder and making small sketches can be surprising—in a good way! Having something concrete to look at, especially a sketch made by your own hand, makes compositional choices easier and more intuitive. Chances are, even if two artists work from the same still life *and* vantage point, they will come up with very different paintings. Their choice of how to frame the scene determines which objects will be the "star players" and which will become supporting characters.

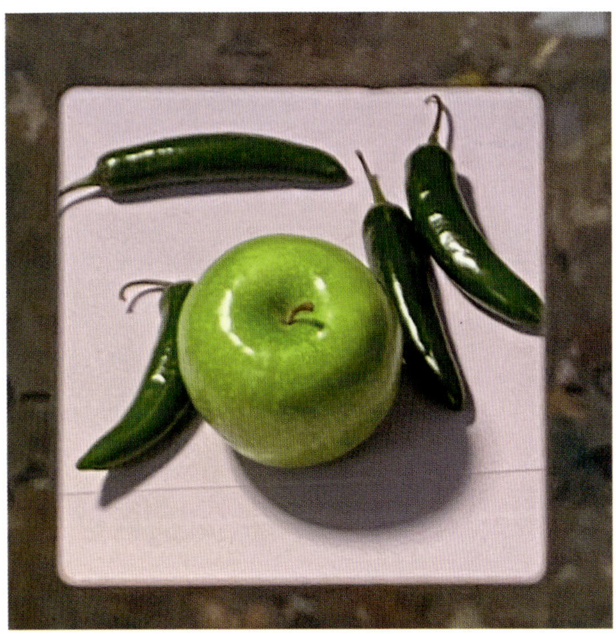

A viewfinder helps us visualize the still life as a painting and experiment with cropping to create a variety of interesting shapes in the negative space.

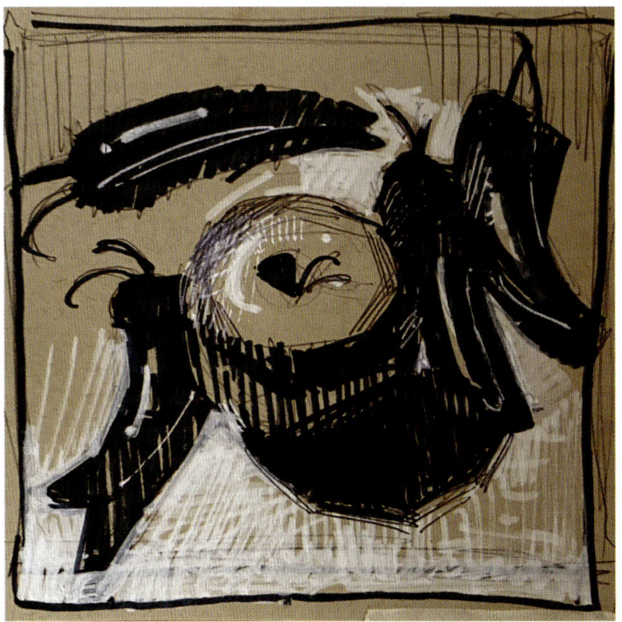

Even a quick, simple sketch can be a powerful decision-making tool. For visual thinkers (which most artists are!), a sketch is more helpful than a photo when thinking about composition.

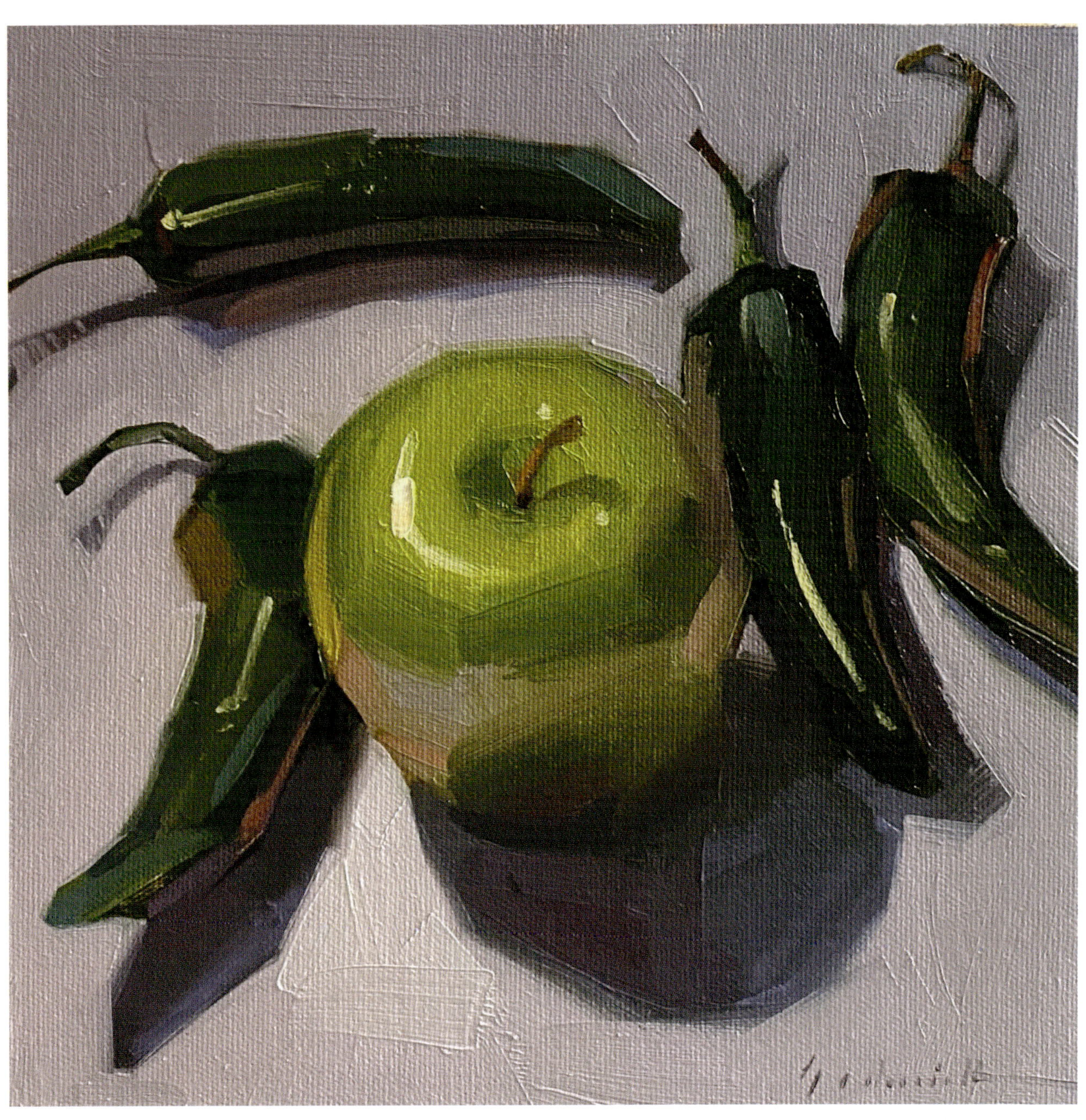

Sarah Sedwick, *Spicy Granny*,
oil on canvas, 8" × 8" | 20.3 × 20.3 cm

USING A VIEWFINDER

Once we've got a still life setup that "clicks" with repetition, variety, and a pleasing combination of colors and textures, it's time to create a composition. The first step is a much overlooked part of the painting process: visualizing. And not just with our eyes. A viewfinder frames the scene, helping us see the still life setup as a finished painting. The viewfinder also shows us how to create interesting shapes in the negative space with cropping. Cropping may sound like a bad thing–chopping that poor object off halfway into the painting–but it is actually the key to dynamic composition. Letting something partially exit the canvas extends the action beyond the frame and can emphasize the overall feeling of movement through the piece.

Holding the viewfinder up to your face with one eye closed, the farther you extend your arm, the closer in you'll crop the scene, like zooming in with a camera lens. The closer the viewfinder is to your eye, the more of the scene you'll see, meaning less cropping and more space around the objects.

Once the scene through your viewfinder starts looking like a painting to you, check in with your "sweet spots" using the rule of thirds (see page 72). Is anything happening in those spots? They are prime locations for your focal point, so if something in one of them is attracting your interest, that's a great sign! This reaction is intuitive, so don't overthink it. As long as you've got something going on in one of your sweet spots, you're in good shape.

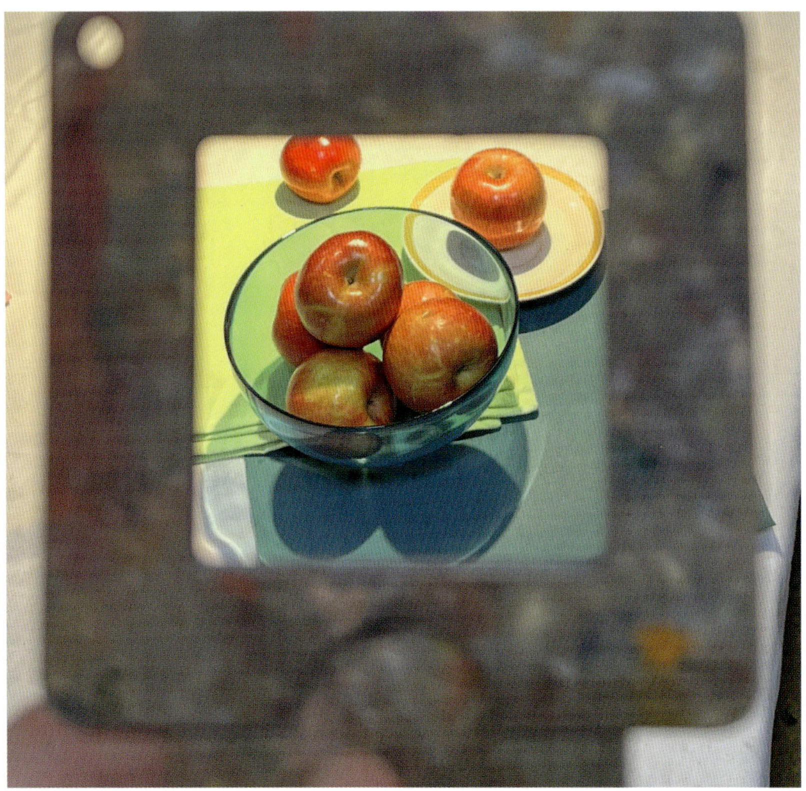

The shiny top apple in the bowl and the beautiful green color around it created by the yellow paper seen through the bowl were definitely what attracted me to this still life setup.

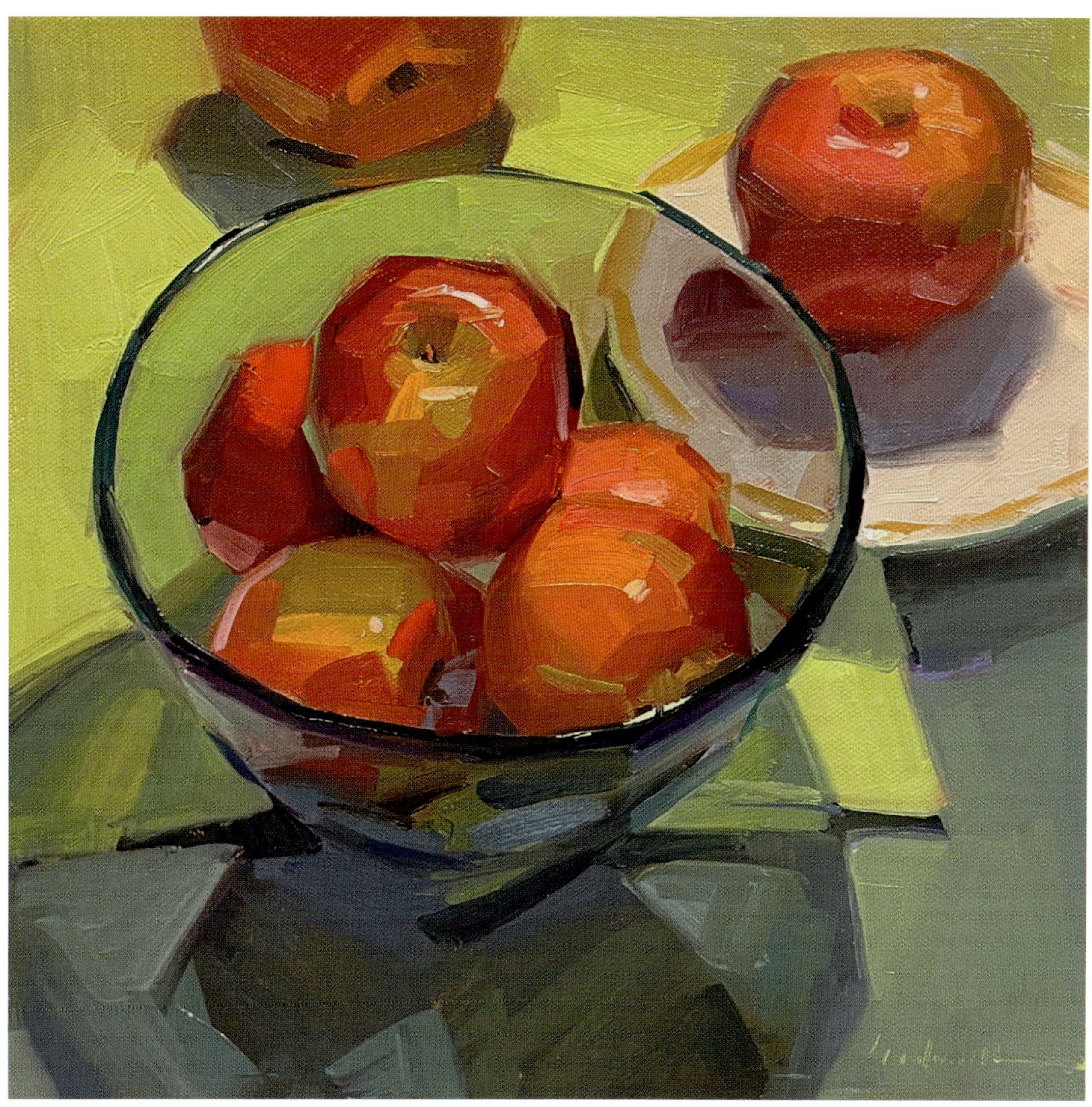

Sarah Sedwick, *Apples in Teal Glass*,
oil on canvas, 10" × 10" | 25.4 × 25.4 cm

Deciding which elements of the still life were most strongly attracting me helped me decide how to compose this painting and where to spend the most time and attention to detail, creating a focal point between the top apple in the bowl and the green glass around it.

THE RULE OF THIRDS

A good way to choose a location for your focal point is to use the "rule of thirds." If you divide the canvas into thirds horizontally and vertically, the four intersecting points of those lines are your "sweet spots." These are prime locations for a focal point—well within the composition and great starting points from which to move around the rest of your painting. If you consider nothing else about composition while looking through your viewfinder—not cropping, not shapes in the negative space—check in with your sweet spots. Ask yourself, "What's happening in my sweet spots? Is *anything* happening in my sweet spots?" If the answer is yes, and one of those things is the thing that's attracting you most strongly to your setup—better yet, if it's also your area of highest *contrast*—you're in great shape.

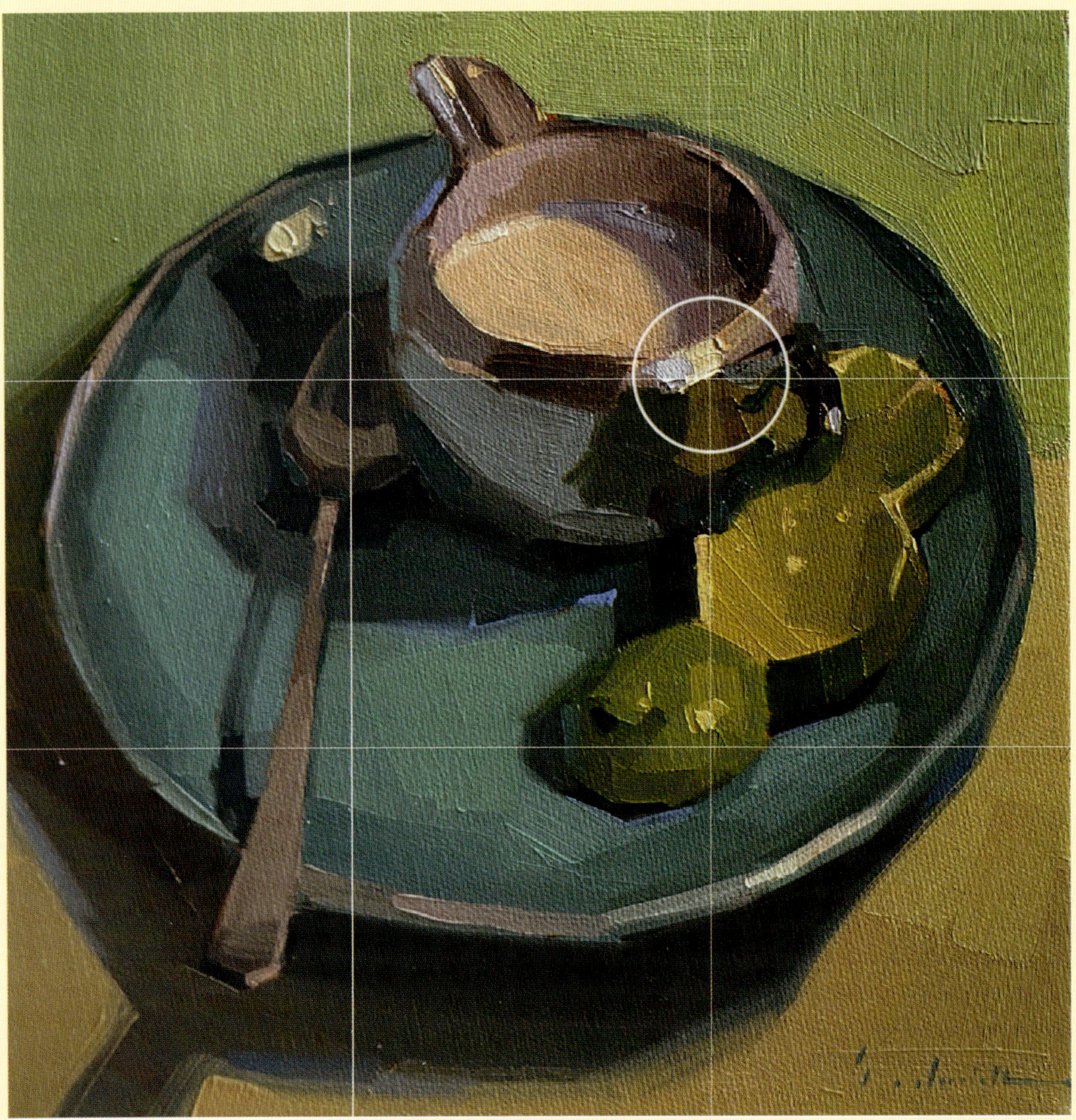

Sarah Sedwick, *Silver and Lime*, oil on canvas, 8" × 8" | 20.3 × 20.3 cm

A rule-of-thirds grid shows that my intended focal point—that gorgeous highlight on the silver creamer—is safely placed in a "sweet spot."

CONTRAST: THE KEY TO CREATING A FOCAL POINT

The focal point is the place that you want the viewer's eye to land first, and return to as they move their eyes around your painting. Just because an object is your "star player," or the subject of the painting, doesn't mean it will be your focal point by default. Our eyes are drawn to strong contrast, so the area of highest contrast will likely become your focal point automatically.

There are several types of contrast we can use to create or reinforce a focal point. The biggest is value contrast—the darkest dark in a piece next to something very light, or vice versa. Color contrast—particularly complementary colors—can also strongly attract the viewer's eye. And size—both the size of shapes or objects and the size of the marks you make—is another type of contrast that creates a focal point. A concentration of small shapes or marks creates a focal point in a piece full of broad strokes and larger objects.

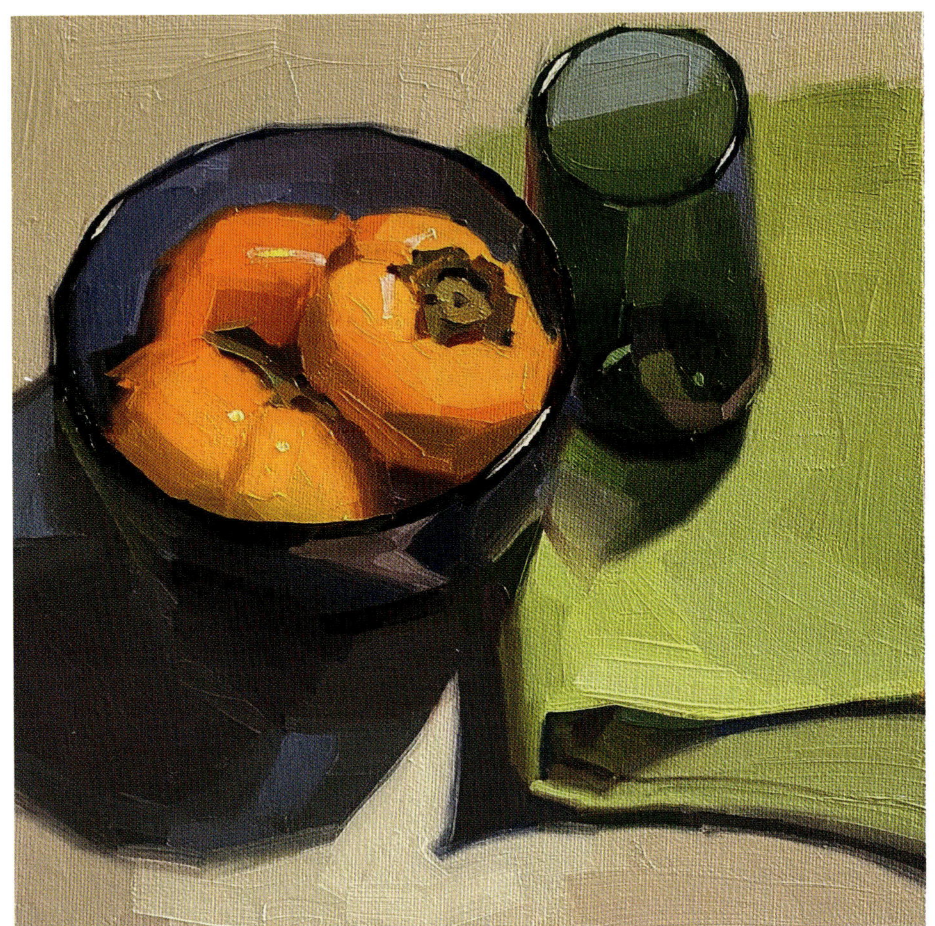

Sarah Sedwick, *Paintable Persimmons*, oil on canvas, 9" × 9" | 22.9 × 22.9 cm

Both the strong blue-orange complementary color contrast between the persimmons and the bowl and the placement of the smallest shapes and details in their stems make the persimmons the focal point of this piece.

THUMBNAIL SKETCHES

Once you've visualized your painting, framing it in the viewfinder, it's time to lock it down, both on paper and in your mind, with sketches. The easiest way to do this is to find *landmarks*—the spots around the edge of the frame where objects enter and leave. These will be anchors for your next step: thumbnail sketches.

A thumbnail sketch is a little study focused on the general elements of a composition—placement of the star player and supporting characters, shapes in the negative space, and simple value structure. It's not drawing practice! Leave rendering for later, and focus on three or four values, locating lightest light and darkest dark. Draw a rule-of-thirds grid over your sketch before you begin or after you finish. There are lots of ways to make thumbnail sketches, so-called because they are often very tiny, but don't need to be, by any means. Graphite, ballpoint pen, Sharpie, pens, markers, charcoal—your preferred sketching medium, or a combination of two or three, will work just fine!

Many artists prefer to use the camera for this—maybe even taking several pictures and cropping them in different ways. This is a great use of the camera as a studio tool. It can

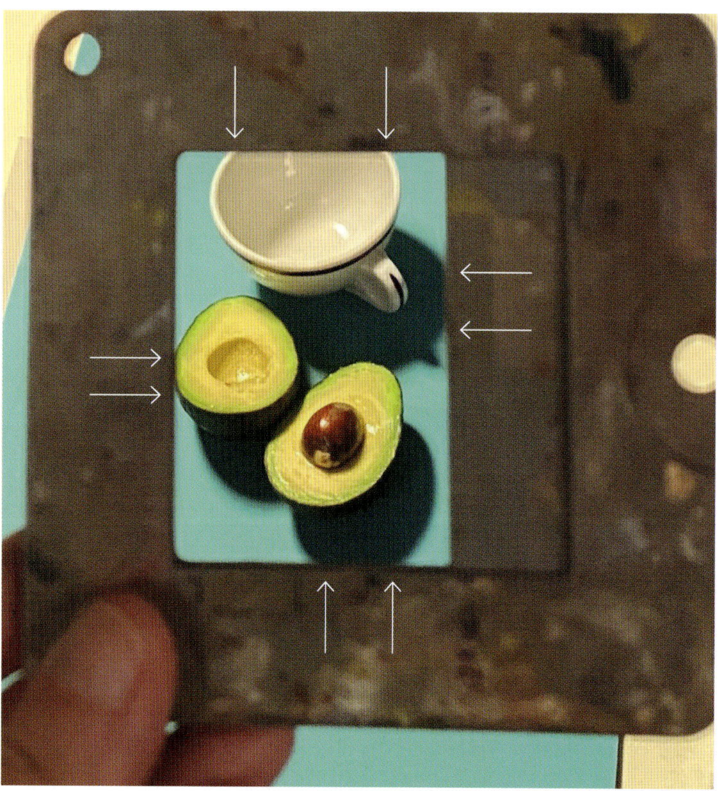

"Landmarks," the spots around the edge of the frame where objects enter and leave, are great places to start a thumbnail sketch.

backfire, however, if the goal is to practice working from life because too often, the photo becomes a crutch that is difficult to let go of moving into the "painting" stages of a painting. I get asked a *lot* about the camera conundrum–why working from life is better than working from photos. The best, shortest answer is that the camera simply does not give us the information we need to work in a painterly way.

Keep in mind that even the best camera lens distorts the scene–it draws lines where none exist. It focuses either in the light or in the shadows, skewing the values relationships, and photo reference is notoriously untrustworthy when it comes to color. It is also difficult to match our eye's natural vantage point when taking a photo, so when switching from framing a still life with a camera lens to painting it from direct observation, some correction will need to occur.

I find that creating a sketch, taking a photo of my *sketch*, and then experimenting with cropping that in several different ways is much more effective than cropping a photo of the still life. It also gives me just a little bit of drawing practice, visually getting to know my subject and building muscle memory before my brush hits the canvas. But the best, most thorough way to use thumbnail sketches is to make three of them: a square, a horizontal rectangle, and a vertical rectangle.

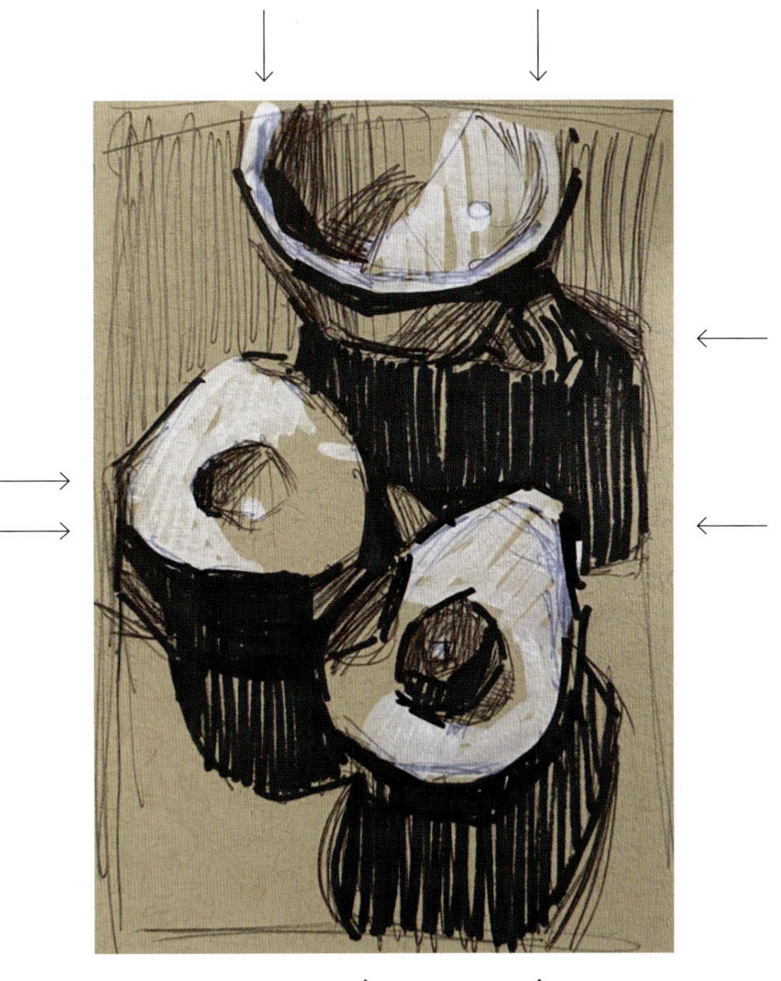

In evaluating potential compositions, the thumbnail sketch is a decision-making tool. As visual thinkers, we painters often have an easier time accessing our intuitive compositional sensibility when we are looking at the work of our own hand rather than a set of digital images. Plus, the added familiarity we gain with our subject through sketching can only help us as we transition to the canvas. That said, the thumbnail sketch is not *really* drawing practice (even though I just said it was). The goal is to figure out big value shapes and general placement of objects and their interactions with the picture plane (cropping), rather than rendering the form of the objects themselves.

We don't need to put a lot of pressure on ourselves at this stage. The goal is to discover a design that feels good to us, today. And the ultimate goal is to have an enjoyable and successful painting experience. Planning really does pay off!

COMPOSITION DOS AND DON'TS

Do

- Check in with your "sweet spots." Is anything happening there?
- Look for your area of strongest value contrast. Where is it?
- Experiment with cropping. "Zoom" in and out with your viewfinder.
- Squint and look for the "big dark shape."

Don't

- Let any objects or lines directly intersect a corner. This leads the viewer's eye straight out of your painting.
- Create a tangent or "kiss" by letting two objects touch at one tiny tension point.
- Space everything too evenly. Variety is the key to dynamic compositions.
- Set up a sea of empty negative space. Make the star players big on the canvas so you can have more fun painting them!

Sarah Sedwick, *Split Avocado*, oil on canvas, 5" × 7" | 12.7 × 17.8 cm

The cropping in this piece creates five distinct shapes in the negative space—all of different sizes. To ensure that I've got variety in my negative shapes, I imagine filling each one up with sand. Do I need a different amount for each one?

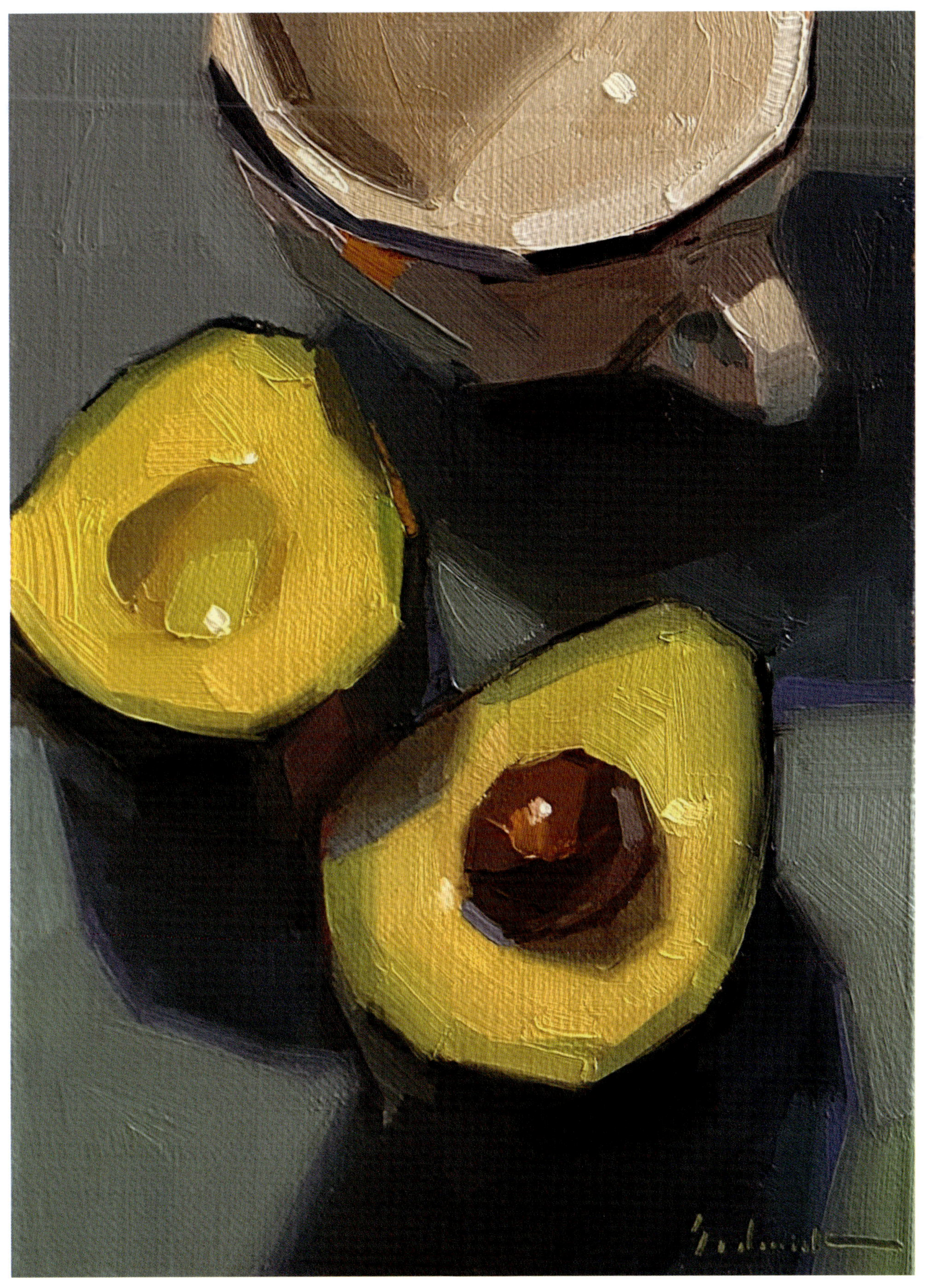

EXERCISE:
ONE STILL LIFE, THREE FORMATS: CREATING THUMBNAIL SKETCHES

GOAL: Using the still life you set up in the Exercise on page 62, look through your viewfinder and visualize your setup as a painting. If you like, try taking a photo and cropping it several different ways.

Next, create three thumbnail sketches. Begin with the frame—sketch out a square and two rectangles, one vertical and one horizontal. They can be any size you like, but keep them small enough that you can complete them in about ten minutes.

Working on white paper, first use a pencil to place or block in your objects, establishing the general layout before moving on to midtones in pencil, followed by black Sharpie for the darks.

The place to start is your landmarks. Look through the viewfinder and locate one or two. Mark them on the outline you've just drawn for your sketch. Once you establish a few of these, begin blocking in your sketch, putting the viewfinder down—or putting your photo away—and working from direct observation.

Drawing a rule-of-thirds grid over your sketches, check in with your "sweet spots." What is happening there?

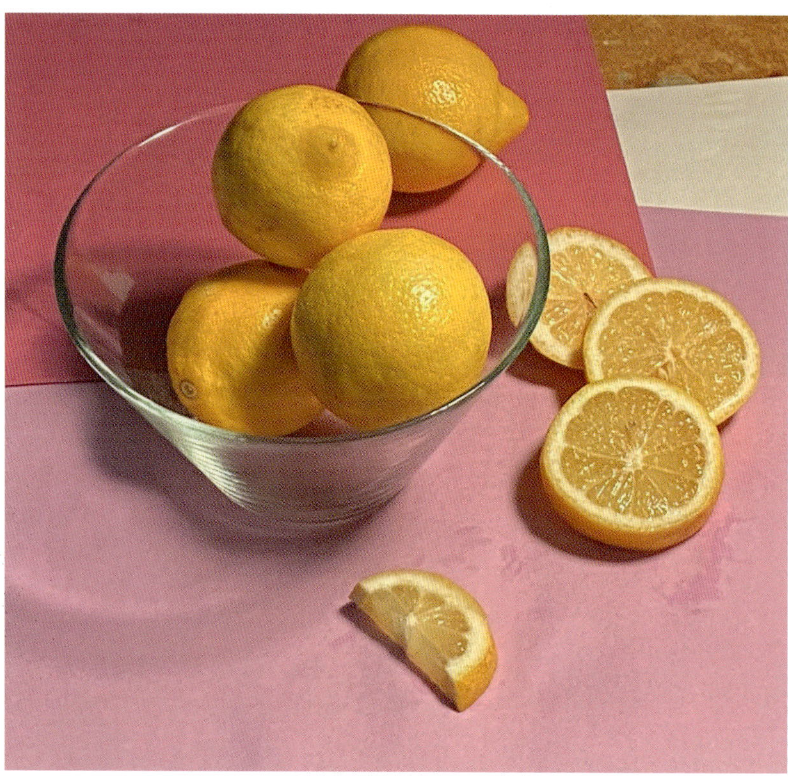

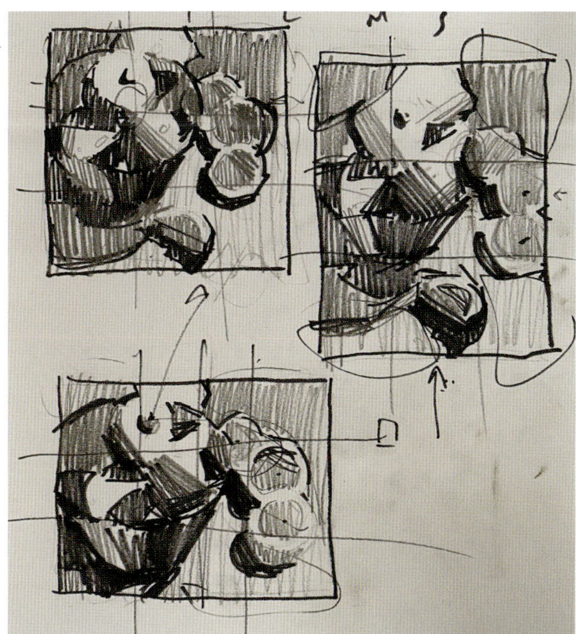

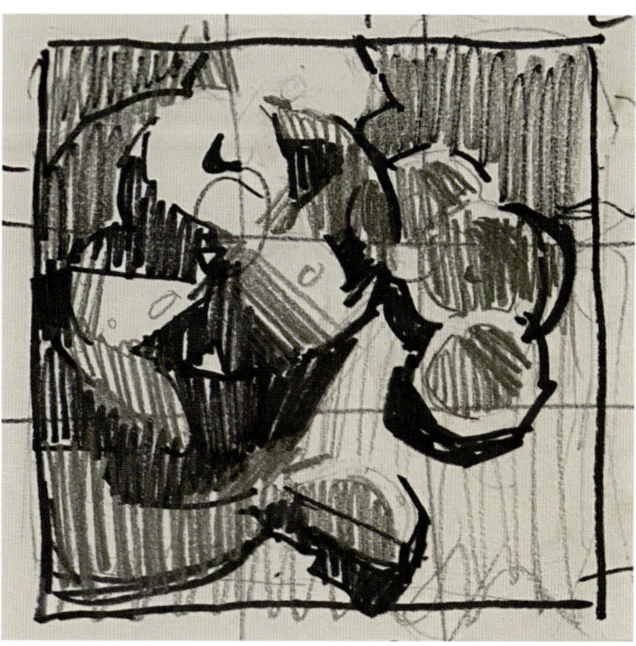

Creating three compositional options with my thumbnail sketches helped me decide on the square format for my final painting. You can see my rule-of-thirds gridlines overlaying the sketch, checking in with my "sweet spots."

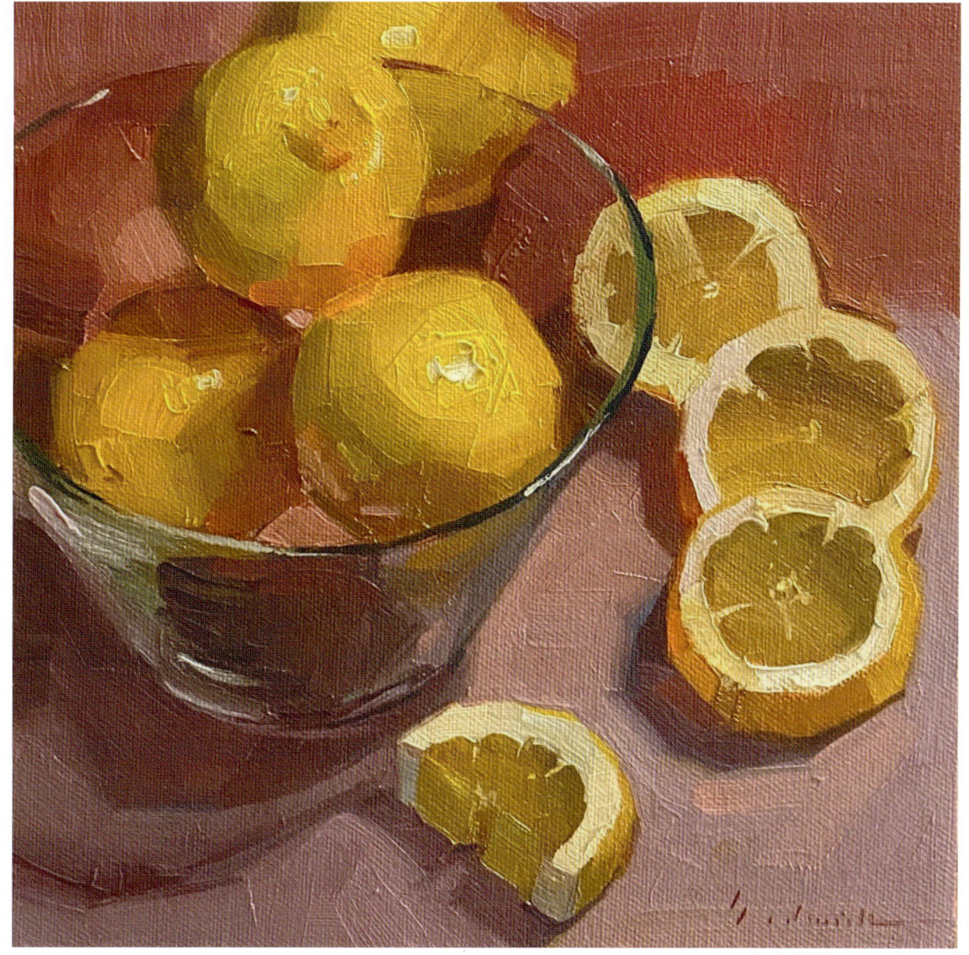

Sarah Sedwick,
Hot Pink Lemons,
oil on canvas,
10" × 10" | 25.4 × 25.4 cm

USING TONED PAPER

Another way I love to sketch is on toned paper—tan or gray. I begin with pencil or ballpoint pen (drawing without an eraser is oddly freeing—try it!), then add my darkest darks in Sharpie and my lights with a white marker, like a Faber-Castell Pitt pen or Posca pen. My favorite paper for this is Strathmore Mixed Media Toned Tan; it's nice and thick, so the Sharpie doesn't bleed through.

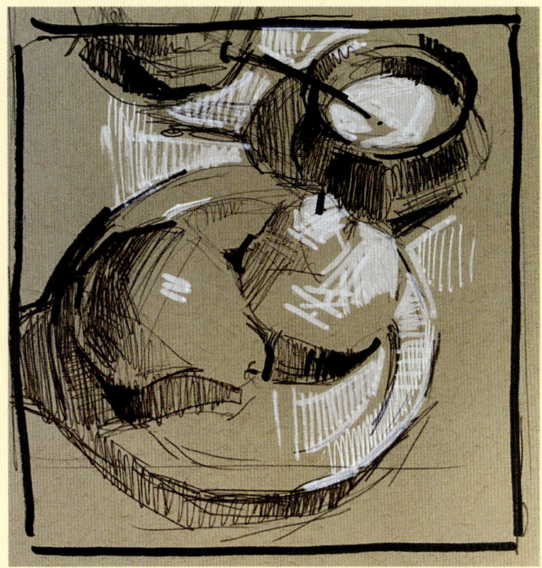

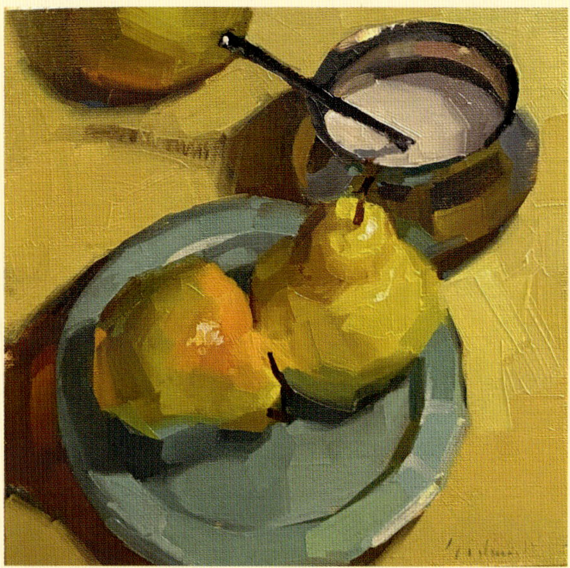

Sarah Sedwick, *Sugar Pears*, oil on canvas, 8" × 8" | 20.3 × 20.3 cm

FORMAT FIRST, THEN SIZE AND SCALE

Now that you've determined what shape your painting will be—square, horizontal, or vertical rectangle—what size will you paint it? Any composition you create using a thumbnail can be painted tiny or huge—the only difference will be how much larger or smaller than life-size your subject will be. (And how much paint you will need to mix!)

Scale has a big impact; it's equally impressive to see an artist take a huge jumble of objects and depict them flawlessly on a tiny canvas as it is to see one small object blown up to ten times life-size.

We all have our comfort zone when it comes to canvas size. Don't assume that a smaller painting will be either easier or faster to accomplish than a larger one of the same subject. There doesn't seem to be much correlation at all between the size and simplicity of a painting and the amount of time it takes. Some paintings happen faster than others, without much rhyme or reason. And

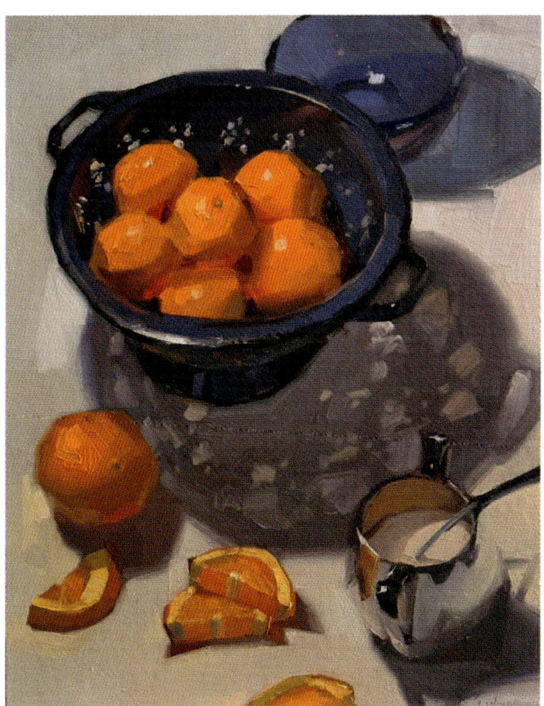

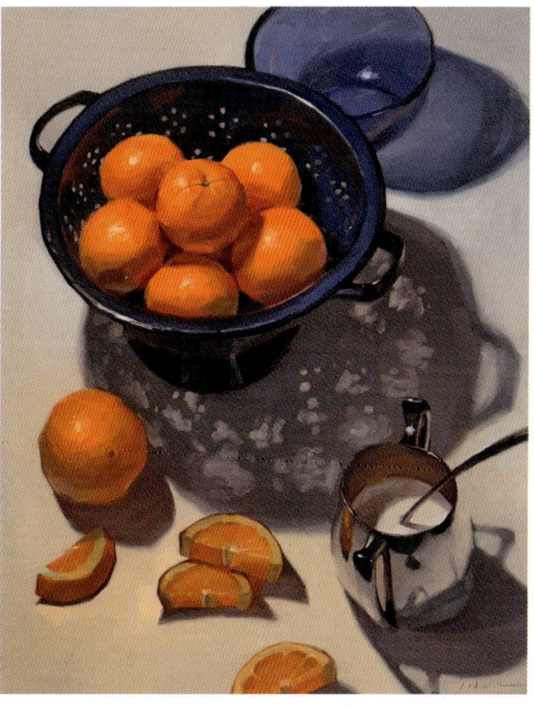

▲ Sarah Sedwick, *Sugar and Shadows* study, oil on canvas, 9" × 12" | 22.9 × 30.5 cm

▶ Sarah Sedwick, *Sugar and Shadows*, oil on canvas, 22" × 28" | 55.9 × 71.1 cm

As part of the painting-planning process for this larger piece, I created a swift color study, staying loose by working quickly and using a large brush relative to the size of my canvas—a #6 flat. I used a #10 flat brush on the larger painting to keep from tightening up.

similarly, there's no way of knowing whether your canvas comfort zone is modest or grand until you try both and see what suits you best.

I have had the goal of creating larger paintings for many years, and I'm making slow progress—sizing up, making myself uncomfortable, and then getting comfortable and sizing up again. Keep in mind: to work in a loose, painterly style, the size of the brush needs to be large *relative to the size of the canvas.* A #4 flat (one of my favorite brush sizes) feels large and satisfying on an 8-inch (20.3 cm) canvas and tight and tiny on a 24-inch (61 cm) canvas.

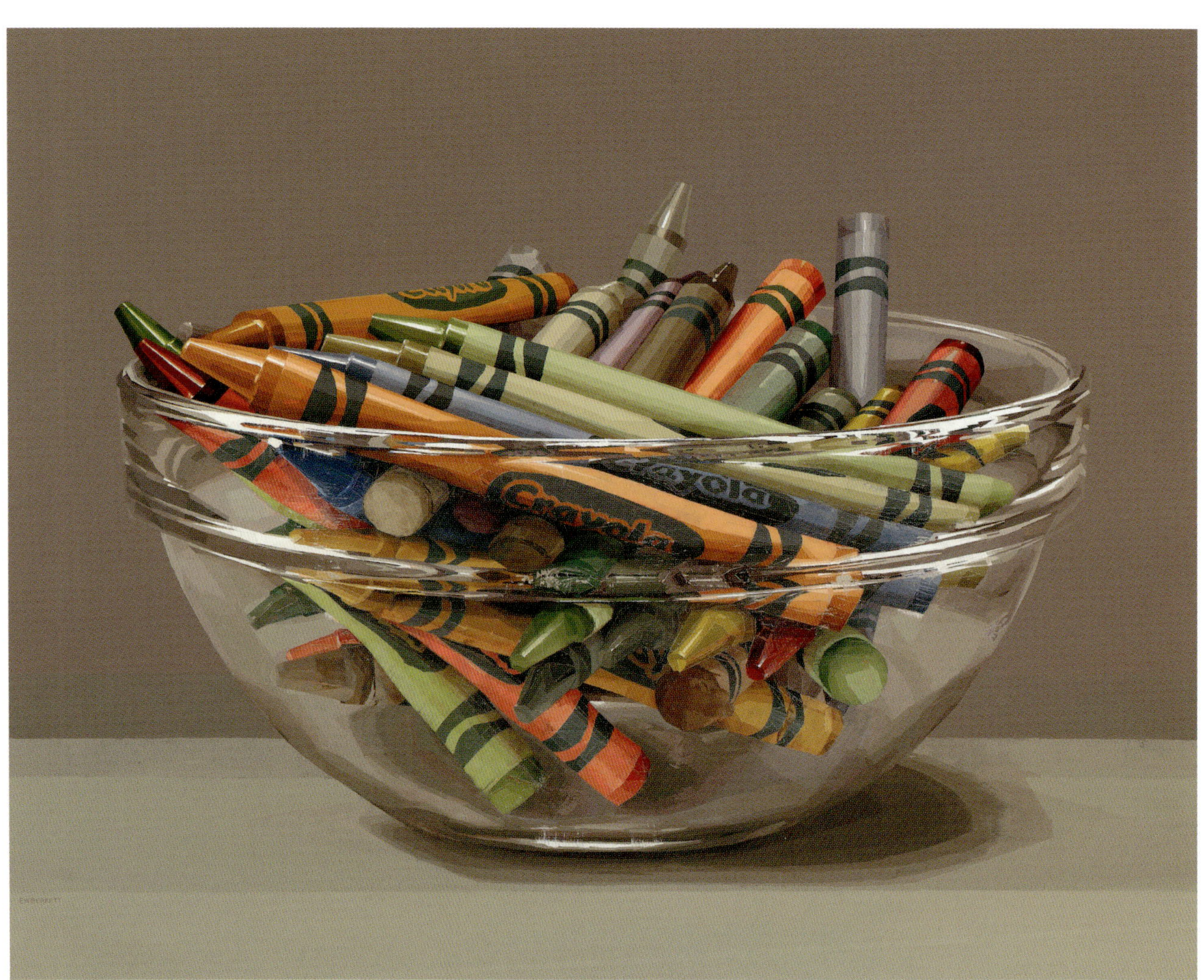

Erin Berrett, *Beginnings*, oil on canvas, 48" × 60" | 121.9 × 152.4 cm

Size matters! In this impressive painting by Erin Berrett, a bowl of crayons is blown up 5 feet (152.4 cm) across. Compressing a large subject onto a tiny canvas can be equally impressive.

VALUE STUDIES: A SOLID FOUNDATION

Still life painting is a decision-making process from start to finish. Which objects and colors to choose? What size and shape of canvas fits them best? Thumbnail sketches take your still life from a jumble of objects on a table to a scene within a frame. To understand the compositional foundation of your painting even more concretely, a study in black and white oils is a great next step. Now you're making decisions not about arrangement or design but about values—more specifically, value *relationships*. Capturing those value relationships is what creates the illusion of three-dimensional form on a two-dimensional surface, *not matching color*. One of my favorite painting sayings is "Color gets all the credit, but value does all the work."

As you squint at your still life, the darkest dark and lightest light stand out. They are not only easy to diagnose, but they are also the benchmarks against which to measure all of

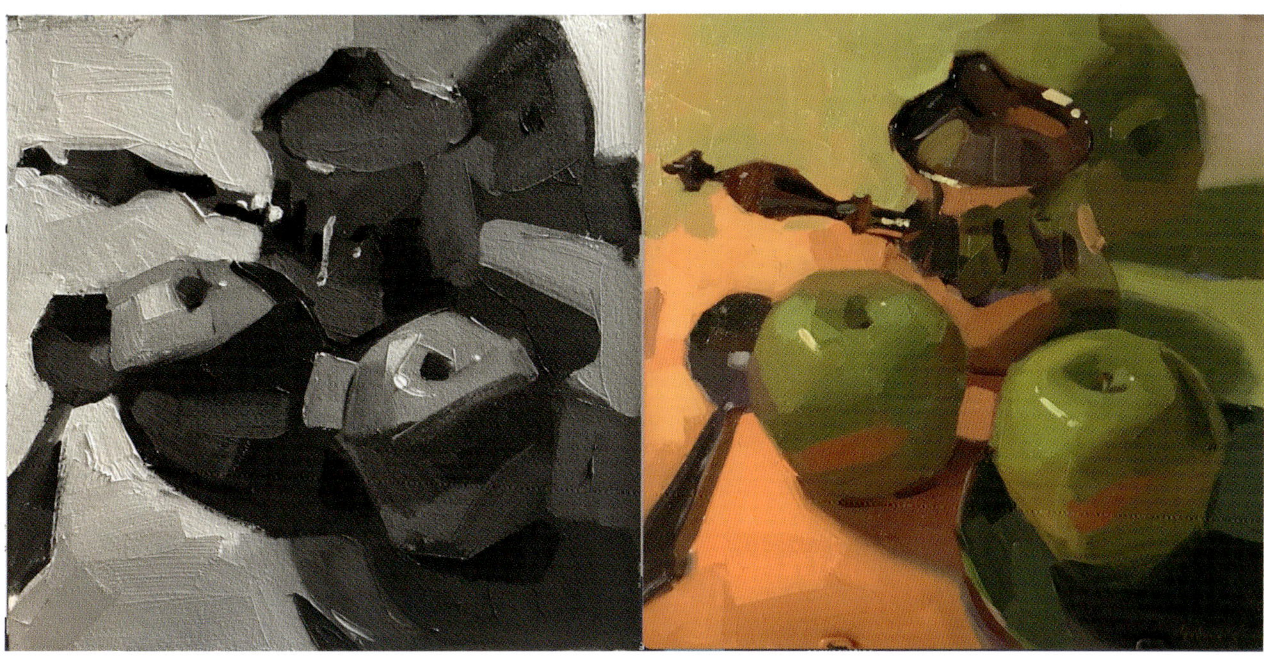

Sarah Sedwick, *St. Louis Silver*, value study and finished painting, oil on canvas, 10" × 10" | 25.4 × 25.4 cm

In this piece, the value study helped me find lost edges—especially between the apples and their cast shadows—and really see how dark those shiny metal objects were.

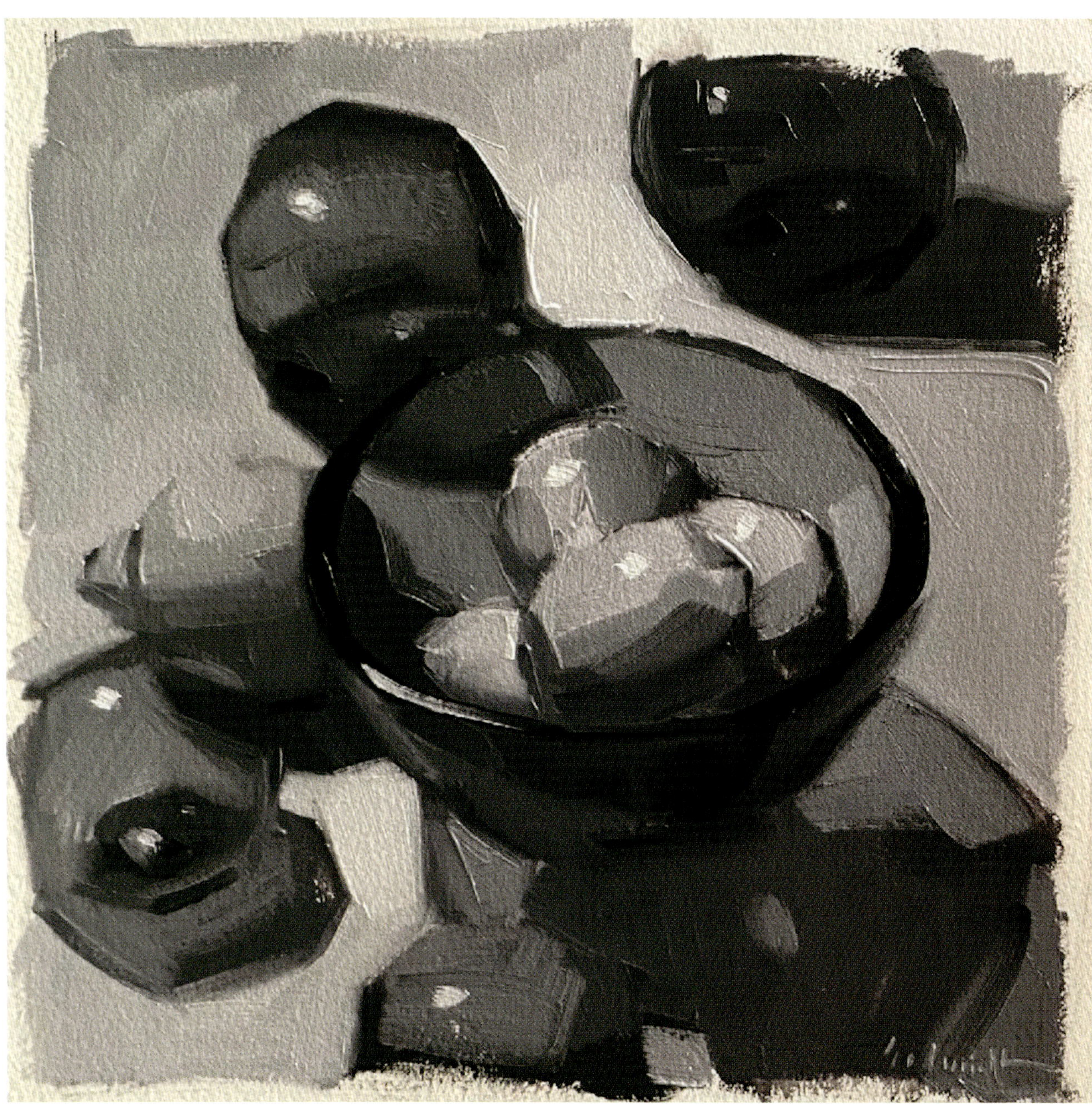

the other values in your painting—the top and bottom of a hierarchy of values that governs the whole world you're going to create on your canvas. It's that range—that hierarchy—in between darkest dark and lightest light where the decision-making happens.

All color has value. If we imagine our eyes are a black-and-white camera and picture a rainbow, we see dark grays and blacks in the reds, blues, and violets, middle grays where green and orange should be, and the lightest values in the yellow band. Still life objects whose colors are mid-value give us flexibility and force us to make choices. If we want an overall darker, richer feel to our painting, we can choose to push them a bit more toward the darkest darks. If we want a light, airy, high-key painting, we can choose to see these midtones as being more in line with our lightest lights.

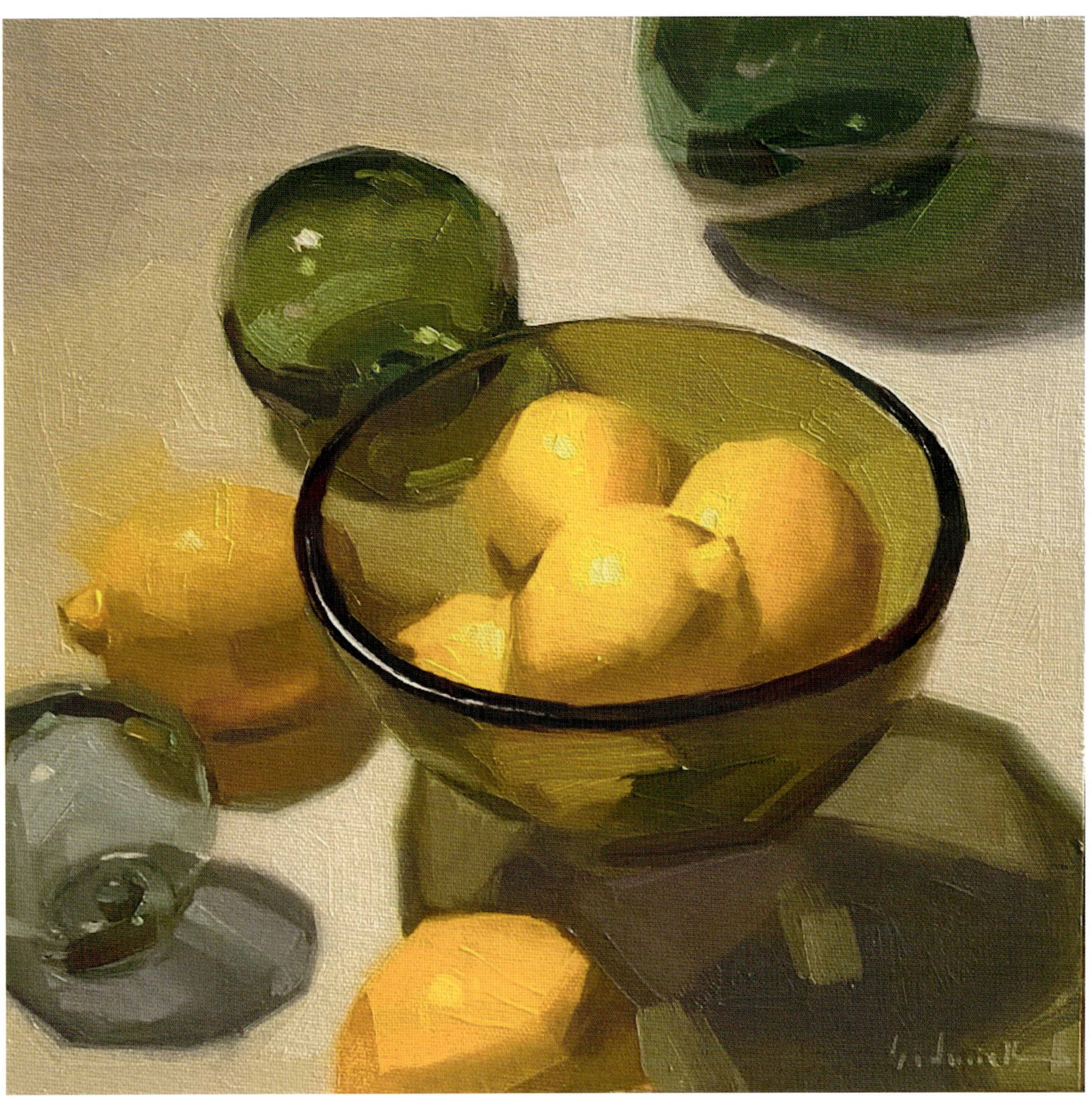

Sarah Sedwick, *Glass Floats and Lemons*, value study and finished painting, oil on canvas, 10" × 10" | 25.4 × 25.4 cm

Even though glass is transparent, what we see through it is often very dark. This value study helped me remember that as I moved into the color painting.

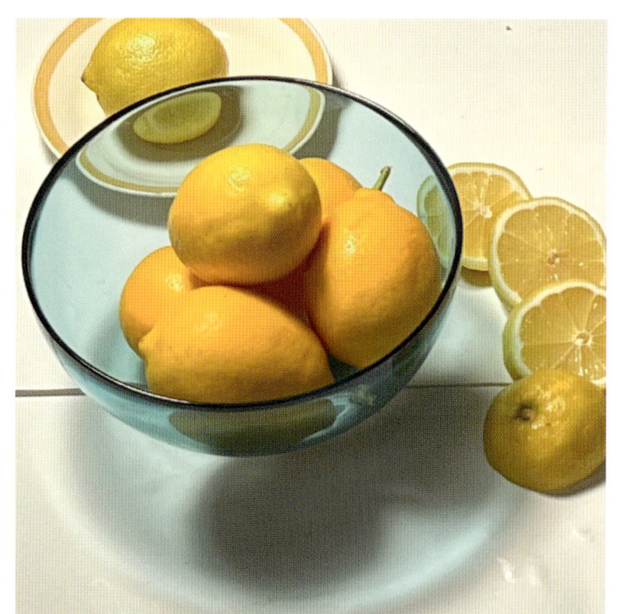

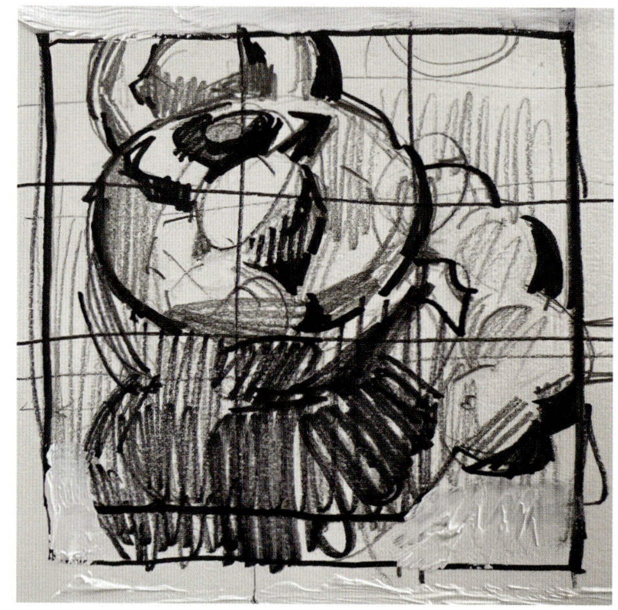

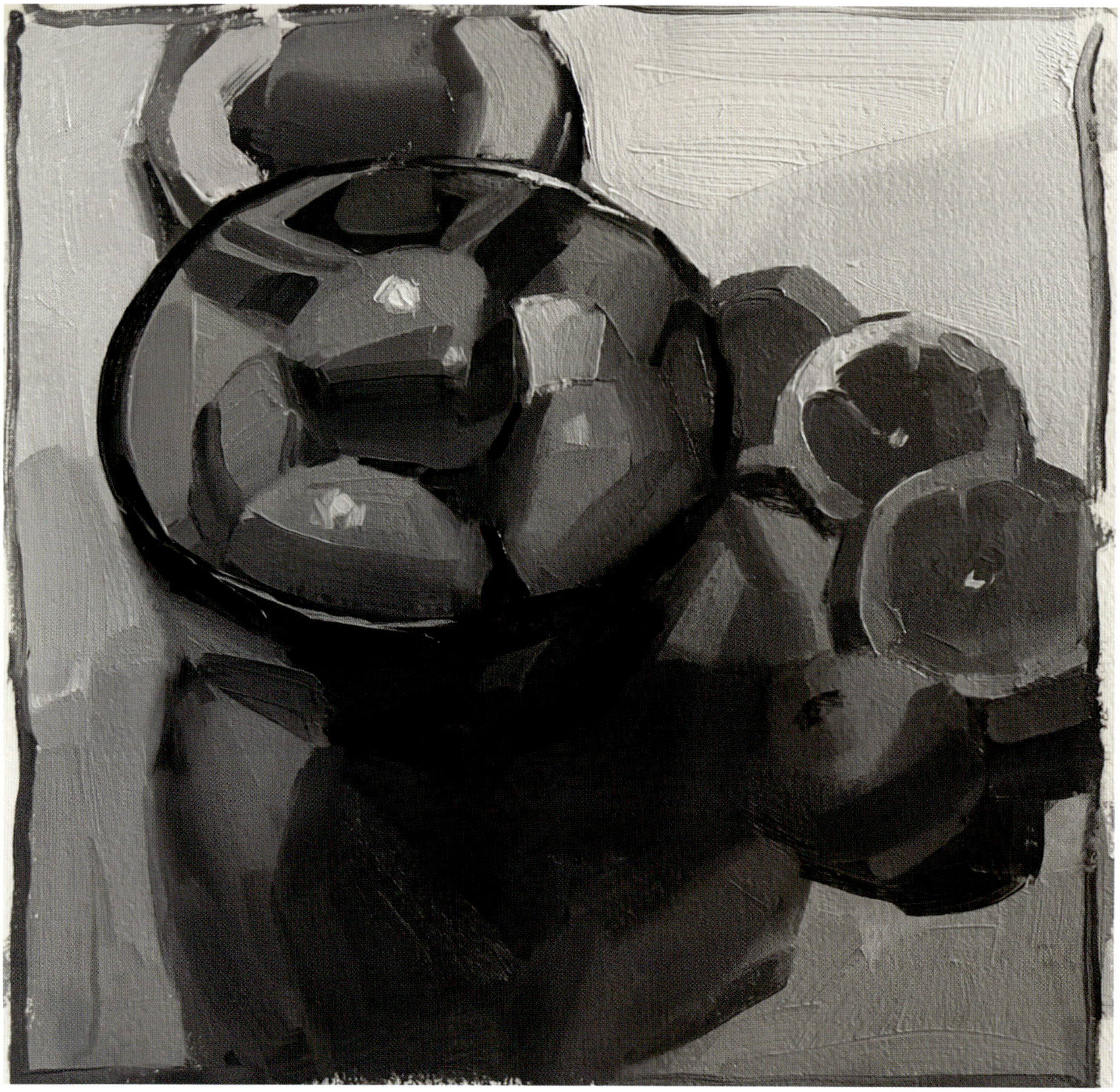

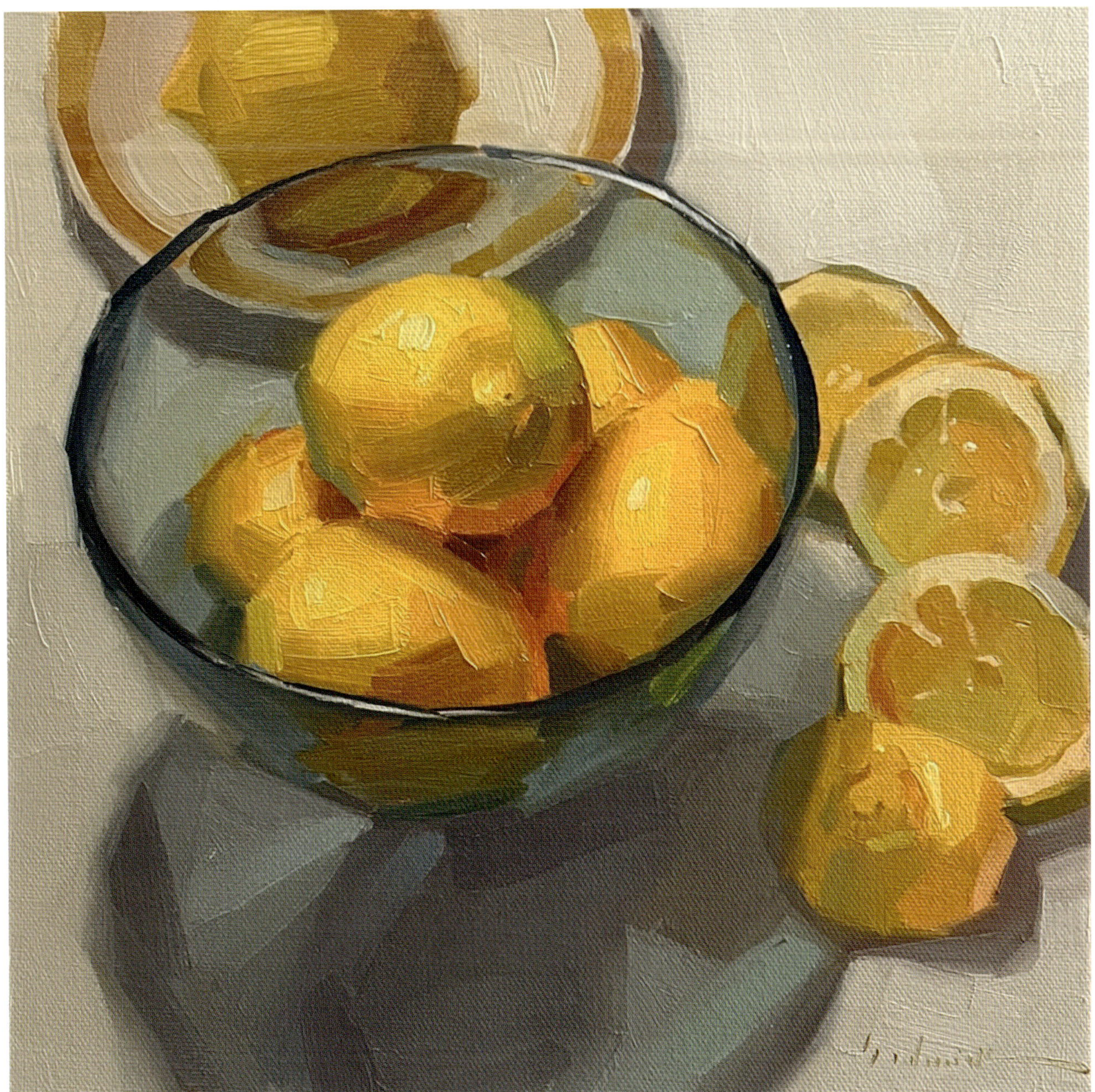

Sarah Sedwick, *California Lemons*, oil on canvas, 10" × 10" | 25.4 × 25.4 cm

The thumbnail sketch on the previous page, done quickly in a combination of pencil and Sharpie, helped me check in with my "sweet spots," ensuring that my intended focal point—the top lemon in the bowl—was well positioned.

Next, the value study in oils helped me see that some of my darkest darks were actually in the lemons—which was counterintuitive since my brain always wants to see yellow as light! It also helped me decide which highlight to make the brightest and to leave the highlight on the lemon on the plate off altogether.

A FIVE-VALUE LIMIT

Creating a black-and-white oil study using only five values—and then keeping it in front of you while you're painting in color—really helps keep your plan in place. You're making decisions about value relationships now, and if you want to experiment, this is the perfect time. Once you've moved on to color—painting on your actual canvas—you might be more reluctant to make changes or look at things in a different way than you would be in a value study.

It's important to keep these simple. Black-and-white paintings are beautiful and can be taken as far as you'd like—all the way to finished, gallery-ready pieces! For a preparatory study, however, keeping the palette to five values, and focusing on loose brushwork and big value shapes—massing values together across contour lines, and working from the general to the specific—is best. With a five-value scale, we have two lights (one and two), two darks (four and five), and a midtone (three). Simple! And three is the most important number. It's the player that bats for both teams. Value three, the midtone, is the light within the shadow side of your object, and the dark within the light sides. Put another way, if we squint to see the "big dark shape," dividing our painting into the light family and the dark family, three is the element we find in both. So, once again, squinting is key!

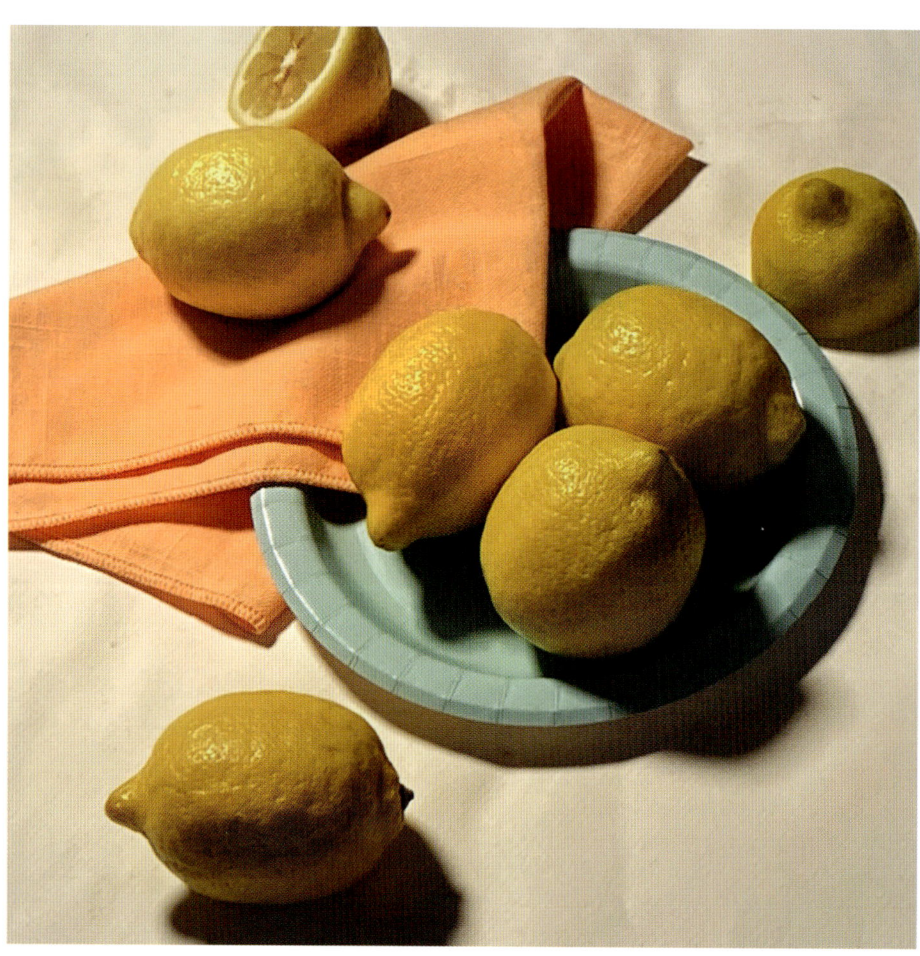

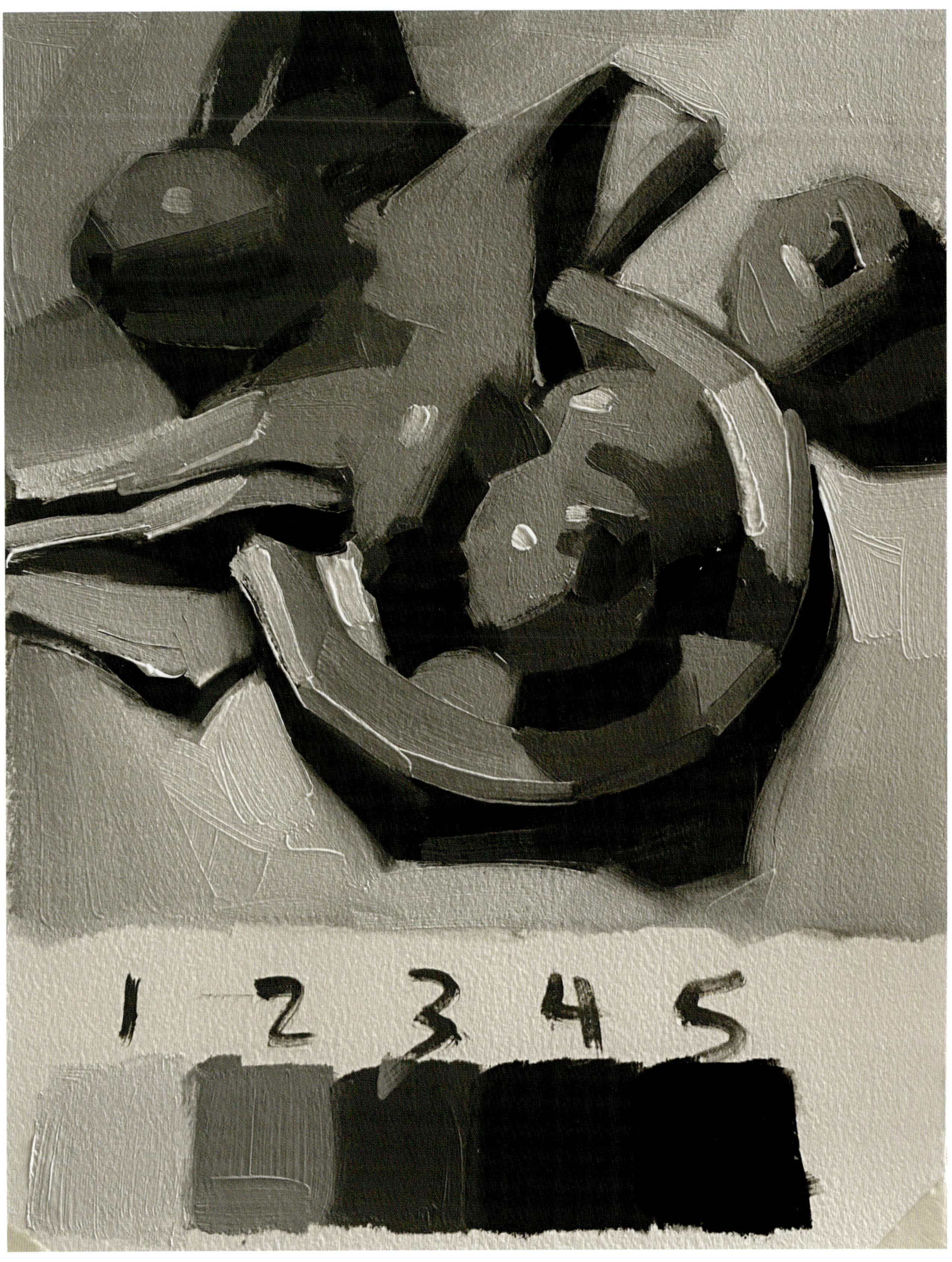

A study in five values can help us gain understanding of a complex setup. It also reveals opportunities for creating lost edges and simplifies seeing the "big dark shape" in our composition.

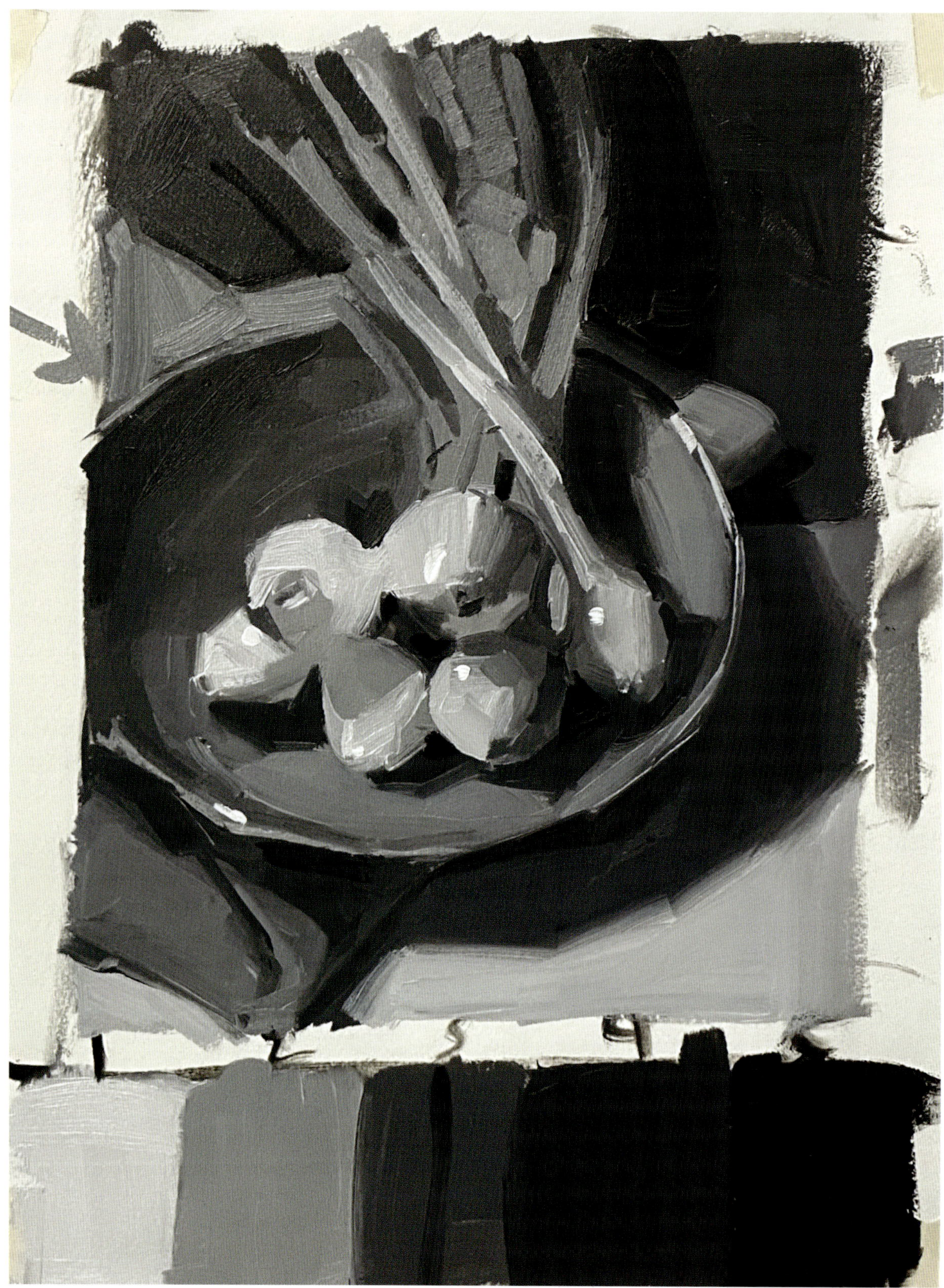

Testing my five values in a strip on the canvas helps make sure I have an even amount of shift from one value to the next. I often go back to the palette and make corrections after testing my mixtures.

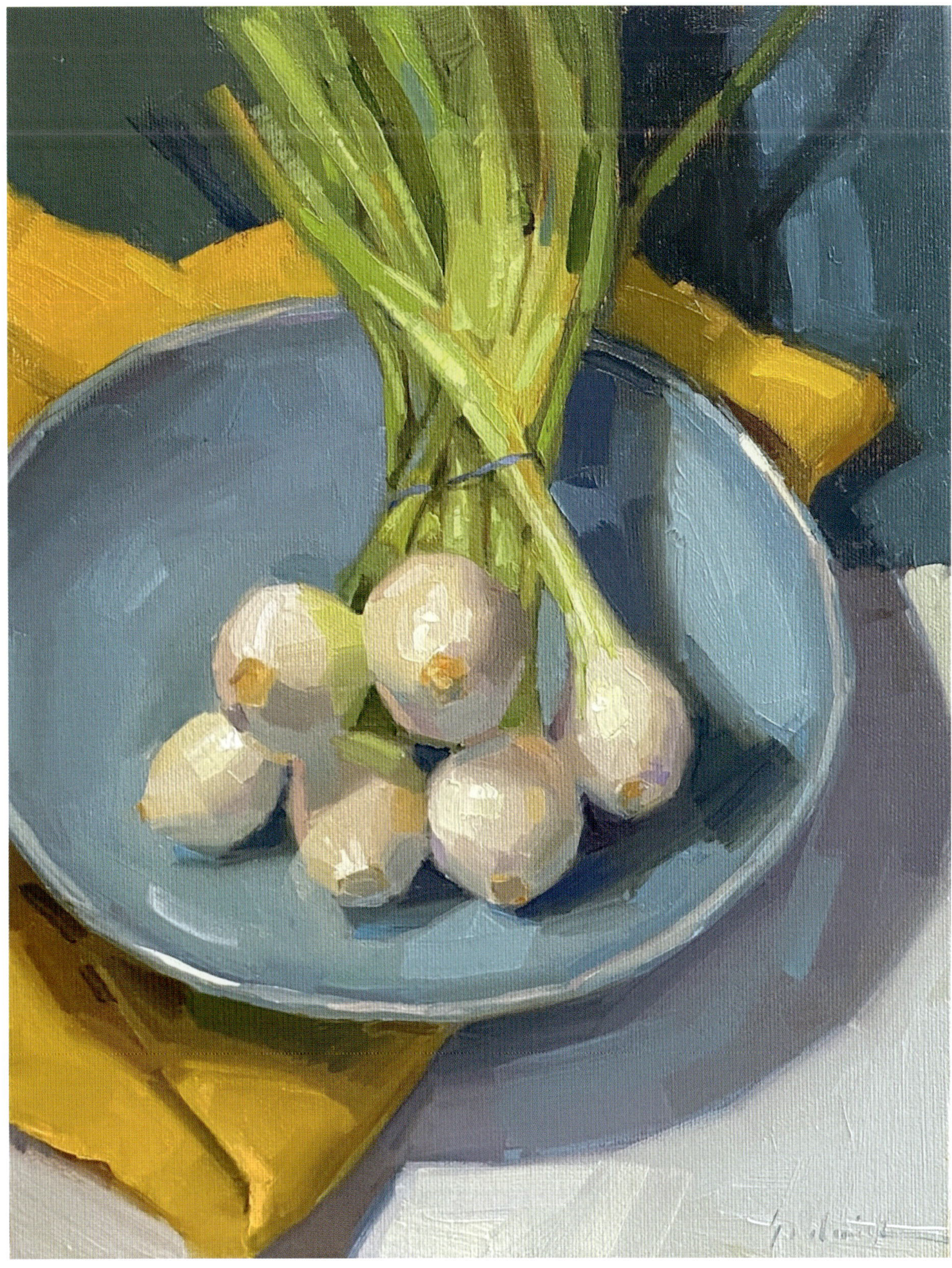

Sarah Sedwick, *Onions on Teal*, oil on canvas, 9" × 12" | 22.9 × 30.5 cm

In this piece, the black-and-white study helped me decide what to simplify—particularly those green tops of the onions—and that the cast shadow on the dark blue paper was much darker than the cast shadow on the white in the foreground.

THE BENEFITS OF BLACK-AND-WHITE PAINTING

Color can be complicated. It certainly takes up a lot of brainpower when we're painting. Working in black and white reminds us that **color gets all the credit, but value does all the work**. When mixing paint, matching color starts to feel very important, but it doesn't have to be. Training ourselves to focus on values by working in black and white—and focus not just on values, but on value *relationships*—later allows us to worry less about matching color and instead focus on color harmony, luscious paint application, and having some fun with color. We all love paintings that feature exaggerated or experimental color—a slash of purple on the face in a portrait, a bit of bright green in the reflected light on a lemon. The artist didn't actually *see* those colors, but because they matched the value that they were observing—the value *relationships* they were observing—their extravagant color choices still create the illusion of three-dimensional form on a two-dimensional surface. We love looking at paintings like that!

Letting go of color means that our attention can shift to how we are loading the paintbrush—how does the paint feel going on? Stiff or soft, creamy or dry? If a little medium is added, does that change the experience? Remember, the paintbrush is just a tool—a little dump truck to move the paint from the palette to the canvas. Next, we can look at value shapes. With only five values to choose from, it becomes easier to group like with like—if two spots are pretty close in value, even if they are on two different objects, can we choose to see them as the same? Can we paint across the contour line, massing them into one big value shape? This is the laboratory where lost edges are born.

One of the best things you can do to improve your painting overall is to practice in black and white. You are working on all the important aspects of painting that don't involve color mixing—paint application, brushwork, and edges—and training your eye and mind to think of color as value. This is a huge step in mastering the art of seeing that is at the heart of painting.

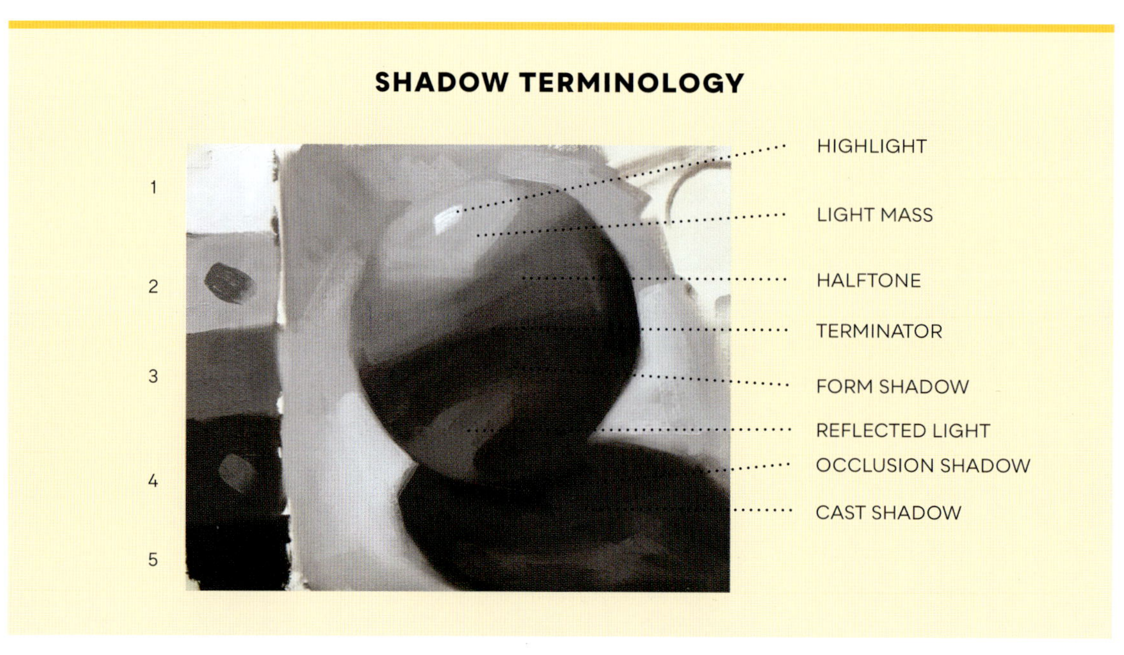

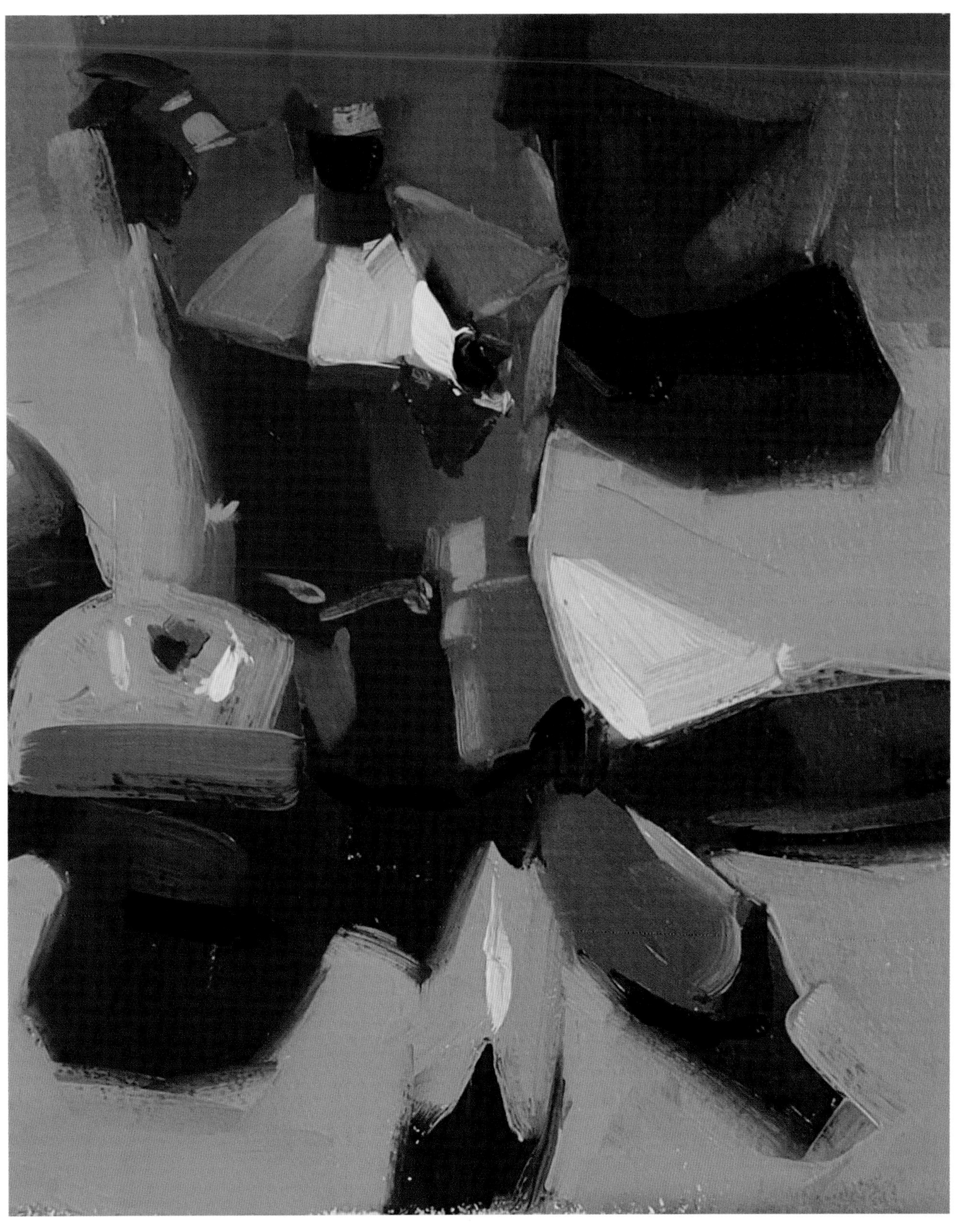

Sarah Sedwick, *Moka Pot* value study (detail), oil on Arches oil paper, approx. 8" × 8" | 20.3 × 20.3 cm

A HIERARCHY OF VALUES: HIGHLIGHTS AND DARK ACCENTS

Your painting is a closed system. It's a universe unto itself—and your **lightest light** and **darkest dark** values are the governing laws of that universe. Locating them early, and then letting everything else fall somewhere in between them, is the key to creating brilliant highlights and establishing a sense of volume, weight, and gravity in your painting.

Paint has limitations, and nature doesn't. Nature's light can create a brilliant specular highlight even on a high-value surface, like a white bowl. But paint can't get any brighter than titanium white. A hierarchy of values has to be established, and to shine like they do in life, highlights must be at the top of the hierarchy—closer to pure white from the tube

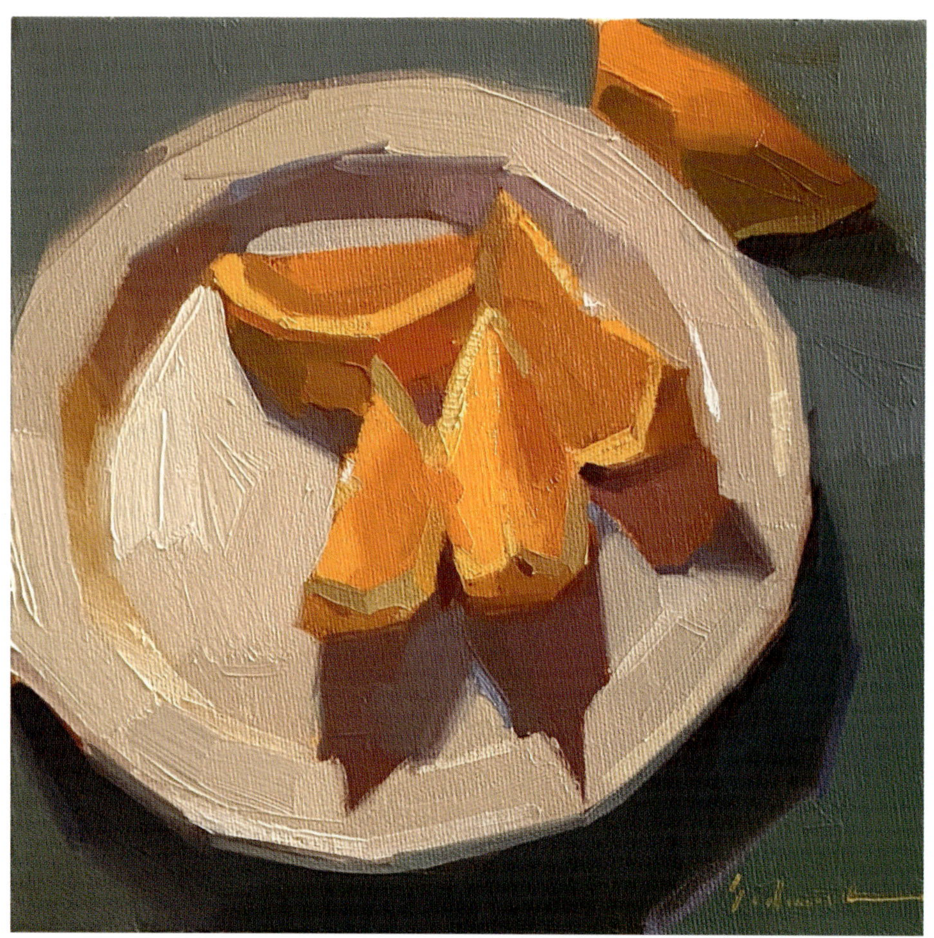

Sarah Sedwick, *Sunny Slices*, oil on canvas, 8" × 8" | 20.3 × 20.3 cm

In order for highlights to appear brilliant on white objects, the lightest "whites" that *aren't* the highlights need to be painted several value steps darker than pure white paint. This creates opportunity for beautiful, colorful neutrals and temperature shifts within those "whites."

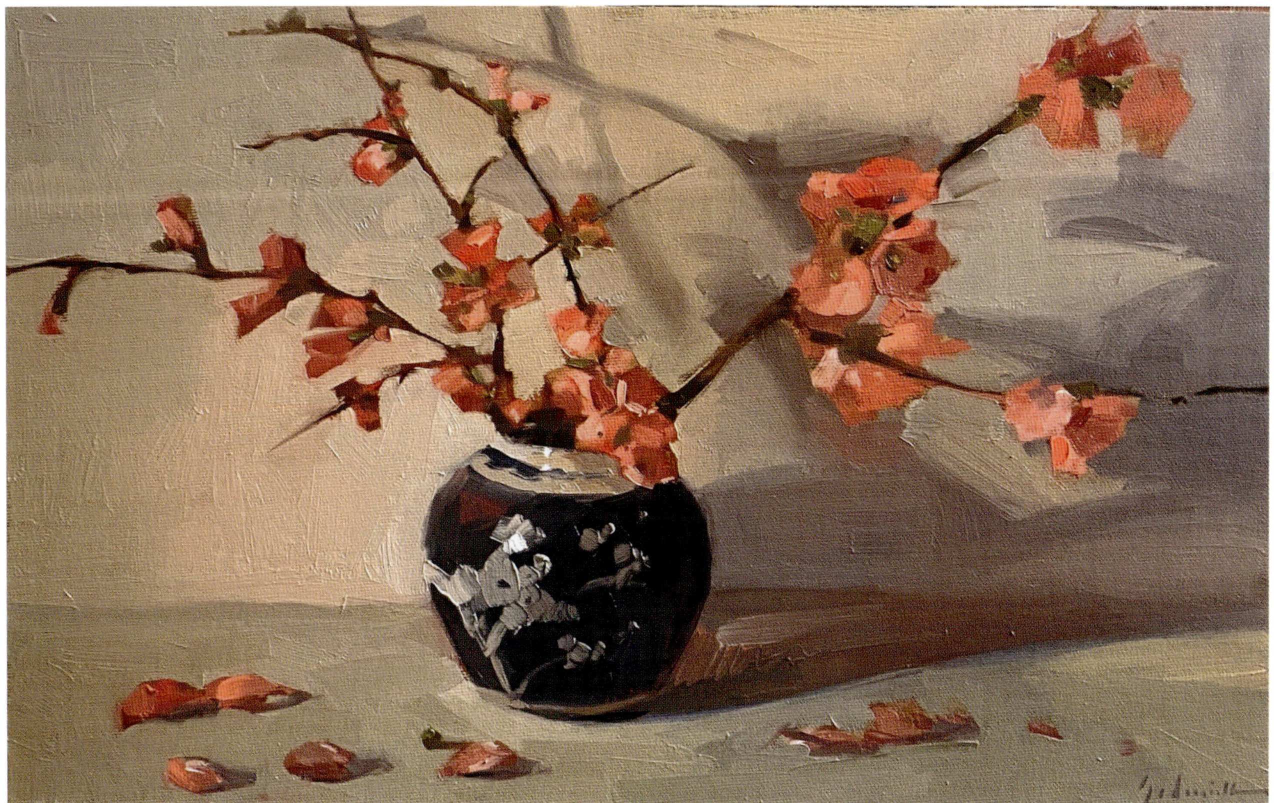

Sarah Sedwick, *Serenity*, oil on canvas, 10" × 16" | 25.4 × 40.6 cm

Pops of darkest dark in the branches, the occlusion shadow, and inside the rim of the vase were the finishing touches on this painting.

than anything else in the painting—and likely *much* closer. That's not to say that I create highlights using pure white—I very rarely do. Highlights have color just like everything else and are affected by both the color of the light source and the color of the object on which they appear. Because I use warm light on my still lifes, my highlights often have a peachy cast, so I add a tiny bit of yellow and red to my white to create them. The *darker* you can keep your lightest large areas of *light*, the more colorful your highlights get to be. So, a white bowl in the light might feel very bright to my eye, but I will paint it farther down the value scale, making my darks darker to compensate and maintain the value relationships I'm observing. My goal is always to paint things just a little darker than they may be in life—the darker they are, the less white they contain. And the less white they contain, the more *colorful* they can be, and the more room I will have to go up the value scale to a brilliant highlight.

Dark accents are usually one of the last things I add to a painting. They are the dark version of highlights and best added after you've established the form of your subjects, to really make them pop. I often find my dark accents in the occlusion shadow—that spot where an object connects with the ground. It's the darkest part of the cast shadow—often a small, subtle mark, but very important for creating a sense of gravity.

EXERCISE:
CREATING A VALUE STUDY IN BLACK AND WHITE OILS

Mix a palette of five values using any white and black pigments. I use titanium white and ivory black. Raw umber and Payne's gray are good black substitutes. Number one should be a slightly grayed-down white and number five will be black. You want an even amount of value shift from one pile to the next, and number three as your midtone—whatever a middle gray feels like to you today.

Lay out your palette with white on the left side and black on the right. Begin by mixing your midtone, three, and then mix one step between that and black, to the right, and one step between that and white, to the left, graying your number one white pile just a bit and setting aside a small amount of pure white for highlights.

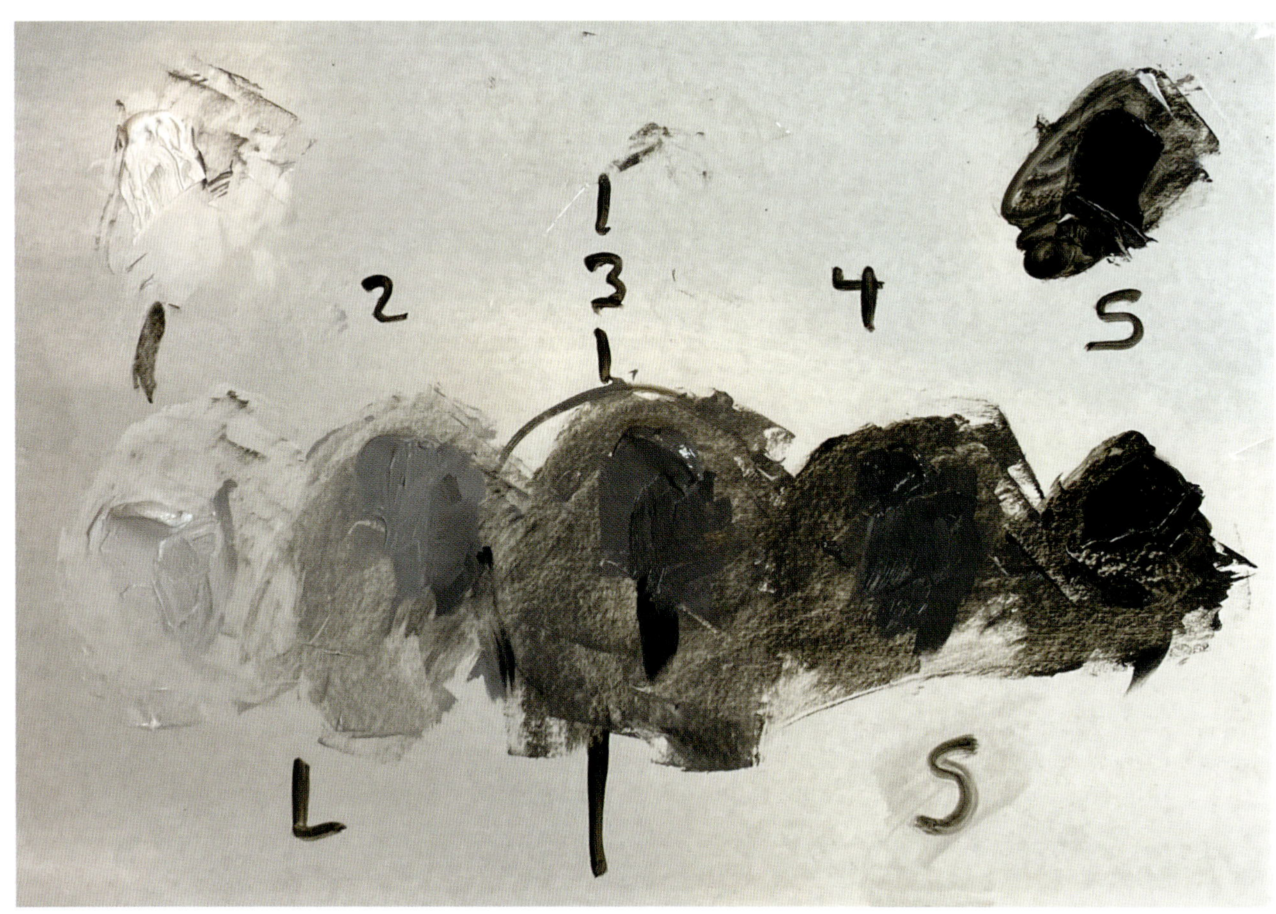

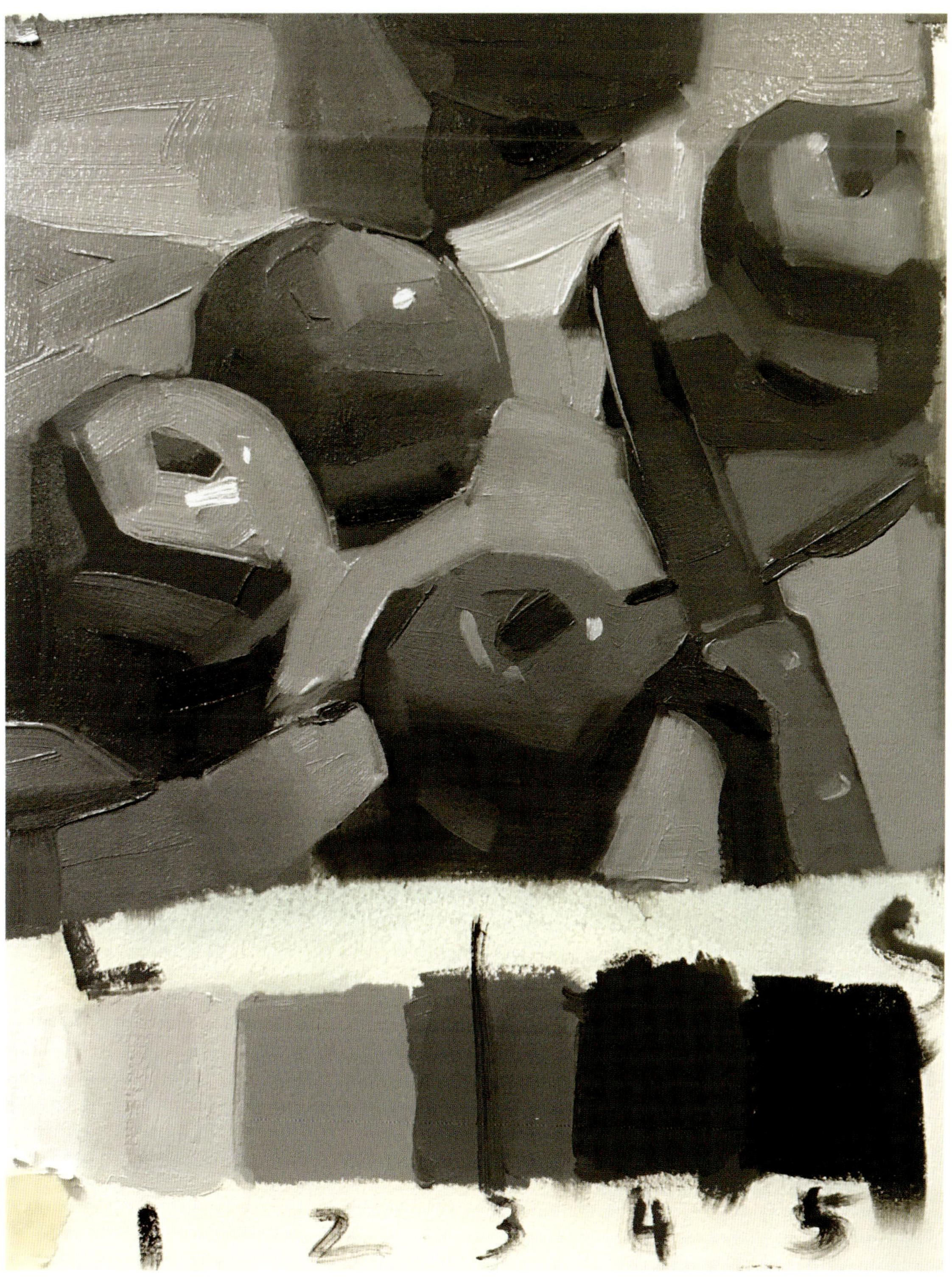

It's a great idea to test your mixtures on a strip of paper or canvas to check your values before beginning your study. You want an even amount of shift from one square to the next. With only five values to work with, they should be as distinct and different as possible, so if two of them are too close together, the best time to catch that is at the beginning! I like to create my test strip on the bottom of my canvas, right underneath my value study.

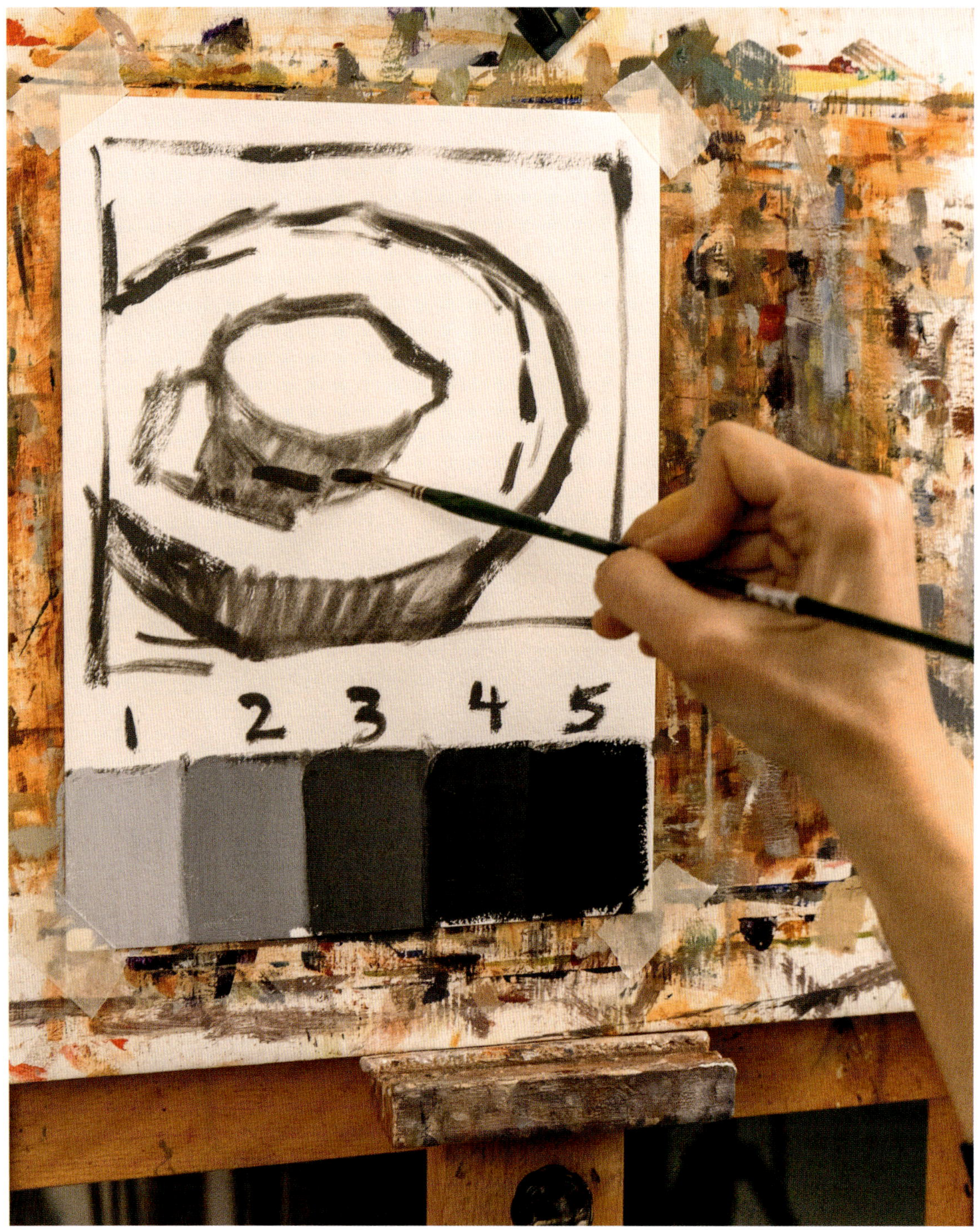

When I work on Arches oil paper, I begin by swiping some clean Gamsol over the surface to cut down on the absorbency of the paper. Then I use a #2 round brush and my #3 value mixed gray—the midtone—to block in my composition, including the general shadow shapes.

Next, referring to your thumbnail sketch, and looking at your still life as well, block in the outline of your composition using your number three value, the midtone. Once you've done that, begin with your darks, using value four. Save value five for last, when you'll paint your darkest dark accents. Work your way from the darks in value four to the midtones in value three, squinting at your canvas and your still life, glancing at

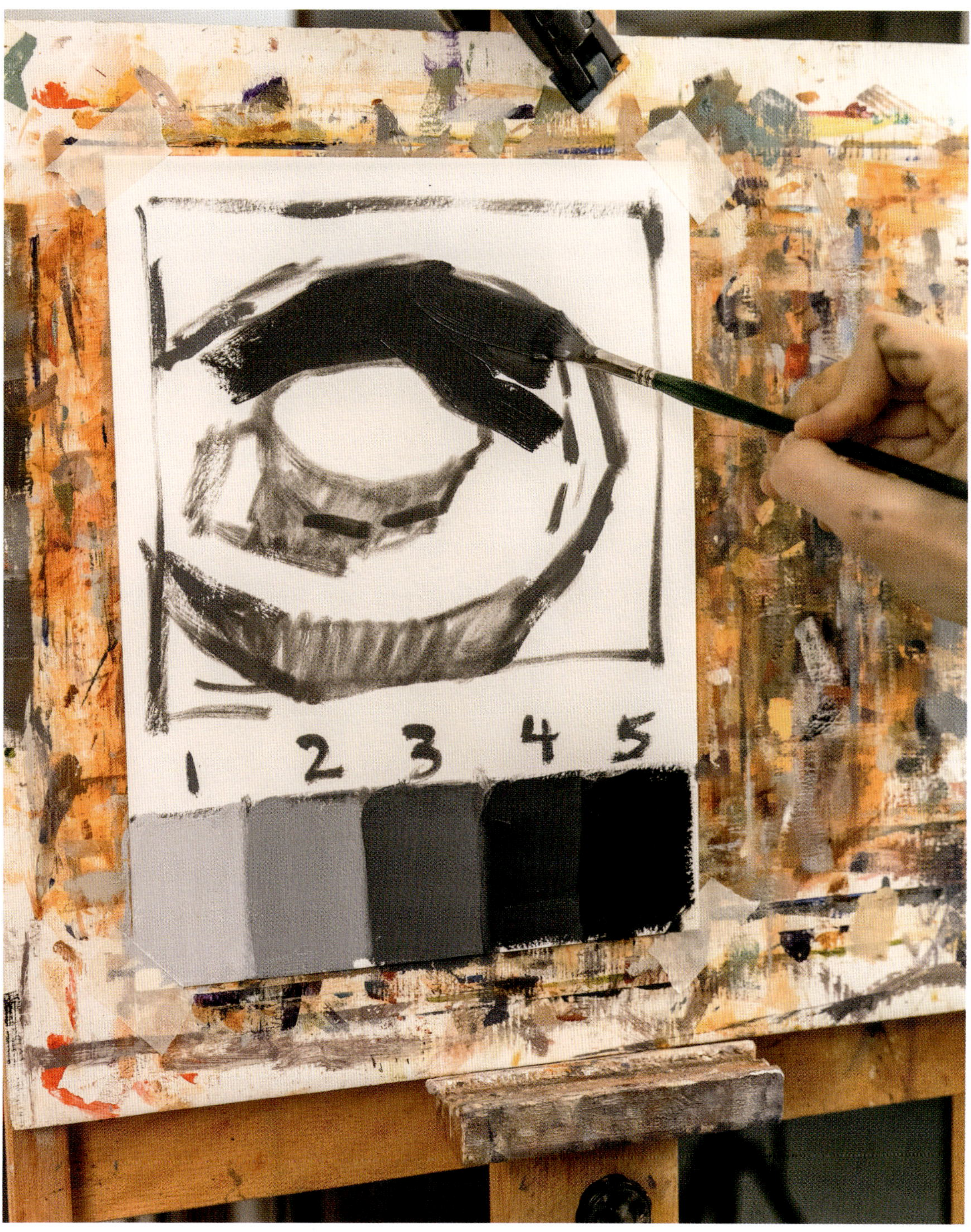

Switching to a larger brush, a #4 flat, and beginning with my #4 value, the mid-dark, I work my way up the value scale toward 1, reserving 5 and pure titanium white for dark accents and highlights, the finishing touches.

your thumbnail sketch as a reminder to keep it simple! Don't blend between value areas too much—apply the paint like a mosaic, in patches of value—and don't be afraid to paint "outside the lines"!

Once you've painted from four to one, use your pure white (not value one, which is a slightly muddy white) for highlights and your pure black (value five) for dark accents.

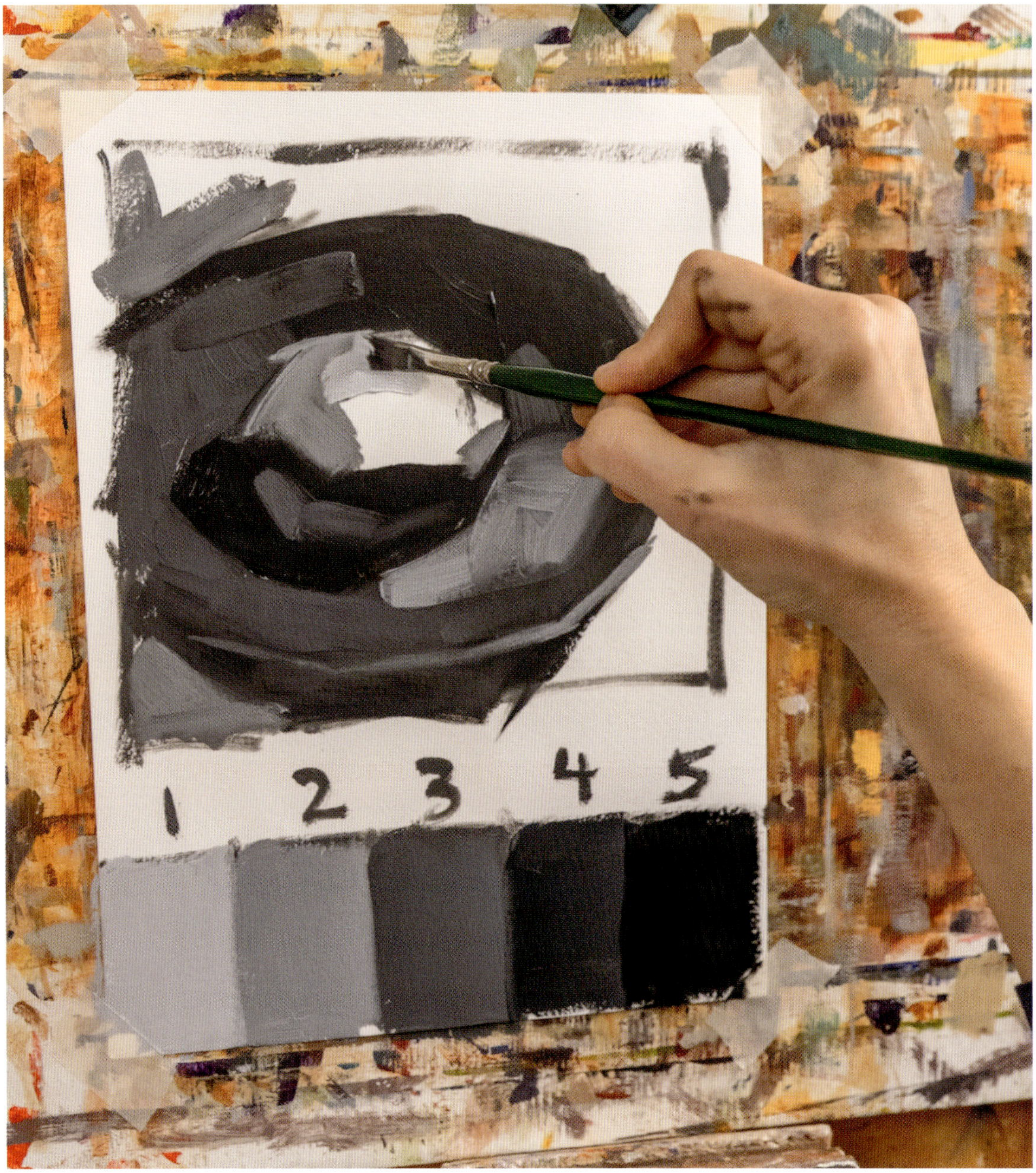

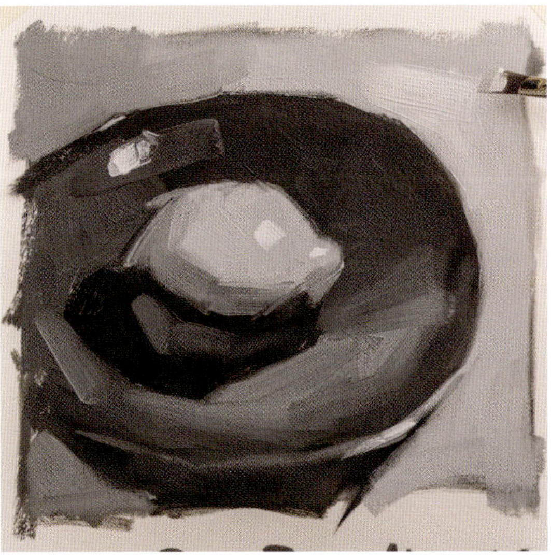

Keep this value study in front of you as you move on to color. You've prepared thoroughly—now it's time to delve into the rest of the process with my three steps for alla prima painting!

THE MECHANICS OF MIXING WITH A PALETTE KNIFE

I mix with the palette knife as though it's a spatula and I'm flipping pancakes! First, I scoop the paint onto the top of the knife blade, then I flip it over by turning my wrist in toward me, pushing firmly down against the palette to mix, instead of working the bottom/back of the palette knife against the palette. Both techniques work, but I feel that mine is more efficient. Give it a try! With time and practice, keeping the pile of paint toward the tip of the knife blade becomes easier, and you will be able to scrape all of the paint off, without having it build up near the handle, simply by pushing it off firmly against the palette with a rolling motion.

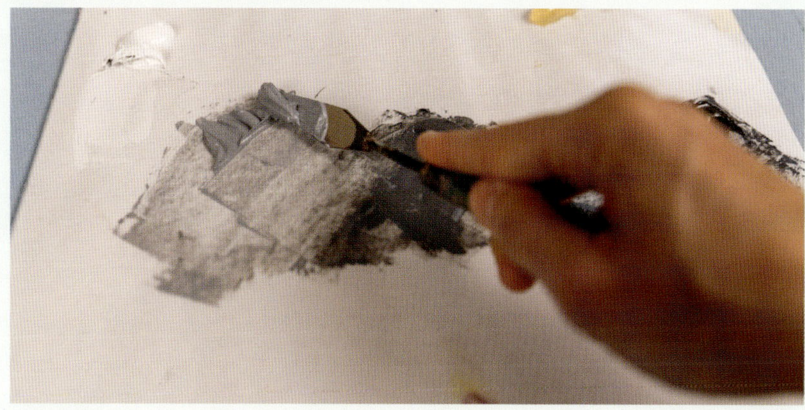

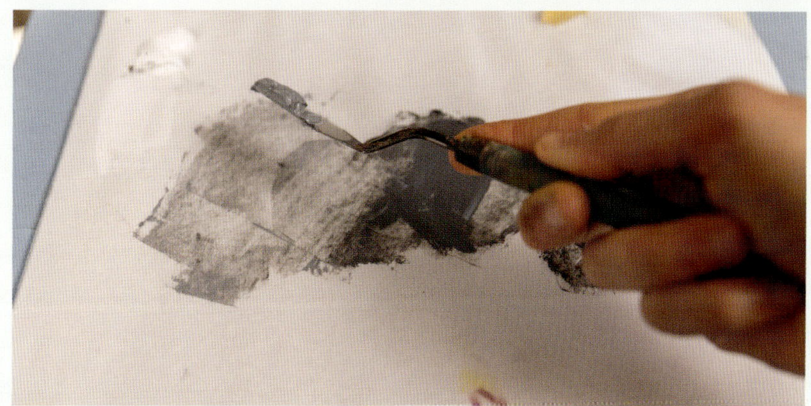

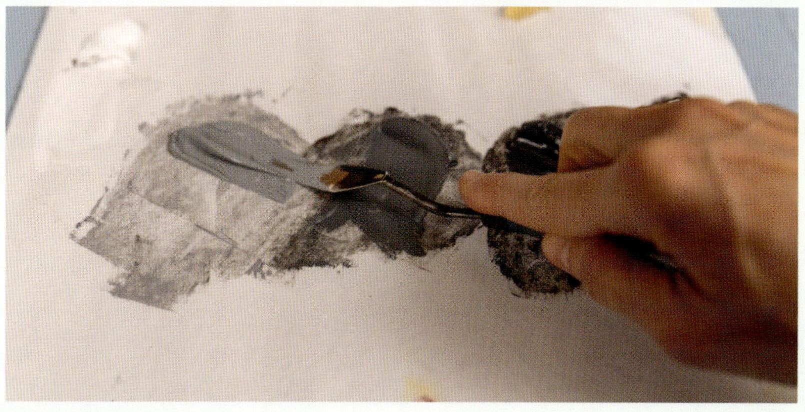

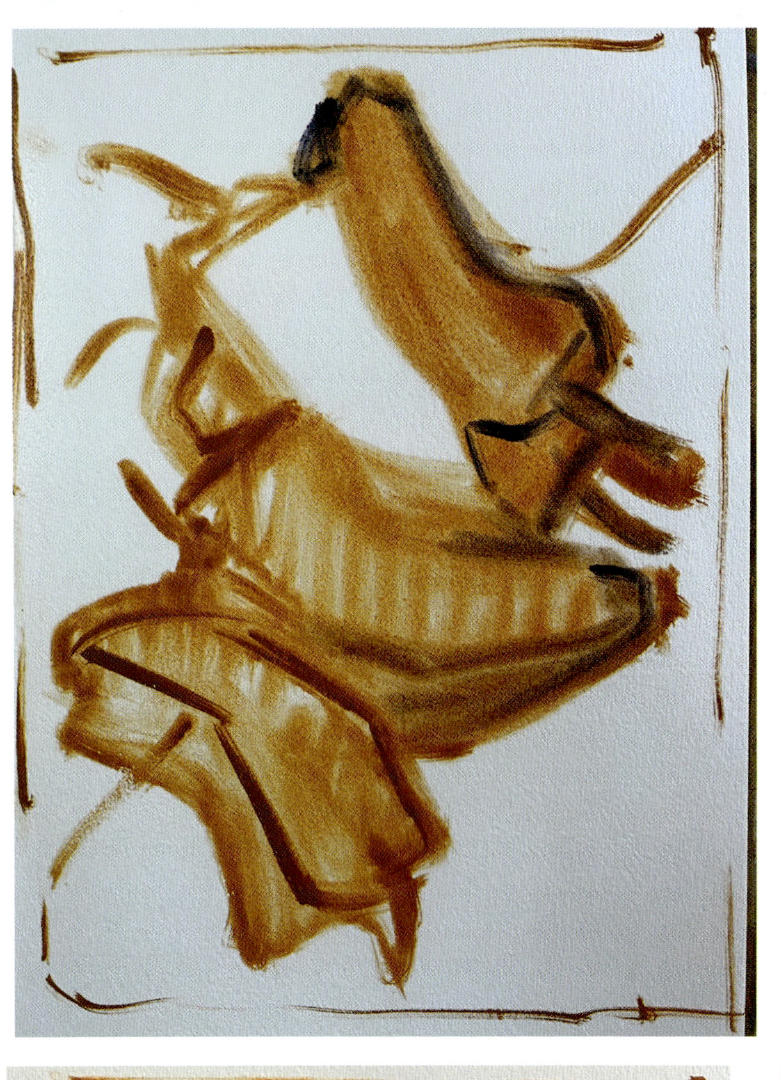
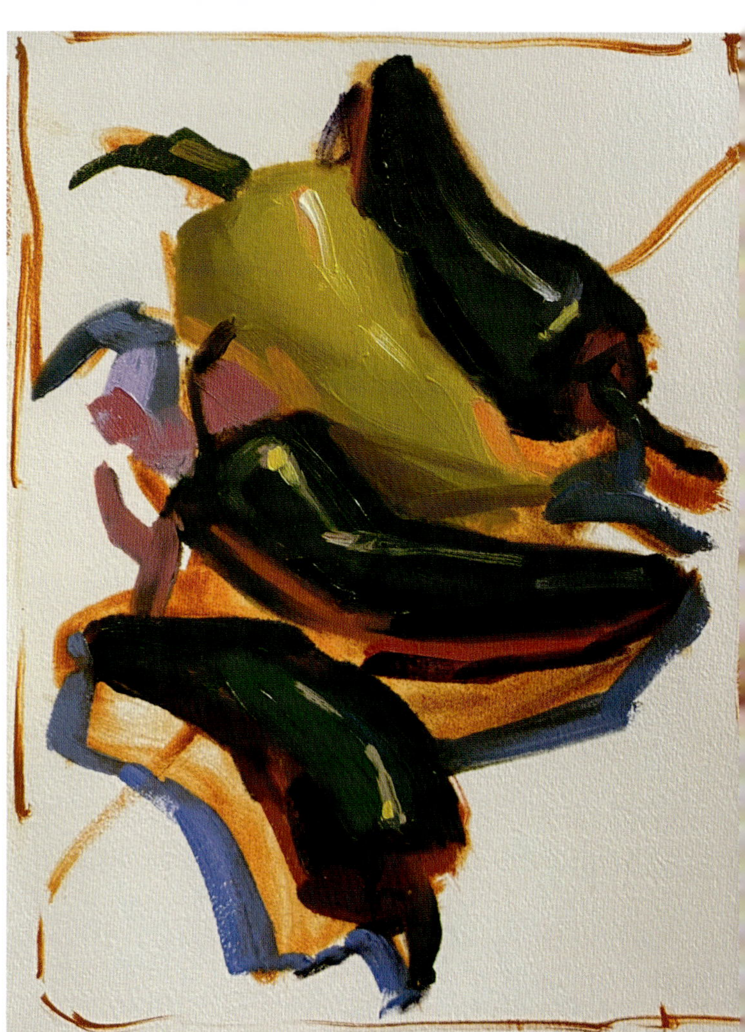
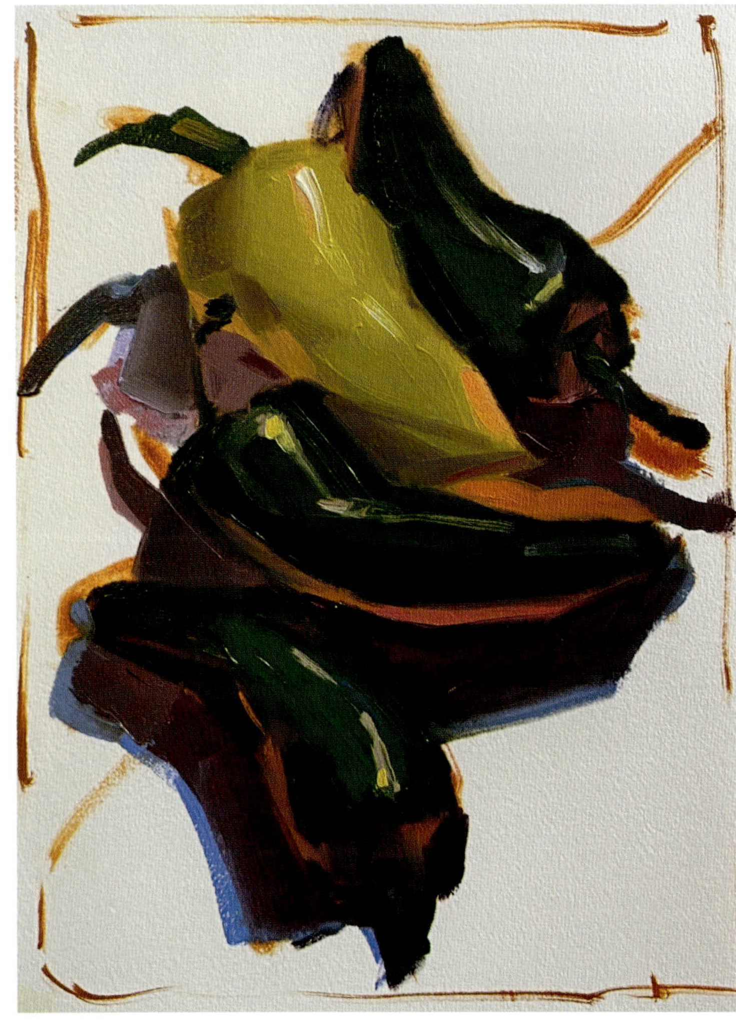
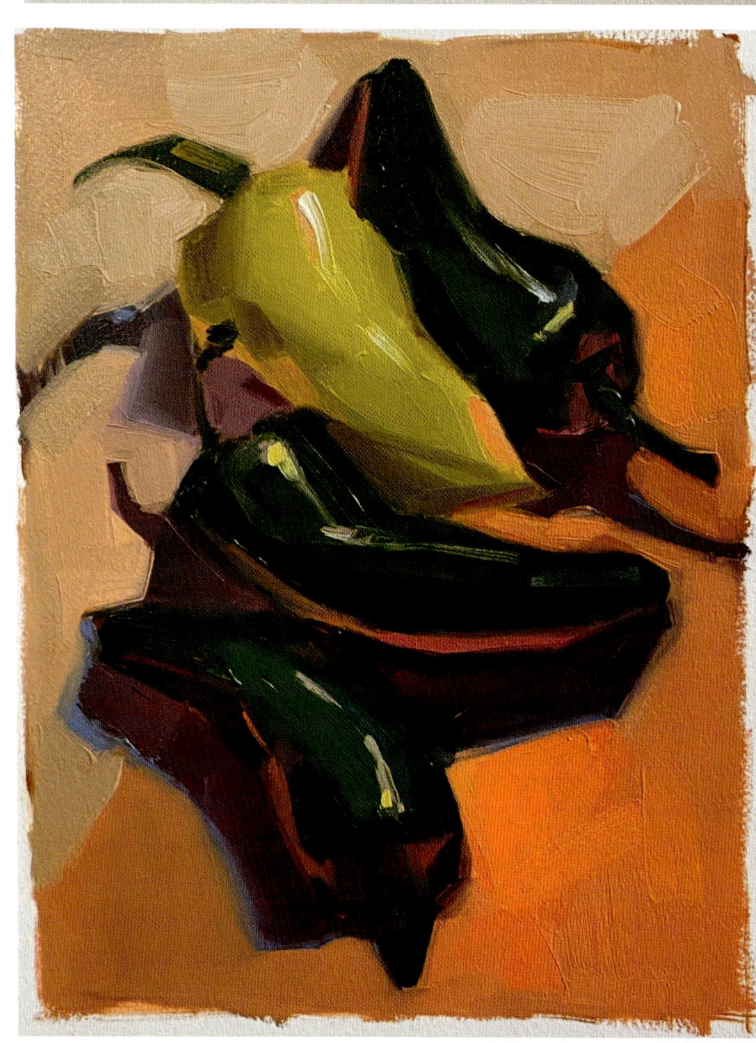

4

PAINTING YOUR DYNAMIC STILL LIFE: ALLA PRIMA IN THREE STEPS

"Alla prima" is an Italian phrase meaning "all at once." The French call it "premier coup," and in English we say "wet-on-wet" or "direct" painting. It generally means that a small painting is begun and finished in one sitting, and a larger one is worked on over consecutive days, or in wet-on-wet sections. The opposite approach is "indirect" painting, in which thin layers or glazes are applied over an underpainting and allowed to dry in between, building up a luminous surface. This can be a lengthy process.

Alla prima paintings have a feeling of exuberance and immediacy. Things can get messy and a little out of control—and there's lots of room for "happy accidents" to occur. Often, my riskiest-feeling choices lead to discovering new techniques I will use again and again.

I think of my alla prima painting process in three steps—they are flexible, and I encourage you to explore, experiment, and fit them to your own way of working.

◀ Sarah Sedwick, *Spicy Sequence*,
oil on Arches oil paper, 7" × 9" | 17.8 × 22.9 cm

STEP 1: UNDERPAINTING

The underpainting, or *imprimatura*, is the first pass of paint on the canvas. It provides a skeletal structure underneath the rest of your painting, not only mapping out your composition but also providing a value plan. Thus, light passages of paint have lighter canvas underneath them, and darker passages are reinforced by a dark layer. Because light travels through layers of paint, this can help your lights feel more luminous. If a blank, white canvas feels intimidating, a tonal wash can also be a great way to ease into the process!

Before beginning, lay out your palette with all the colors you're going to use, grab some Gamsol (or your preferred solvent—or none at all), your palette knife, brushes, and rags. I only use **paint and solvent** in this first layer—no medium or added oil—to observe the "fat over lean" rule: thinner paint first, thicker, oilier paint later. This prevents cracking as the layers of paint dry and helps us build alla prima layers, because paint with more "fat" (i.e., oil or medium) sticks well to other wet paint, while "lean" paint (*thinned* with Gamsol) sticks well to the gessoed surface of your canvas or board.

To start an underpainting, swipe a tonal wash evenly over the whole canvas. It should be translucent—not thick and pasty. The white of the canvas should shine through, creating an even mid-value. This can be done in any color, but I recommend that the color not have white mixed in, unless you are planning to let it dry before proceeding. I like to create my own custom "tone color" with a combination of cadmium yellow, cadmium red, and ultramarine blue. Burnt sienna or raw sienna straight from the tube is also a great option. Using a warm brown or orange tonal wash can lend your finished painting a golden glow, especially if you leave a little breathing room between your brushstrokes in spots, or have thinner passages of paint on your canvas. In fact, a huge advantage of working on a toned canvas is that you won't necessarily need to cover every square inch of the next layer with thick, opaque paint—that bright white canvas will be covered!

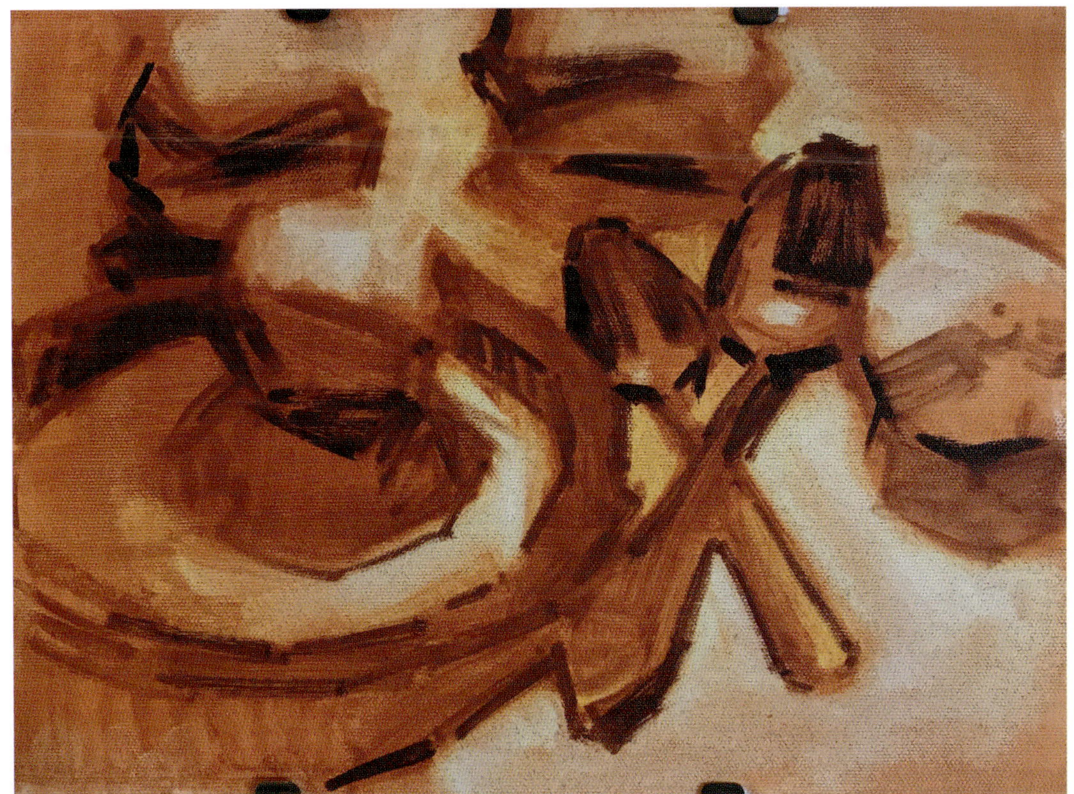

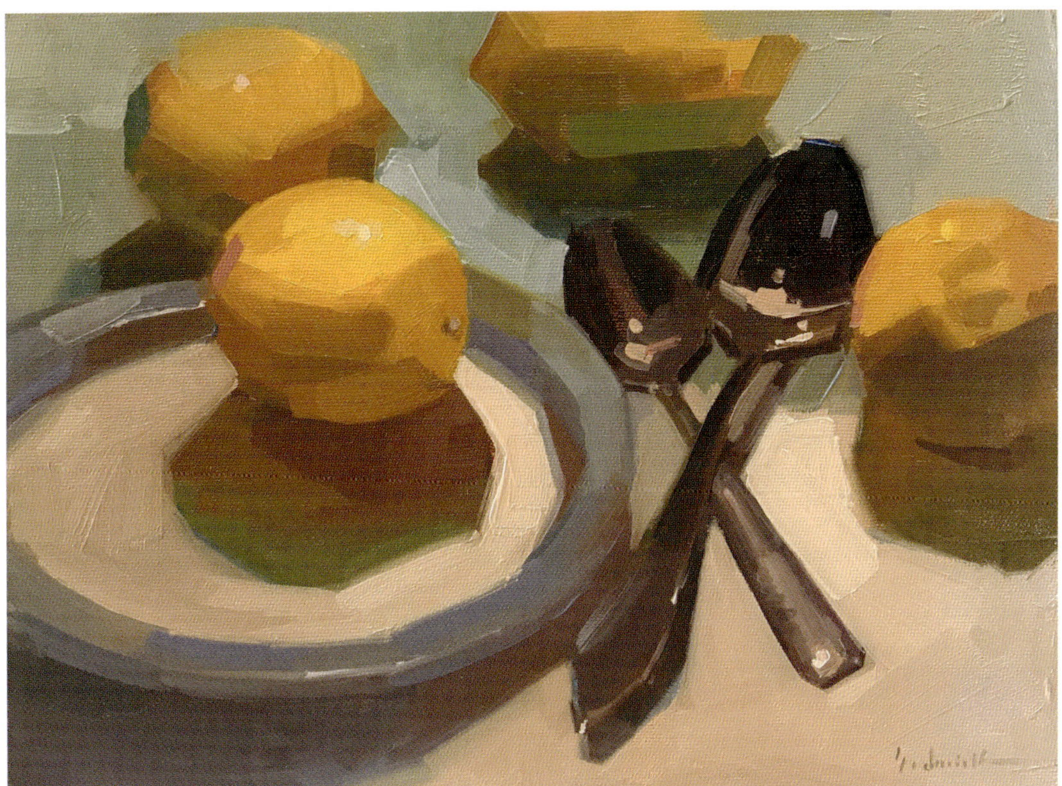

Sarah Sedwick, *Crossed Spoons*, oil on canvas, 9" × 12" | 22.9 × 30.5 cm

Using a neutral brown/orange-like burnt sienna for your underpainting—or mixing your own from colors like I do—can give your finished piece a warm feeling, even if the color scheme is cool!

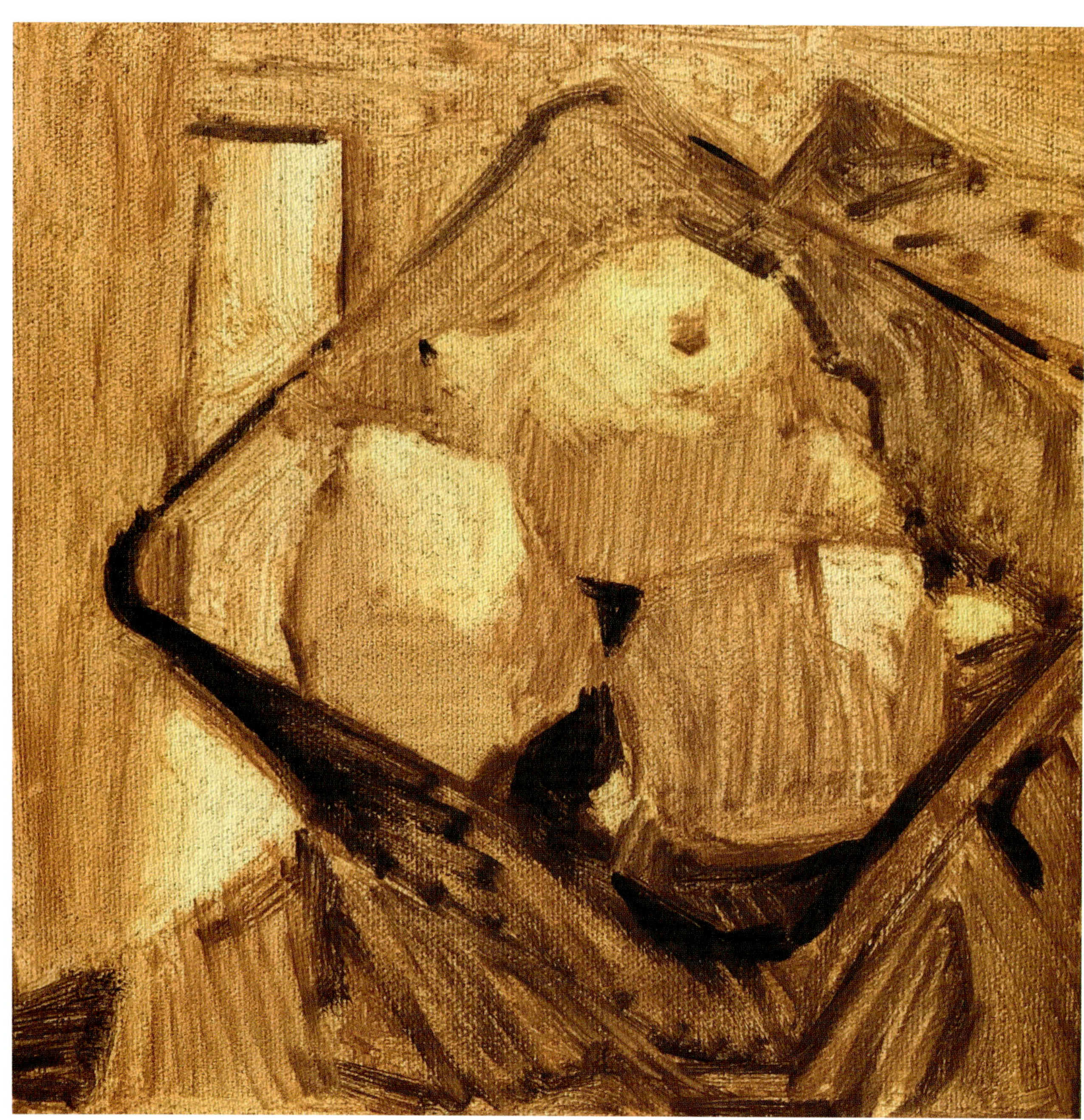

In this underpainting, I am leaving myself little notes, reminders for later on when I am consumed by and concentrating on seeing and painting in color. For example, the values of everything seen through the blue glass are darker—a lot darker—than when they're not seen through glass. And the cast shadow in the foreground is darker where it passes over the blue paper and lighter against the yellow.

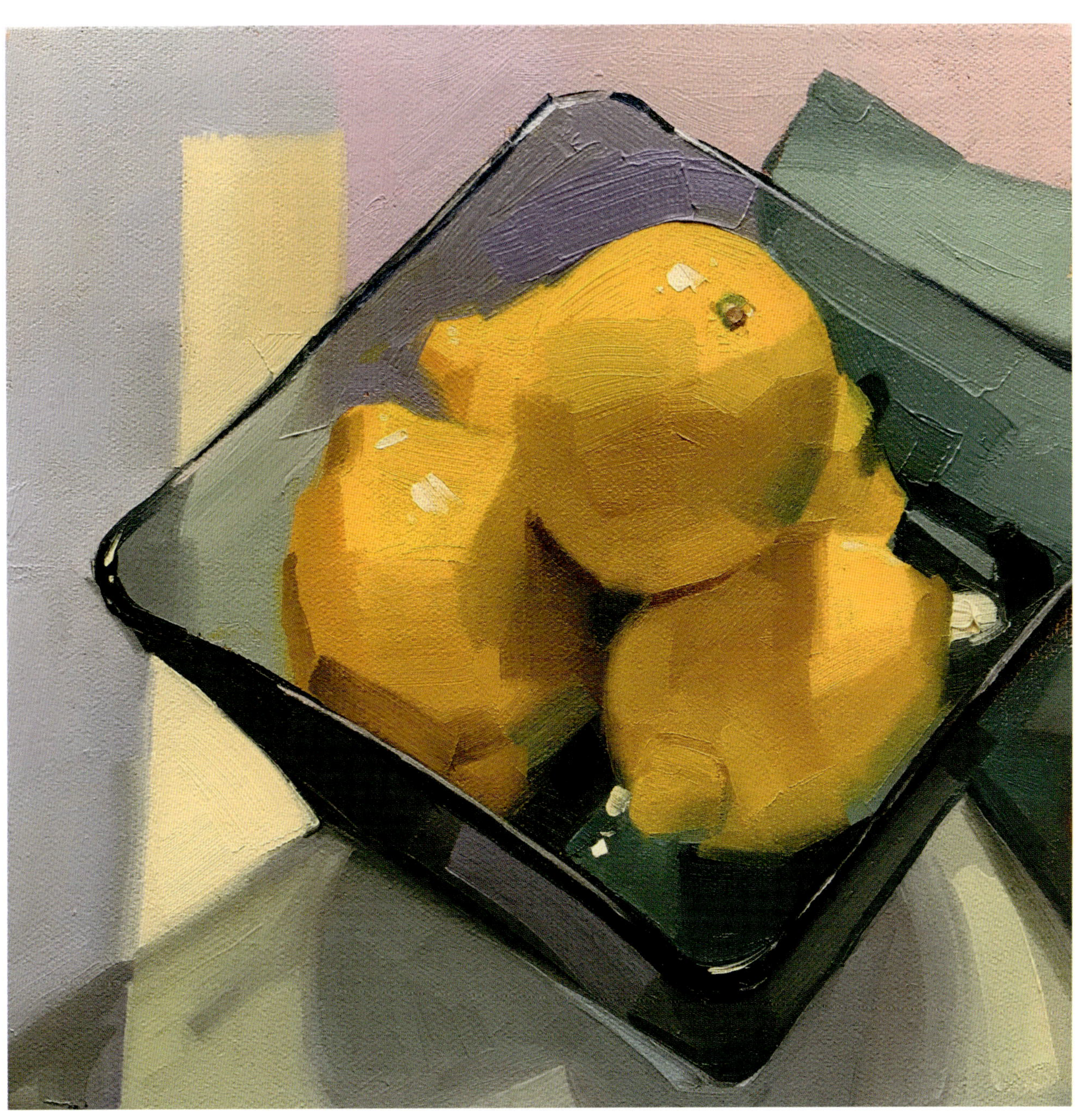

Sarah Sedwick, *Lemon Geometry*,
oil on canvas, 8" × 8" | 20.3 × 20.3 cm

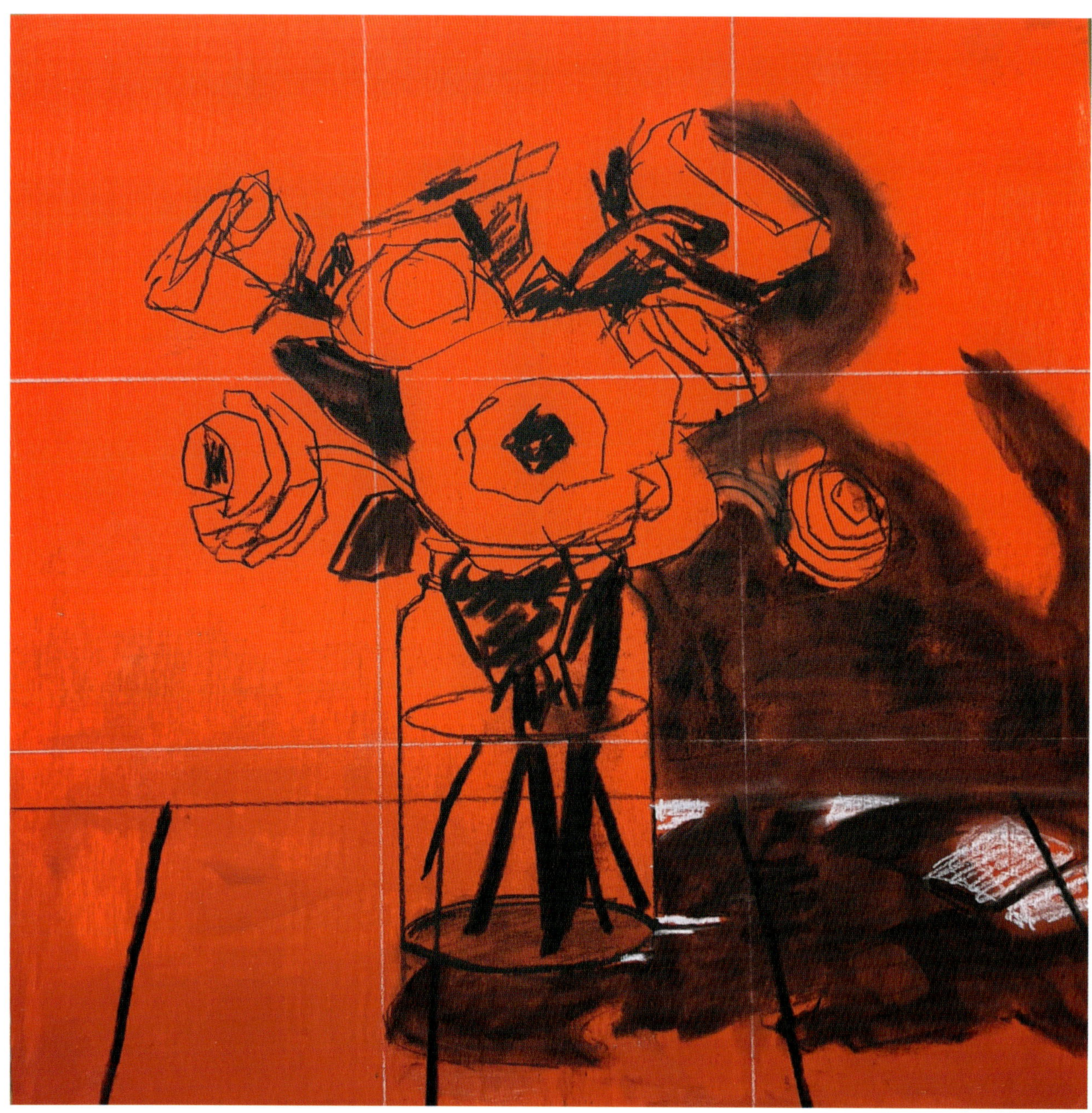

Whichever color you choose for your wash can act like a photo filter on your work, so go ahead and experiment! If working on a wet-toned canvas doesn't appeal to you, try acrylic paint or even colored gesso for a fast-drying color base for your painting.

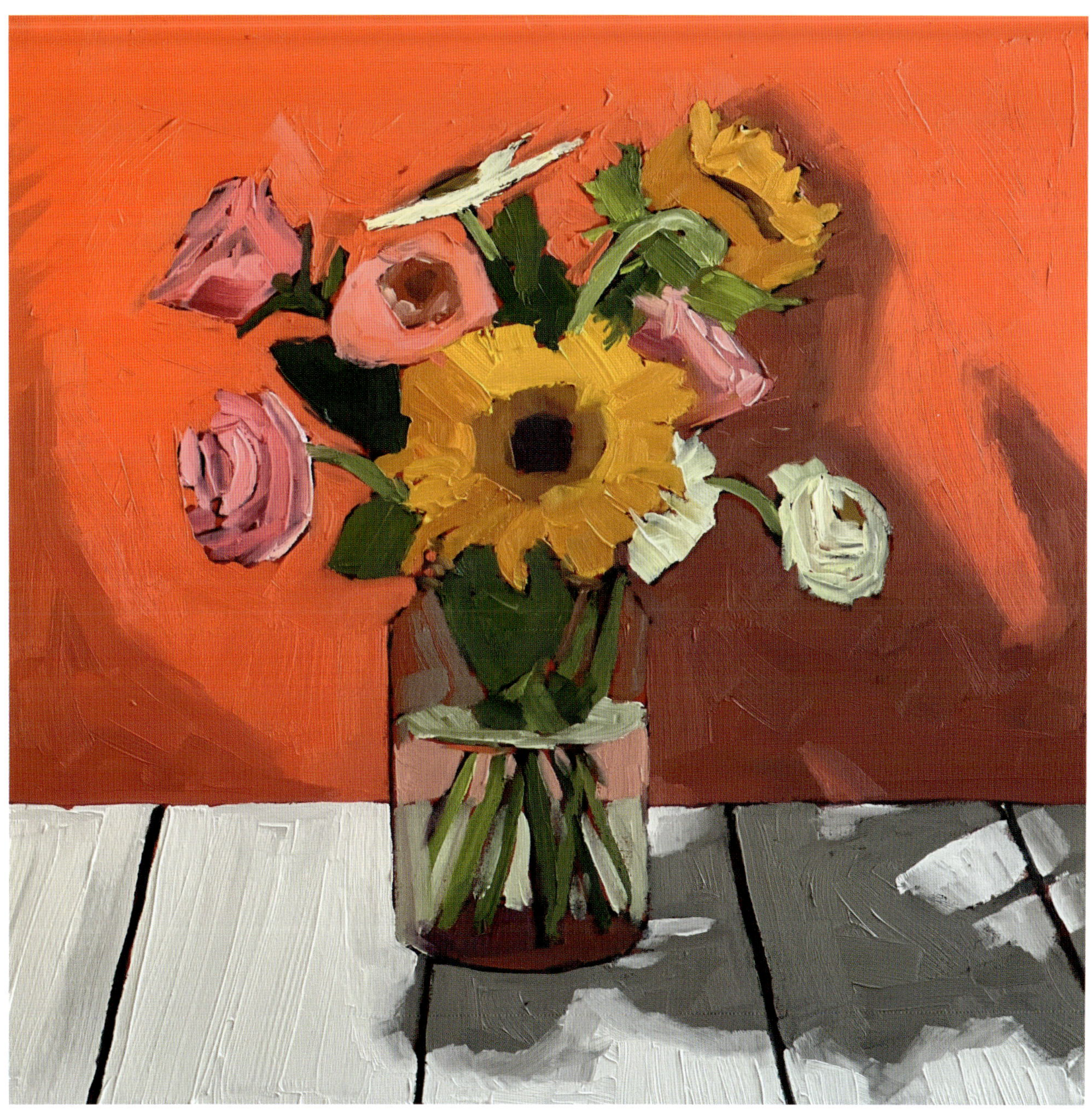

Debbie Miller, *Red Hot Mama*, oil on panel, 12" × 12" | 30.5 × 30.5 cm

Gesso is an acrylic-based primer that can be used on any paintable surface and comes in many colors, including black! Debbie Miller prepares her panels with red gesso before painting her cheerful, engaging floral still lifes.

After I've toned my canvas using my mixture of cadmium yellow, cadmium red, and ultramarine blue, I begin blocking in my composition by looking at my thumbnail sketch or value study to locate the "landmarks" around the edges. Once those are established, I switch to working from my still life setup, refining my drawing as I go along. Remember to keep squinting at your still life and checking in with your big value shapes. Don't get too involved with any one area of the drawing before you've got the whole composition blocked in loosely. Bring it all up together. If something is tricky to draw, switch to drawing the space around it. I like to block in curved objects and ellipses with a series of straight lines, using shorter strokes rather than a continuous, curved brush mark. I also like to break up my ellipses; I might place an object on a plate so that it crosses the rim or contour line. Then I only have a series of small curves to render, not a complete ellipse. Check your blocked-in drawing by looking at it in a mirror. This will show you, all too clearly, where things are lopsided.

This method of creating an underpainting is a lot like charcoal drawing—additive and subtractive. So, alternate between blocking in lines, pulling out lights with a rag or a clean brush dipped in Gamsol, and emphasizing darks by adding a bit more ultramarine and some alizarin crimson to the tone color. No white is used in this stage. Wiping off paint creates lighter passages, and darker paint—not thicker paint—creates darker passages. Keep your paint to an even consistency by mixing in some Gamsol as you're loading your brush. This part of the process is almost like watercolor!

There's no white used in the underpainting, because I'm going to paint on this thin layer while it's still somewhat wet, but while I pause for color mixing in the next step, this layer will sink into the surface of my canvas a little. It won't "dry," but I'll be able to lay paint over it without mixing in. If I have white paint in the underpainting, that sinking in will not occur, and my first step will mix into whatever I put over it, turning everything pastel! So keep the white out—for now. All other colors, thinly applied, are okay!

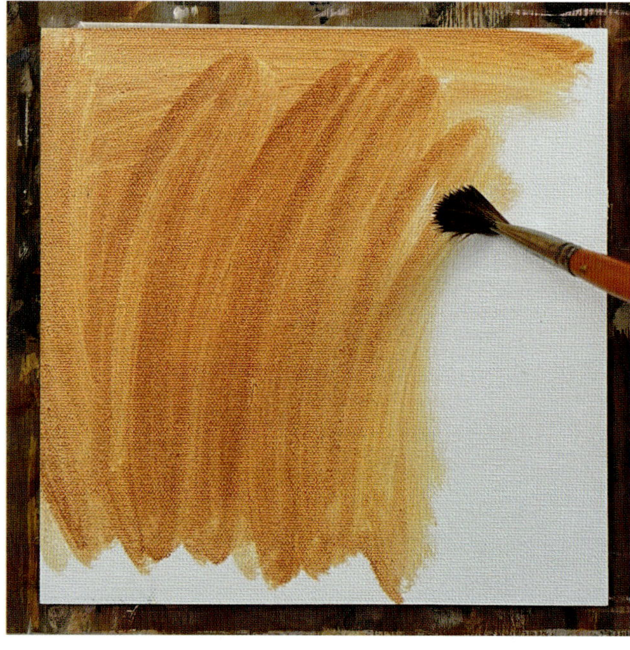

An underpainting in three steps: tone, put in darks, pull out lights. The underpainting is an additive and subtractive process, much like charcoal drawing. It's my favorite step of the three, because everything is fluid, nothing is set in stone, and there are no mistakes.

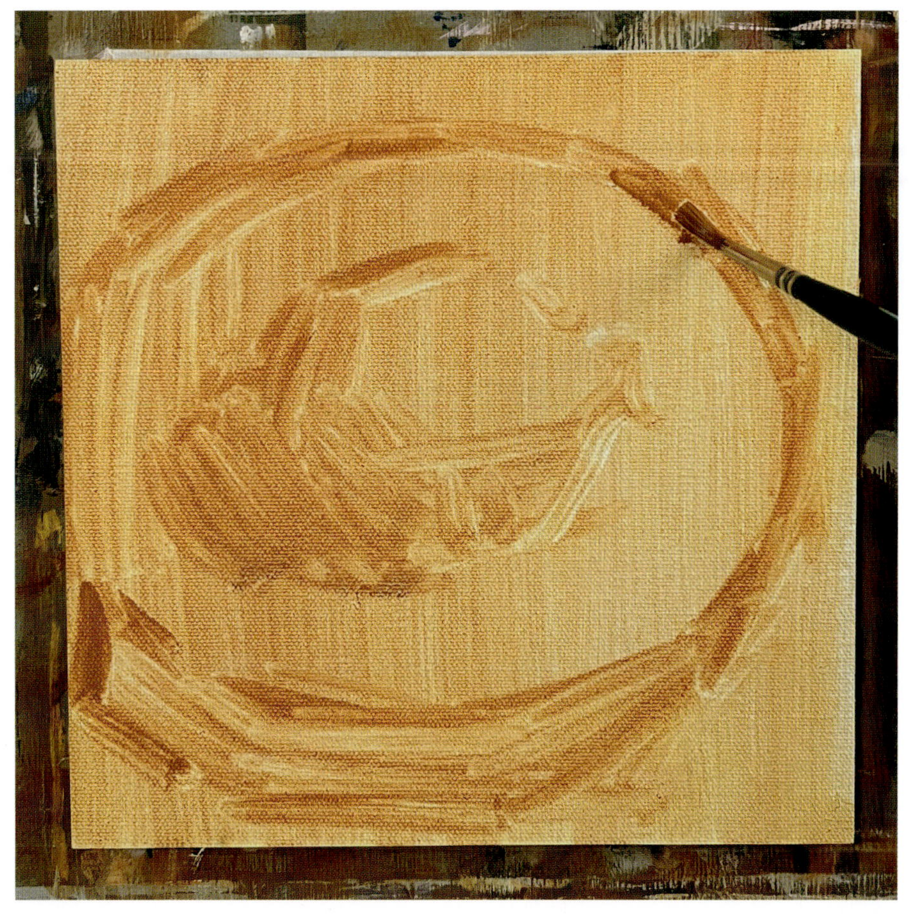

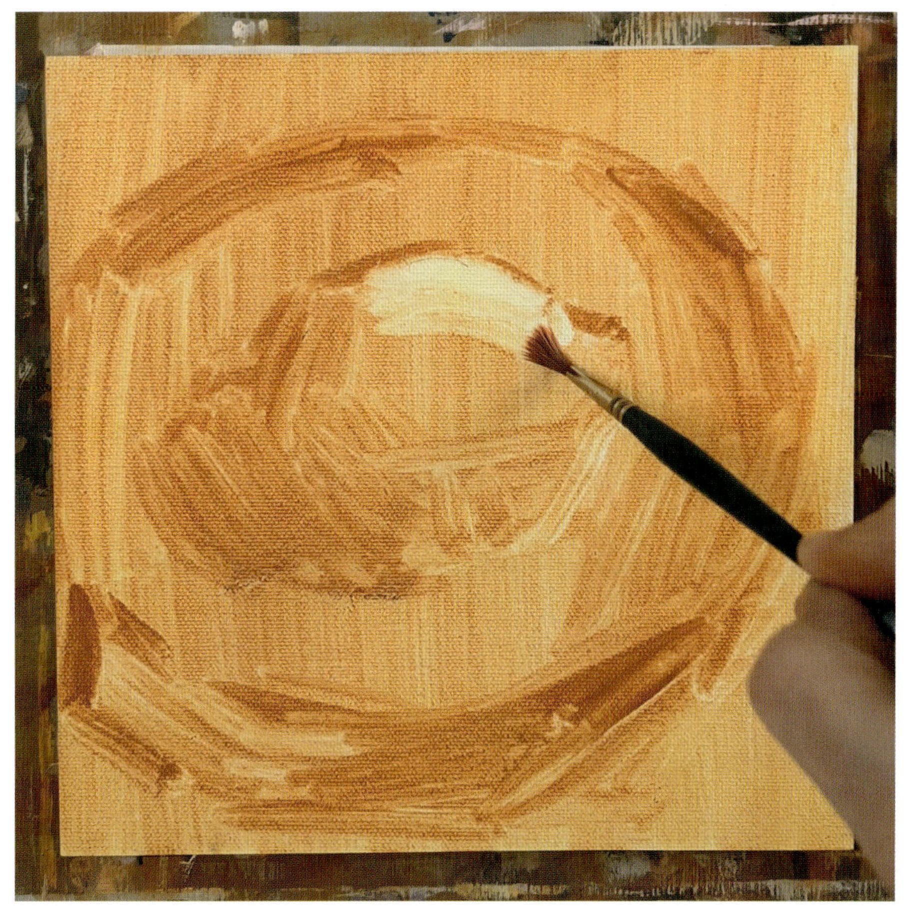

STEP 2: COLOR MIXING

I am a big believer in premixing colors. Time spent mixing is time spent painting! And that time is going to get spent at some point during your painting process. So, if you like to mix with your brush as you go, great! Your mixing time will be spread out through the entire painting session. I like to take some of that mixing time up front so I can focus more on paint application and edges later. Possibly the biggest benefit of premixing is that it saves time and energy that might be spent on *re*mixing—backtracking to recreate a color that's been used up, fix a mistake, or tweak an edge. It can be difficult to remember which pigments went into a particular mixture, so having a premixed pile in reserve can be a lifesaver in the later stages of a painting.

Painting alla prima, or wet-on-wet, doesn't mean not painting in layers; it just means not waiting for the layers to dry in between. Adding mediums and thickening the paint can help wet paint stick to other wet paint, but before we get there, the next step is to mix some colors. During this color mixing time, the underpainting has a chance to set up. It won't dry, but it will settle into the gesso on the canvas or panel, just enough to easily paint over without lifting or mixing into the paint, even if we only spend ten or fifteen minutes mixing color. (Note: If the underpainting is still very wet after color mixing, or if you mixed your colors previously, try blasting your underpainting with a hair dryer to help it set up. A quick fix!)

I don't mix a color for every single spot that I see—there could never be a palette big enough! (That said, choose the biggest palette you can—at least 12 by 16 inches [30.5 by 40.6 cm]). I want to mix a pile or two for the light and for the dark values of every hue family in my still life. So, for a lemon on a purple plate, I mix at least six piles of color: lemon in the light, lemon in the shadow, purple plate in the light and in the shadow, and the color of the negative space, in light and in shadow. Because color mixing is a journey, not a science, I often end up with mixtures that aren't exactly what I intended, but if they're close, and they're appealing to my eye, I keep them. (If they're not, I continue mixing them into something else.) It's lovely to have a range of warms and cools for each value area, and some mixtures for the midtones as well.

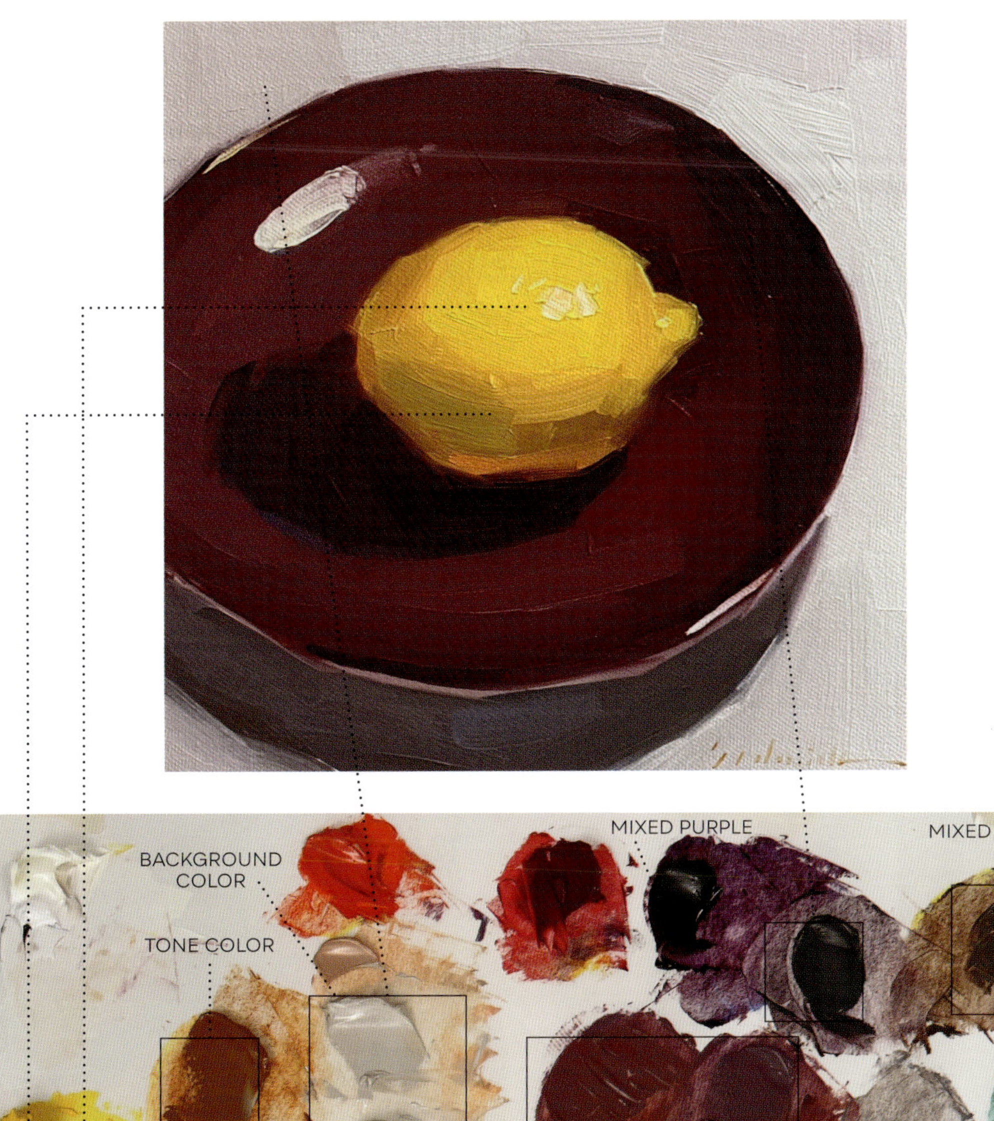

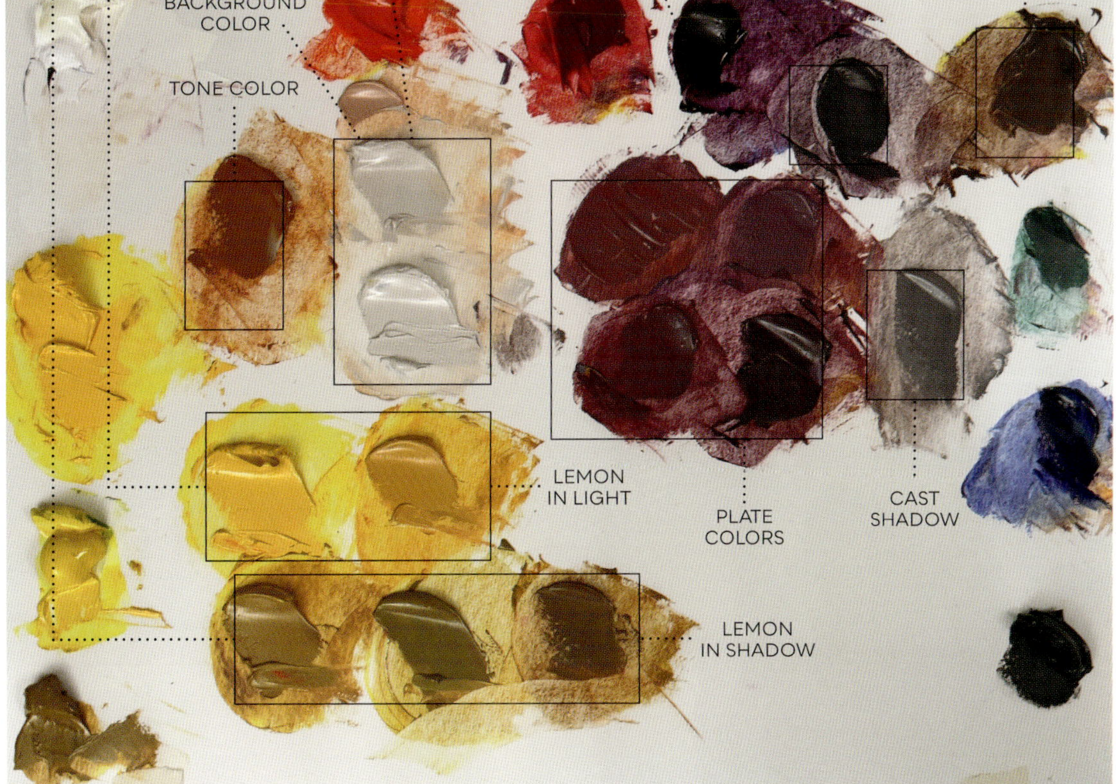

It's a good habit to get into to keep your premixtures for each area of a painting close together on the palette. So, my lemon mixtures are all together, my purple plate mixtures are together, and so on, forming "color clouds." The "tone color"—a mixture of cadmium yellow medium, cadmium red light, and ultramarine blue—is what I will use for my underpainting in step one.

Because I use a split-primary palette, I don't have any secondary color pigments to work with—I mix them all. So, my oranges, greens, and purples are less intense than they would be if I were to use, say, cadmium orange from the tube or dioxazine purple. I *do* use those colors sometimes, but generally, I like the slight neutralization that comes from mixing them from the primaries. All colors get more neutral, and more naturalistic, by being mixed rather than taken straight from the tube. The more ingredients in a mixture—the more steps a color mixture is taken from the tube—the more neutral it gets. Adding white is also a neutralizer—it reduces chroma as it increases value. Neutralizing colors is not a bad thing—it's desirable. It creates natural-feeling colors. When I am mixing, my goal is to have at least a little of the third primary involved, so if I'm mixing an orange from red and yellow, unless it is for the brightest, most saturated orange spot in my painting, I definitely want at least a whisker of the complement, the third primary—blue—in the mix.

Just as I lay out my palette with the pigments in the same spot around the outer edge each time, I tend to organize the central "real estate" of my palette consistently as well. So, I mix warm colors toward the left, near my red and yellow pigments in the outer ring, and cooler colors on the right, near the blues and greens. However you organize your mixtures, try to be consistent. Over time you'll develop a method that works for you, and every time your brush goes back to the palette, you'll eliminate the extra thought-step of hunting for a color. If forgetting what part of the painting your mixtures were made for is a problem, keep your colors together—so, lemon colors in one area of the palette, plate colors together in another, and so on. I think of these as "color clouds," loosely organized but distinct.

The larger the painting, the more paint needs to be mixed. For one of my larger paintings, I could be mixing for over an hour! I try to let this be a relaxing, meditative time. Mixing colors and watching what happens as the pigments combine is the *active study of color theory*. Move your eye around your still life. Compare one color spot to another, and remember to keep squinting and thinking of color as value. That dark yellow on the shadow side of the lemon is a lot darker than you think it is! Comparing that value to the value of the cast shadow can help you gauge just how dark it is. And lastly, no matter the size of your canvas, mix a lot of paint. Mix more paint than you think you need to. Painting is a lot more fun when there's plenty of juicy paint to use, and the leftovers can always be stored in the freezer for the next studio session.

STEP 3: APPLYING COLOR

The first brushstrokes on a painting are decisions that set the tone for everything that comes after. They don't have to be perfect, but they should be as correct as possible, because they're a benchmark against which to judge the next steps. That's why I like to begin applying color with an "easy win," or a color I think I understand—its hue, value, and intensity—and can mix easily. This is often the lightest, most saturated color I see. Starting with the lightest, most intense color also has the added benefit of helping keep that color clean and fresh as I fill in the rest of the elements around it.

Returning to my lemon on the purple plate: If I begin with the plate, working from background to foreground, when it's time to paint the light yellows in the lemon, it will be very difficult to keep them clean with all that purple around. If I paint the yellow first—and even paint a bit outside the lines—any extra yellow can be covered with purple later on, refining the edges of the lemon by cutting into it. Yellow paint will not cover purple as well, so I think of it as a "vulnerable color." It's vulnerable to getting muddied up by a darker, complementary color right next door. So, where to begin? With an "easy win," or with a "vulnerable color."

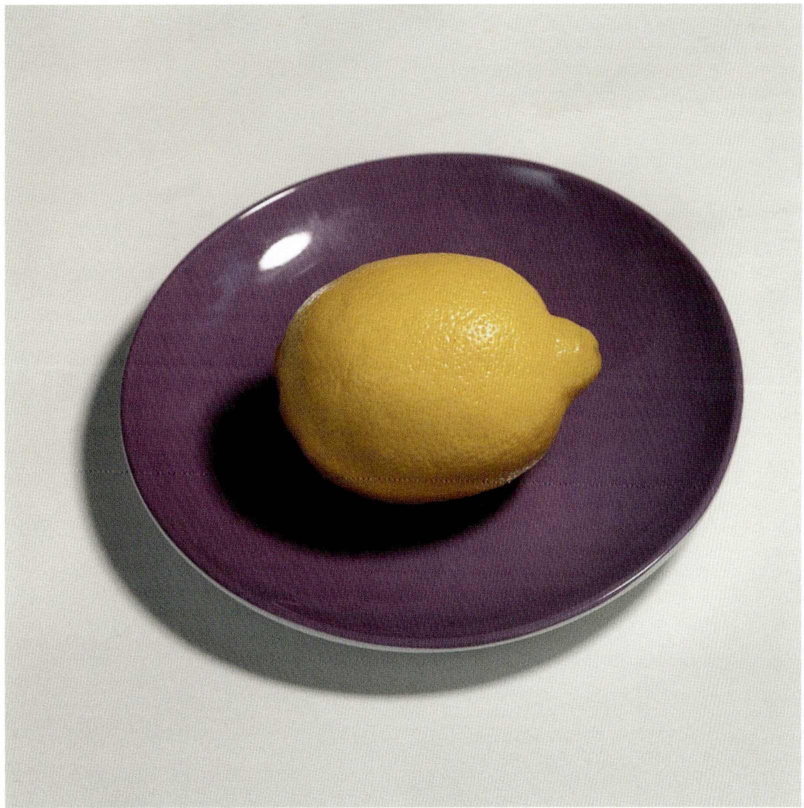

Lemon on a purple plate. The yellow is a "vulnerable" color since it is surrounded by its much-darker complement. The light yellows are also a fairly easy color to diagnose and mix; they are close to the tube, possibly not neutralized at all! So, those light yellows are an "easy win," a good place to start applying color.

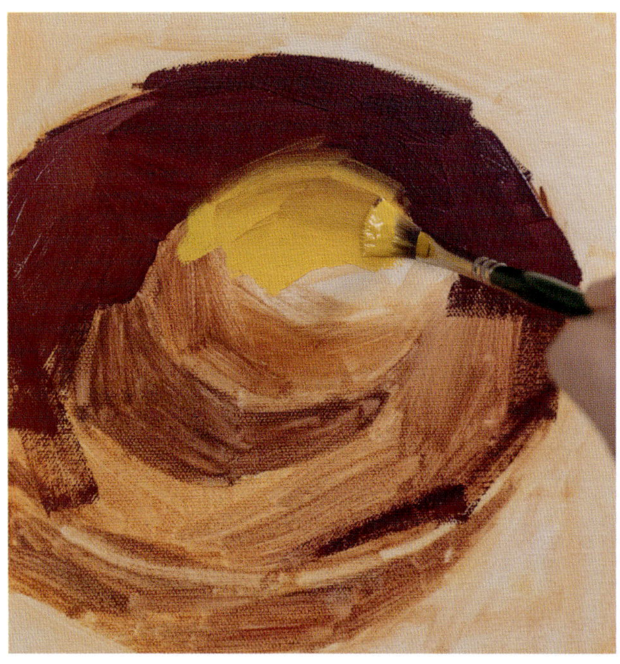

If I begin by laying in purple, the *much* darker complementary color to yellow, it's likely that my lemon will get muddy when I add it in.

Achieving loose realism is all about edges, and the best way to control your edges—and get a rich, painterly look—is to use more paint. The key to using more paint is loading the paintbrush. I crosshatch my brush back and forth in the paint on my palette, really packing the bristles with color, to get the most bang for each brushstroke. Using mediums like Gamblin's Solvent-Free Gel, or a little walnut oil, helps the paint load onto the brush and unload onto the canvas in a satisfying way. Think of the paintbrush not as a magic wand, or as a way to "pet" the canvas, but as a little dump truck for transporting paint from the palette to the canvas—and load it up!

As you begin applying color, work from the *general* to the *specific*, big shapes to small details. Form is created by getting the big value shapes of the light and shadow side correct relative to each other, and once you have form, then there is somewhere to place the details. So, begin big and bold with your brushstrokes, working toward smaller marks and greater detail as you go. It's great to begin with a bigger brush than you want to, and then switch to the smaller ones—or maybe never pick them up at all! I like to paint with flats because they create the greatest variety of brush marks—pinpoint highlights with the corners, thinner and rounded strokes with the brush turned vertically on its side, and broad swaths of paint with the bristles flat on the canvas.

How firmly are you connecting with the canvas? Experiment with different pressures, squeezing the paint out of your brush or scrubbing it vigorously onto your surface. Try pushing your paintbrush backward or moving it in a circular stroke. The only "wrong" way to paint is timidly!

Texture can be created with impasto—an application of thick, dimensional paint—or by scratching or scraping into the paint. The ability to backtrack—to remove wet paint when things just aren't working—is a huge advantage of painting alla prima. It's like the Command + Z shortcut for your canvas! And the scraping off can create beautiful effects.

Just because a painting is made "all at once" doesn't mean it doesn't have layers. Layering wet-on-wet brushstrokes by adding mediums to help paint stick to other wet paint builds from a thin underpainting to a richly textured surface.

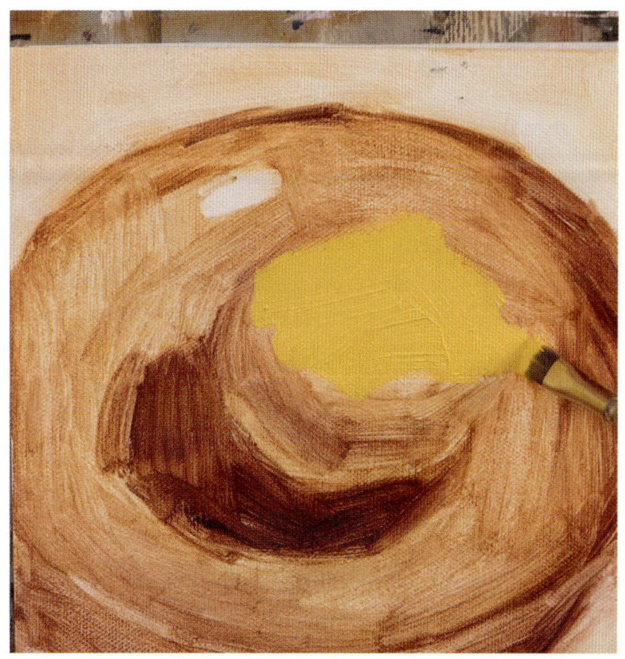

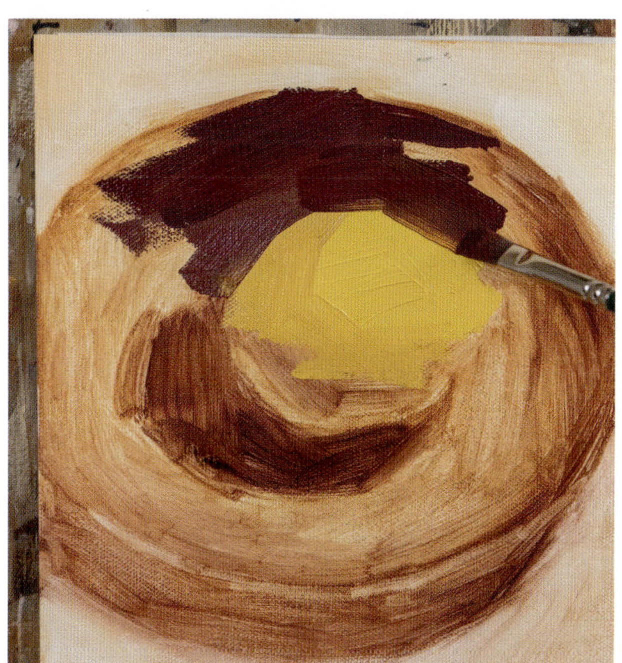

If I begin with my "vulnerable colors," the light, saturated yellows on the light side of the lemon, and paint them *out beyond the contour lines* just a bit, I can cut in on them with the darker purple later on, crafting the richly painted edges that I want.

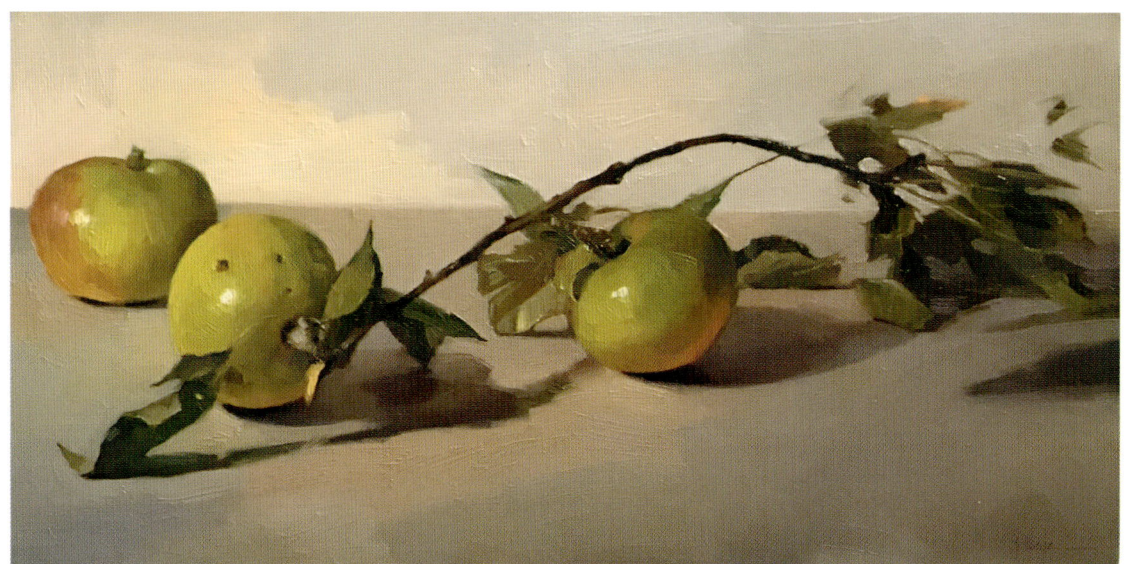

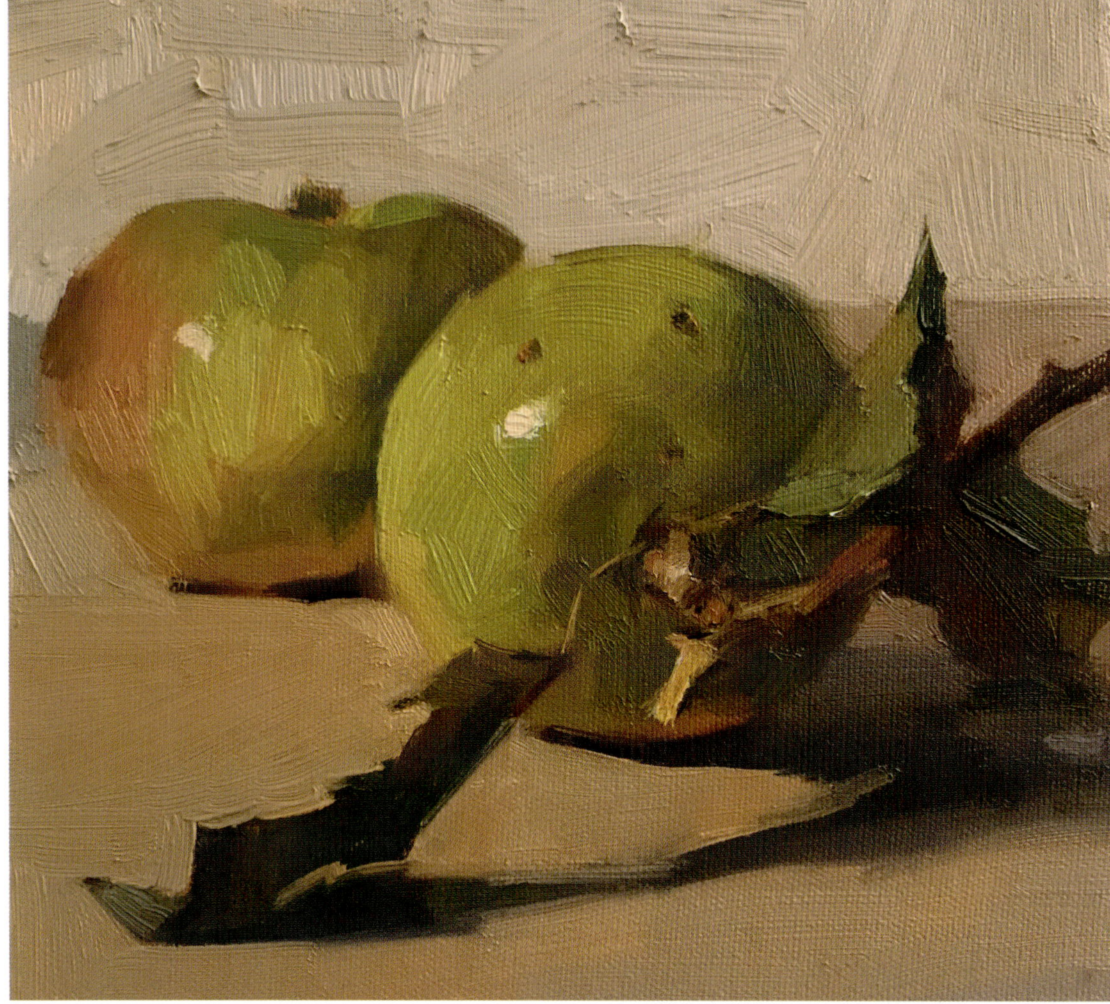

▲ Sarah Sedwick, *Early Apples* (and detail), oil on canvas, 12" × 24" | 30.5 × 61 cm

Experiment with different types of brushes, putting down opaque strokes of paint and then leaving them alone! Often, I paint with synthetic flat brushes. Here, a hog bristle filbert creates gorgeous texture on the canvas.

▶ Scott Conary, *Ruby*, oil on panel, 8" × 10" | 20.3 × 25.4 cm

Periodically scraping and then building the paint back up on the panel creates gorgeous texture in Scott Conary's work. And I love meat as a still life subject!

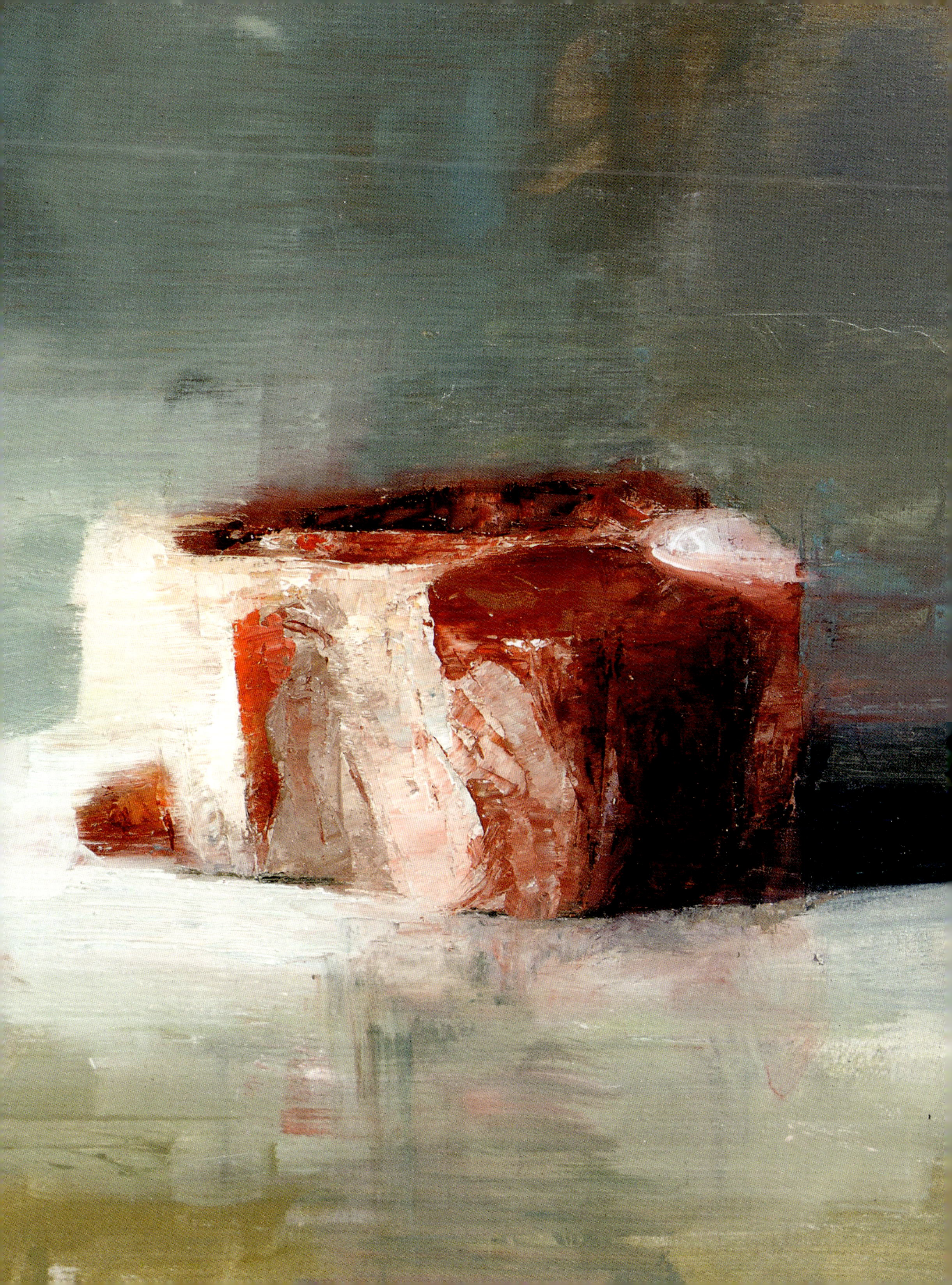

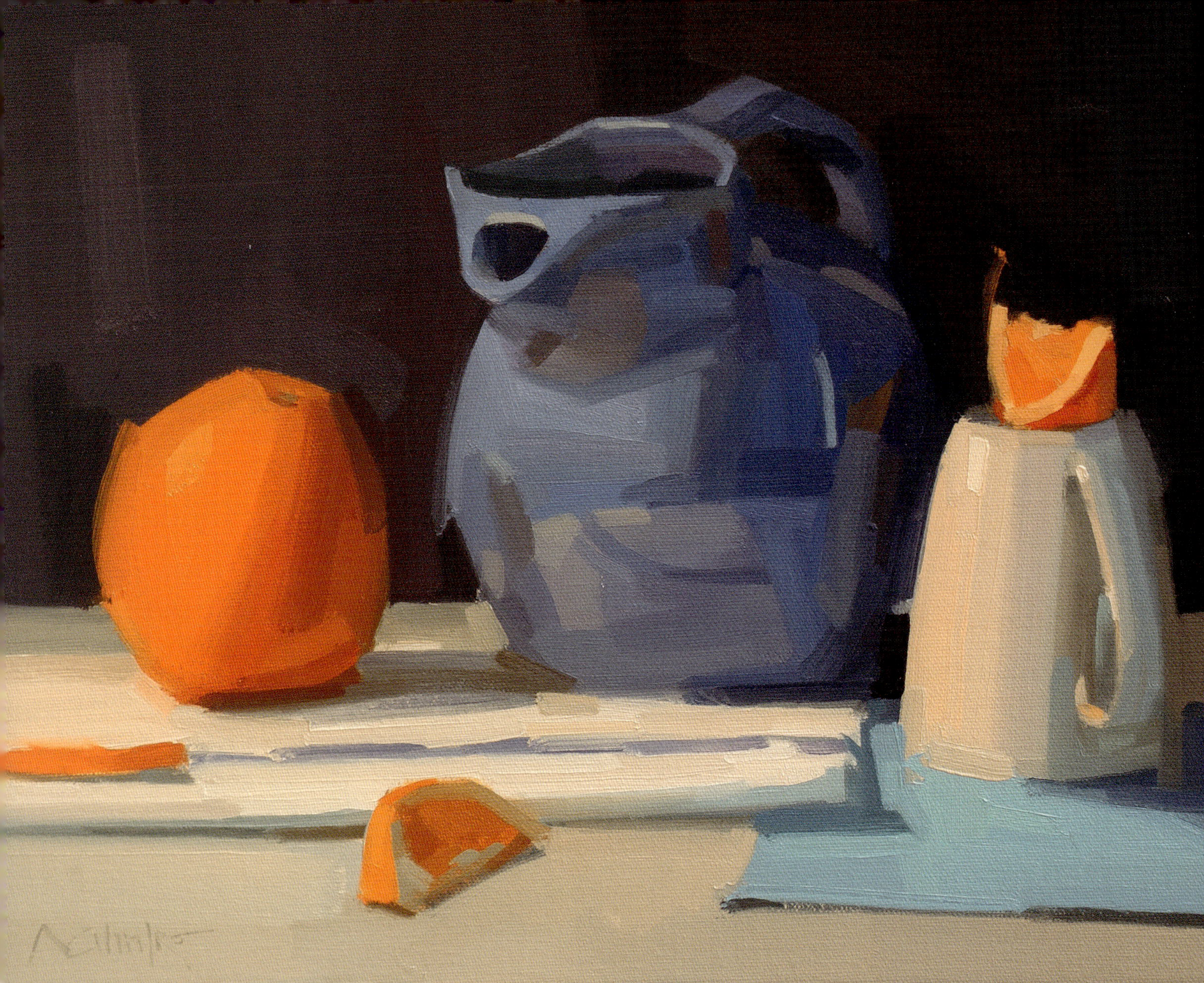

▲ Sarah Calandro, *Orange Reflections*, oil on canvas, 14" × 11" | 35.6 × 28 cm

A variety of edges excite the eye. Hard edges attract us—here, to the mouth of the pitcher, the left edge of the mug, and the orange slice on the ground. Soft edges turn the form, rounding out the orange on the left and the mug on its right. And lost edges, like the one between the rim of the pitcher and the background, give the viewer a mystery to solve, making this painting a joy to look at.

THE THREE TYPES OF EDGES: HARD, SOFT, AND LOST

Hard edge. A crisp meeting of brushstrokes, in sharp focus, unblended. These are great for creating or reinforcing focal points and to use where an object is lit most strongly. They attract the eye.

Soft edge. A broad spectrum. All edges that aren't *hard* or *lost* are soft—to varying degrees. I like to create soft edges by massaging one brushstroke into another, placing paint down and then placing the next stroke so that it overlaps just slightly, wet into wet. Blending with a clean brush can soften an edge. Cast shadows almost always have soft edges, increasingly so the farther they get from their object. Anything in shadow probably has a soft edge—we don't see hard edges in the dark!

Lost edge. The key to loose realism. A lost edge can be *created* where two spots of the same value come together in a painting—even if they are different colors—so that when you squint, no dividing line is visible. The camera hates lost edges and will in fact create edges where none are visible. My motto for finding lost edges: "Squint and combine, don't separate and define!"

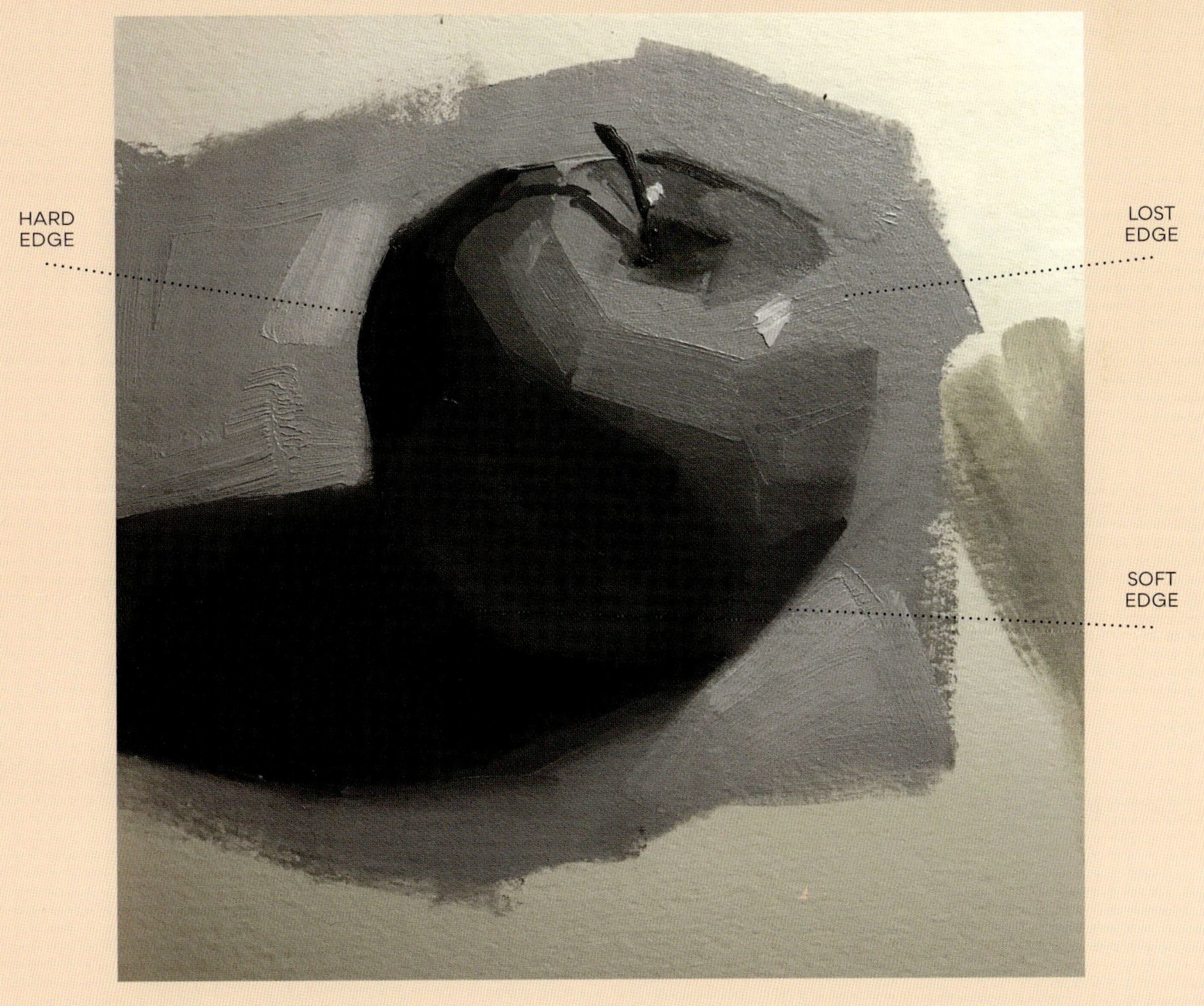

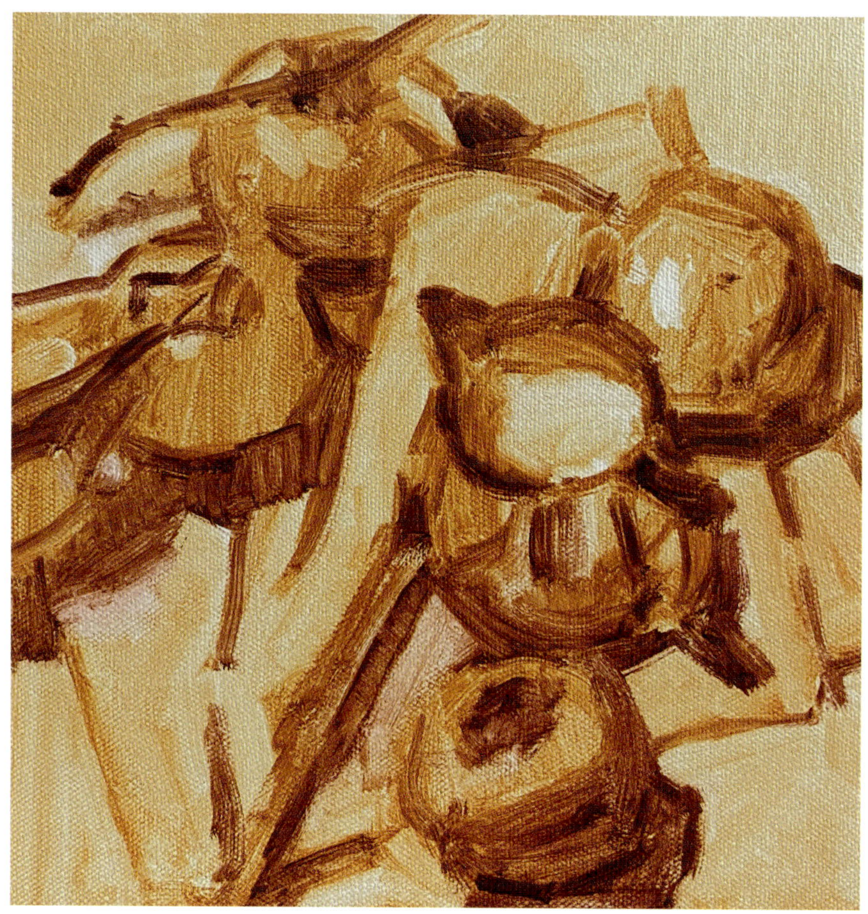

Sometimes it happens that my colors look great on the palette and just feel wrong in the first few strokes on the canvas. With practice, I've learned that I have to get some other colors down—preferably next to the ones I'm uncertain about—before I can judge their rightness or wrongness. It's like an early "awkward stage," those first exploratory strokes on the canvas. One idea is that we should just accept that our first steps are wrong and plan to come back and fix them as we paint our way into an understanding of what's going on in the particular and unique painting we are making today.

Checking in with your palette periodically during the painting process is a great habit to get into. When the palette gets out of control, your painting won't be far behind! The goal is to use up all that luscious paint you mixed in step 2 *and* to notice when it's been used up, put down the brush, pick up the palette knife, and make some more. I call my palette check-ins "mix-downs," as I'm often combining several depleted piles of color into one, and then remixing what I need, starting from there. This process brings more color harmony to my palette, by "marrying" all the pigments I've laid around the outer edge, and gives me a chance to do with my palette knife what I might have been doing with my brush as I was painting—altering my premixed piles to suit my subject.

All the preparation—from choosing a color scheme and setting up a still life, to thumbnails, a value study, and color mixing—has led to this: the main event! And now that preparation is paying off, so let go, have fun, and enjoy!

The first strokes of color you apply to the canvas can feel "off," especially if you're beginning with an orange object over an orange underpainting! Trust your premixtures, and keep going—the more color you add, working all around the painting, the better able you'll be to make judgments about those initial strokes.

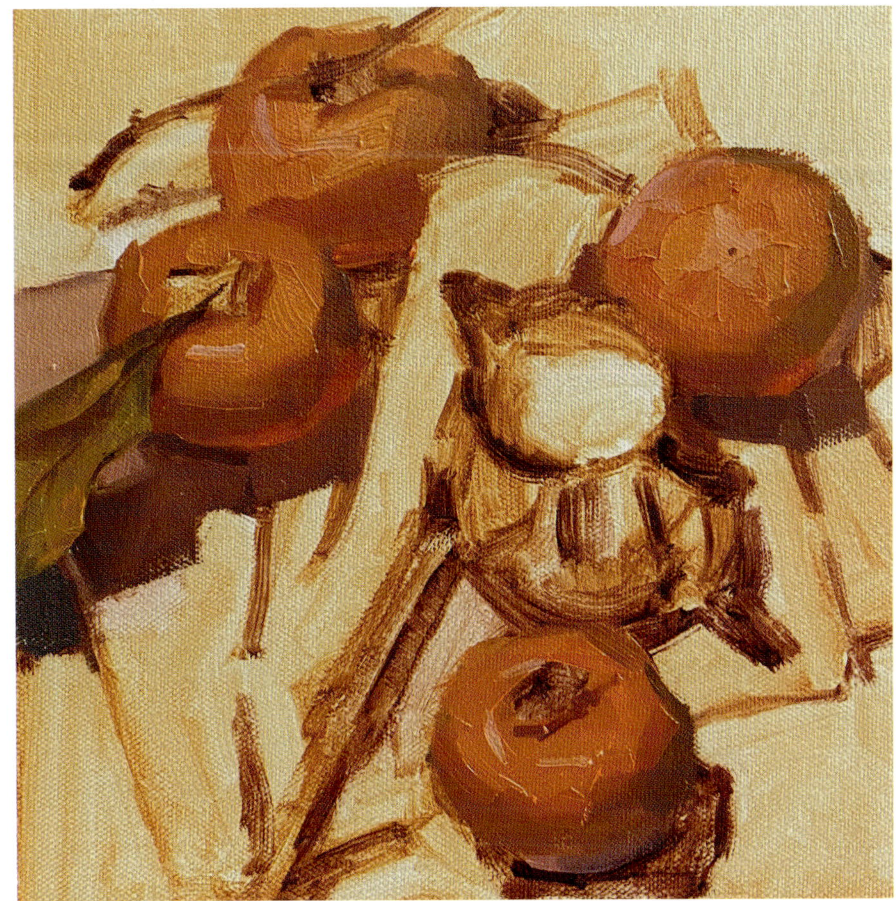

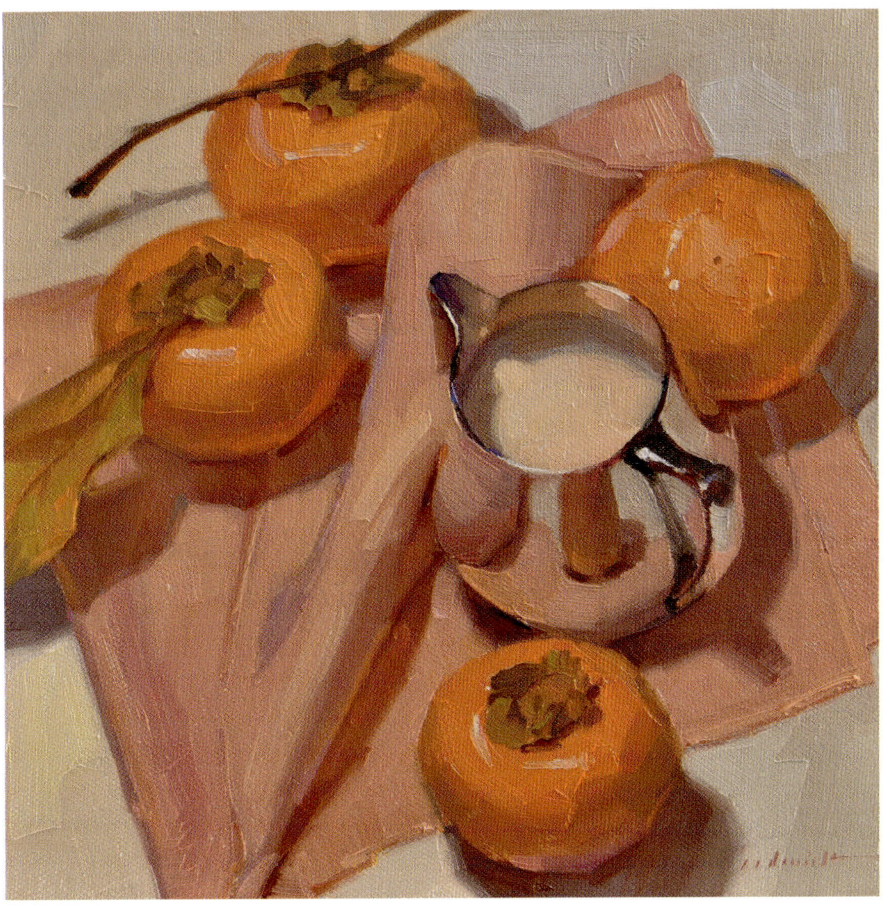

Sarah Sedwick, *Persimmons and Cream*, oil on canvas, 8" × 8" | 20.3 × 20.3 cm

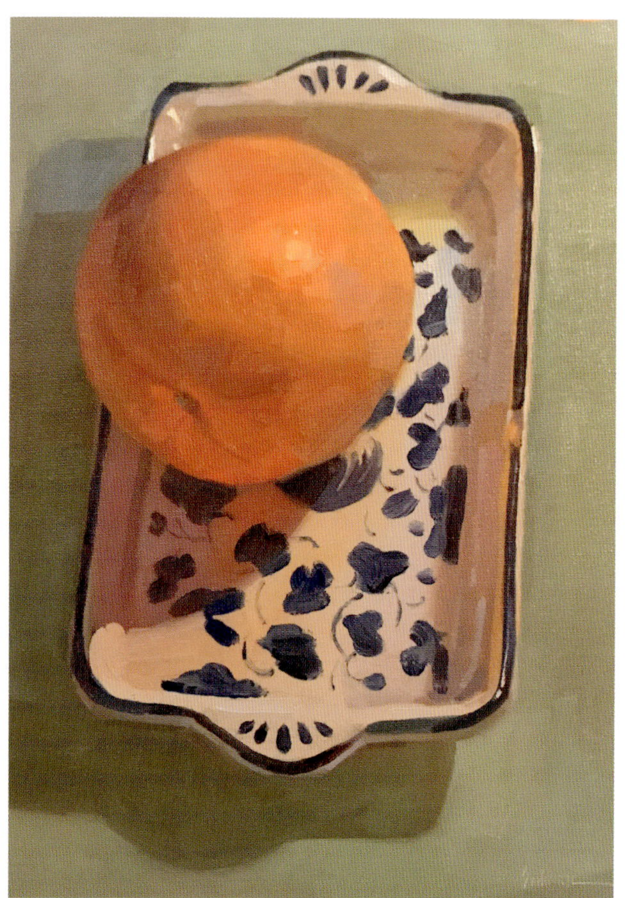

▲ Sarah Sedwick, *Cracked Rim*,
oil on canvas, 9" × 12" | 22.9 × 30.5 cm

“White” is almost never white! Be aware of how the colors in your still life affect one another, particularly when it comes to white. And with a patterned object like this one, I paint the entire form first, modeling it in “white” and then paint the pattern on top. Sometimes I give it a day or two to get semi-dry first, but usually I paint it right on top, wet into wet.

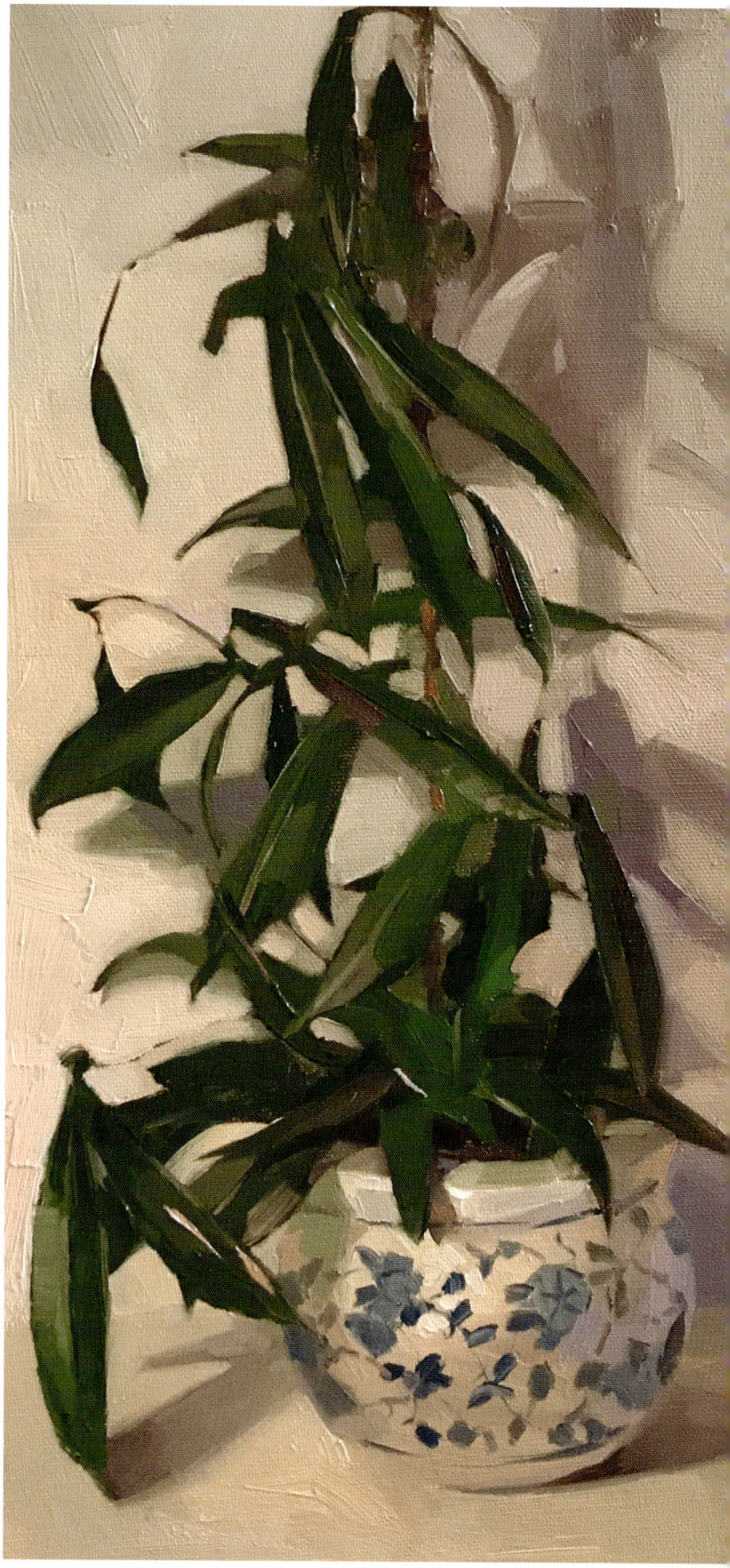

▶ Sarah Sedwick, *Hoya Kentiana*,
oil on canvas, 8" × 16" | 20.3 × 40.6 cm

Another blue pattern on white, this one in two shades of blue. I painted this pattern very loosely, especially where the form turns into shadow, letting the pattern feel clearer and more defined where the pot is in light.

PAINT OUTSIDE THE BOX: ALTERNATIVE MATERIALS

Oil paint is my medium of choice, though the alla prima technique described previously can be enjoyed with acrylics, particularly slow-drying varieties like Golden Open Acrylics. There are also water-mixable oils available from several brands; Royal Talens Cobra is one I've heard highly recommended.

Canvas, linen, and wood are traditional supports for oil paints, and nowadays panels made of aluminum and copper are revolutionizing the way artists think about what to paint on. I love painting on Arches oil paper, which is impermeable to oil and ready to use right off the pad, but any kind of paper can become a surface for oil painting if it is sealed with a coat of gesso or acrylic medium. You can even oil paint right in your sketchbook. Choose one with thick paper and either gesso the page first or just go ahead and paint! Gamsol doesn't warp paper the way water can, so your sketchbook will still close flat. True, paintings on unprimed paper will break down over time, but for practice, an oil painting sketchbook can be great.

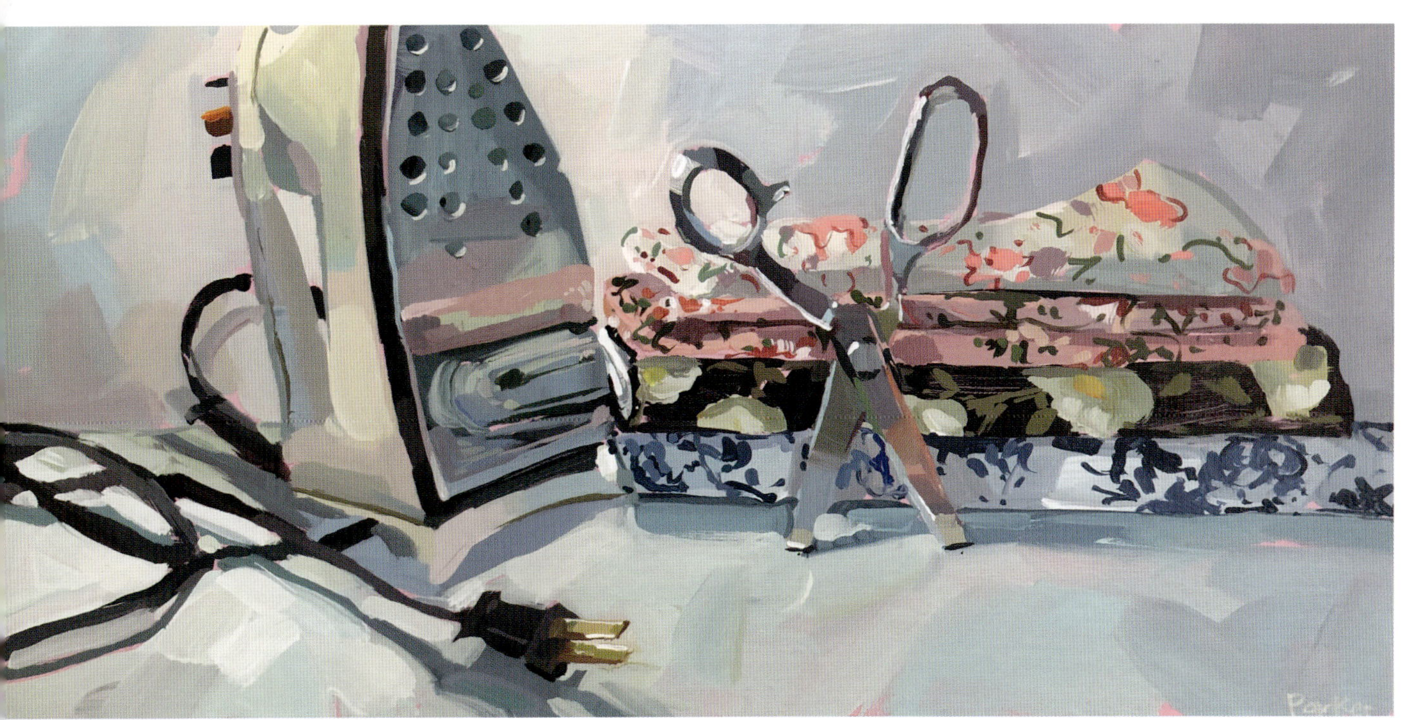

Teddi Parker, *Sewing on the Brain*, acrylic house paint on canvas panel, 8" × 16" | 20.3 × 40.6 cm

Teddi Parker uses acrylic house paint to create her fun, colorful still lifes. Painting quickly allows her to use some wet-on-wet techniques, even with this fast-drying medium.

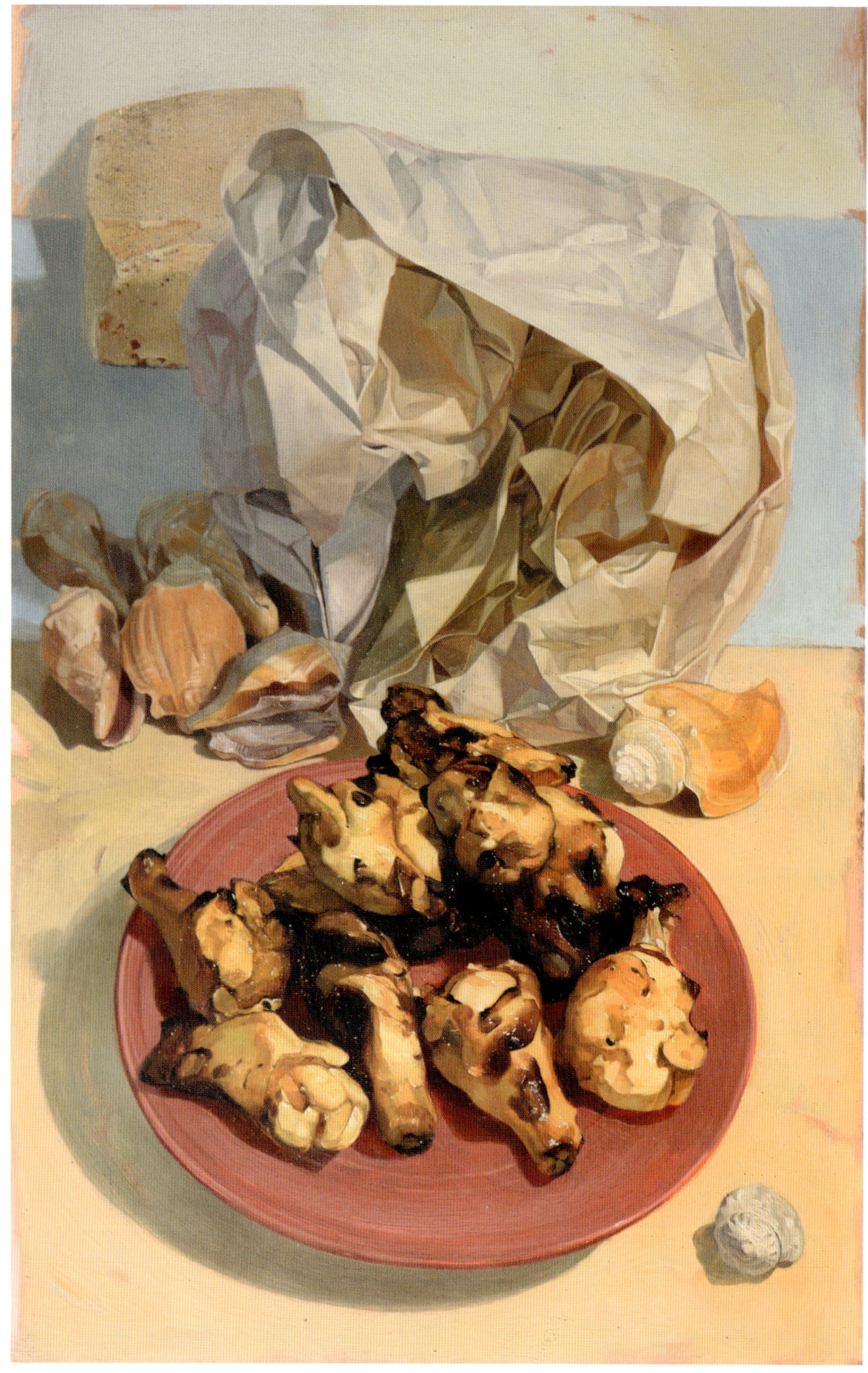

Benjamin Shamback, *Curry Wings*, oil on copper, 18" × 21" | 45.7 × 53.3 cm

Copper and aluminum are catching on as sturdy, archival supports for painters. Benjamin Shamback paints directly on his homemade copper panels, usually using no primer.

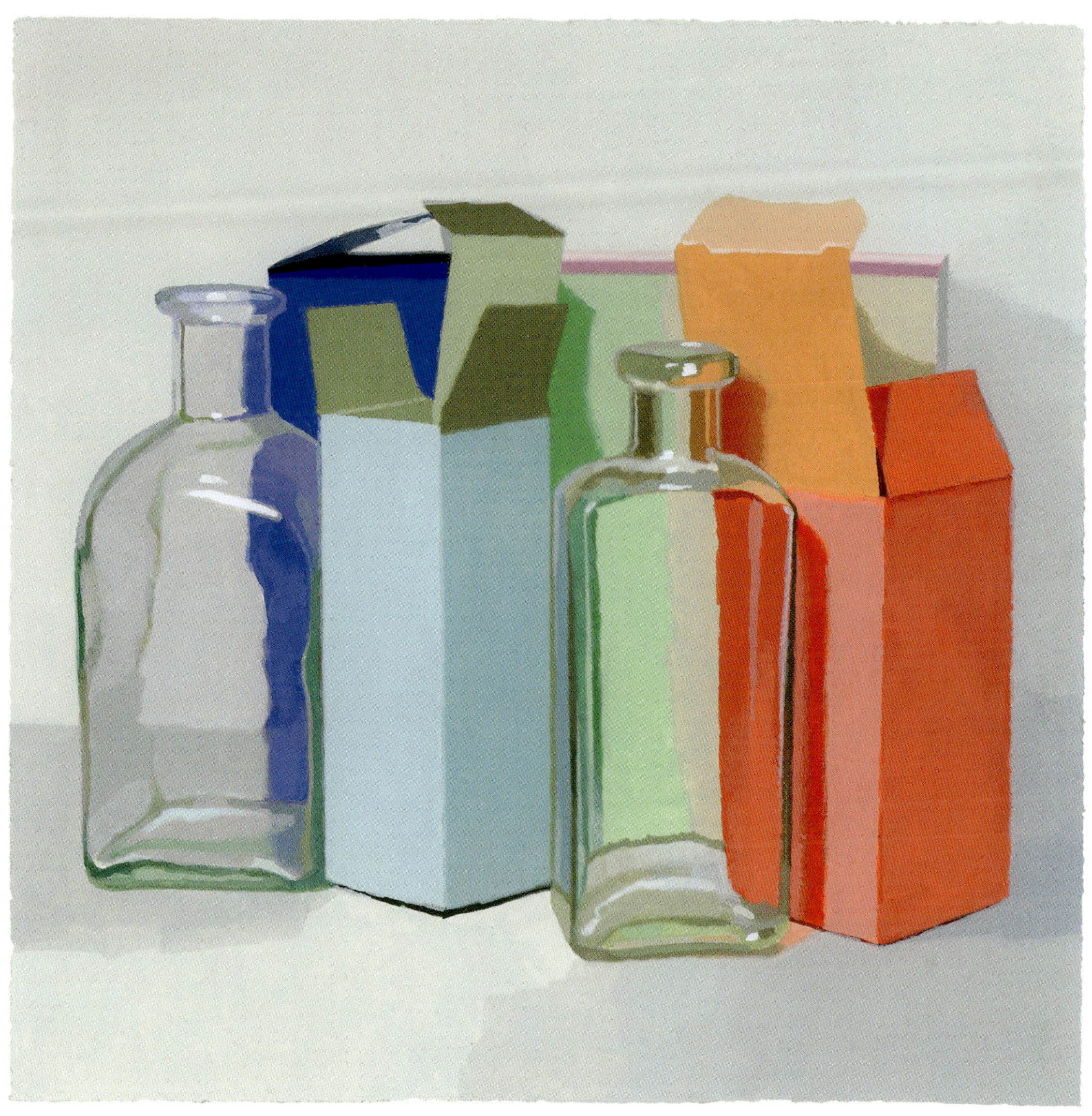

Jaye Schlesinger, *Bottles and Boxes*, gouache on paper, 9" × 9" | 22.9 × 22.9 cm

Jaye Schlesinger's colorful, modern still lifes show the versatility of gouache, an opaque watercolor.

For another alla prima option, give gouache a try. It's an opaque watercolor made from pigment mixed with gum arabic that can be used on any kind of paper—the heavier the better—or illustration board. Unlike watercolor, gouache comes in opaque white, so it can be used a lot like oil paint!

BATTLING OVERWHELM: BREAKING THE PROCESS INTO "BITES"

An uninterrupted studio day is a luxury. Many of us are scheduling our painting time around our busy lives, or vice versa. Breaking your process down into "bites" allows for progress to be made in an economical way.

Here's an example. On Monday, I only have one hour to be in the studio, so I do a little organizing and work on still life "marination," assembling two or three groups of objects and experimenting with color elements like paper and fabric to go with them. If I have time, I start arranging my favorite on the still life table. On Tuesday, I've had a chance to "sleep on" my experiments. With a three-hour chunk that afternoon, I refine the still life I started yesterday and play with lighting. Next, I look at it through my viewfinder and create a set of three thumbnails, or I might just jump to a value sketch in black and white oils. If I still have time, I'll choose a canvas size and do my underpainting. If not, I'll take a picture of my black-and-white value study and look at it on my phone later in the evening, thinking about any changes I want to make. On Wednesday, I can't make it into the studio at all.

By Thursday, I'm excited. I've got a composition I'm satisfied with—or an underpainting ready to go—and I know what my next steps are. I have a whole day to work, so I mix paint for thirty minutes or so and get to it. At the end of the day, I save time for photographing my work. Later that night, after I've given my eyes a rest, I look at the photo and ask myself, "If I were going to spend twenty more minutes on this painting, what are four or five things I'd tweak?" I still have my palette, stored in the freezer, so the next day I can try those tweaks—or not. Sometimes, all it takes is a good night's sleep for a painting to become finished!

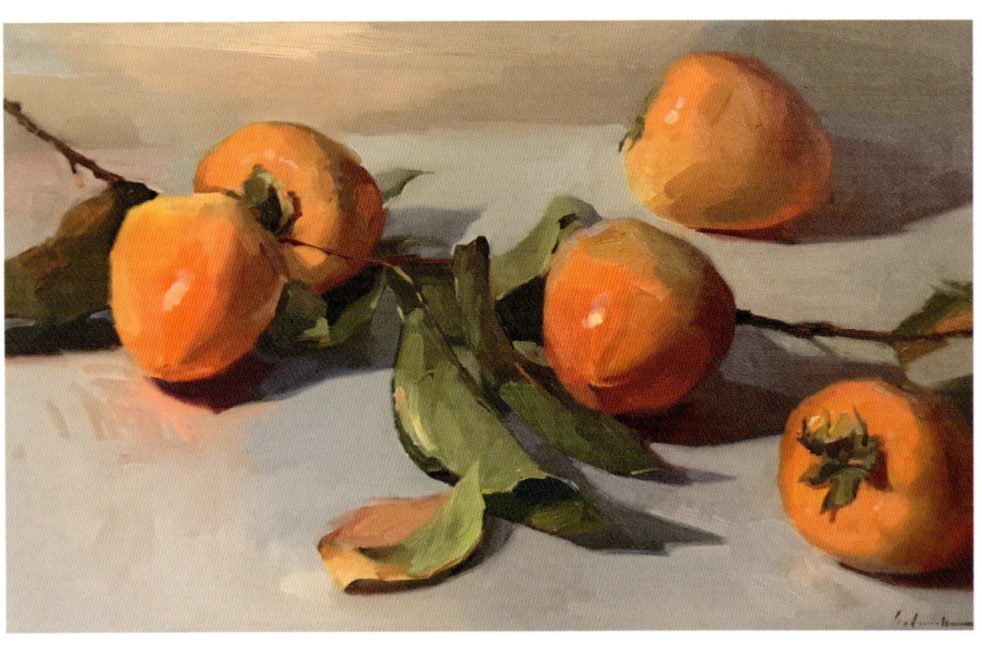

Sarah Sedwick, *November Persimmons*, oil on canvas, 13" × 21" | 33 × 53.3 cm

NO "BAD" PAINTING DAYS

The more we paint, the more "bad" painting days we are going to have. So, less-successful studio sessions are actually a *good* sign. In between times when we are making progress, we are usually on a plateau, which can get uncomfortable. If the level of challenge doesn't stay just ahead of our skills, the reward for success is much less. Conversely, if the challenge is too high compared to our skill level at the time, we will get discouraged and give up.

When I began Daily Painting, I simply looked around at what other artists were doing, and if it looked like fun, I tried it. Things I thought would be easy defeated me, and subjects that looked too difficult fell off my paintbrush with ease.

So, when a subject feels intimidating, attack it with the mind-set that it's just values, shapes, and colors. "Hard" and "easy" are just concepts in the mind, after all. And I'll repeat, keeping the challenge level appropriate is critical to maintaining your dedication to the study of painting. We should be pushing ourselves on a regular basis.

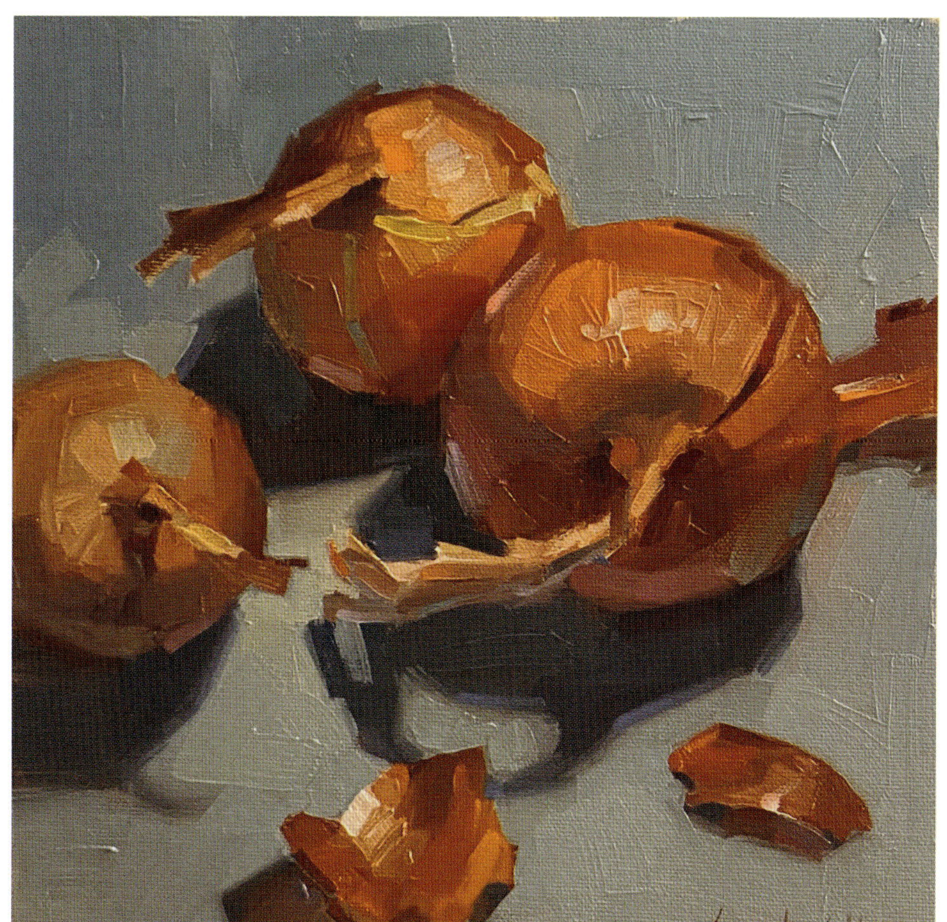

Sarah Sedwick, *Three Onions*, oil on canvas, 9" × 9" | 22.9 × 22.9 cm

Onions only *looked* like an intimidating subject! Once I was brave enough to tackle them, they turned out to be much easier than anticipated—proving, once again, that I never know what will be "easy" or "hard" until I give it a try.

EXERCISE:
THE THREE-STEP STILL LIFE

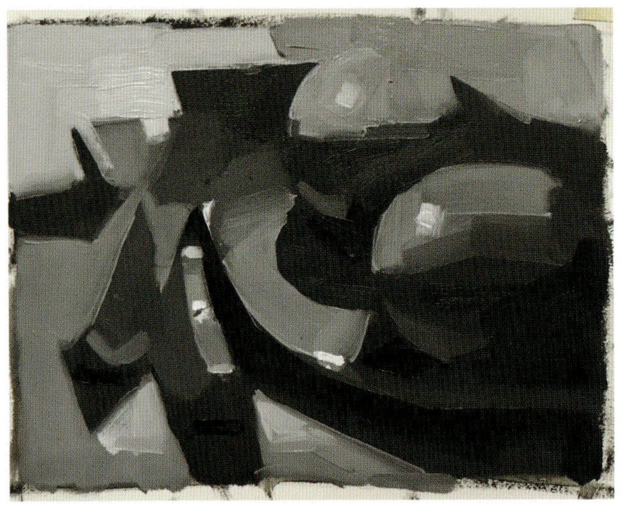

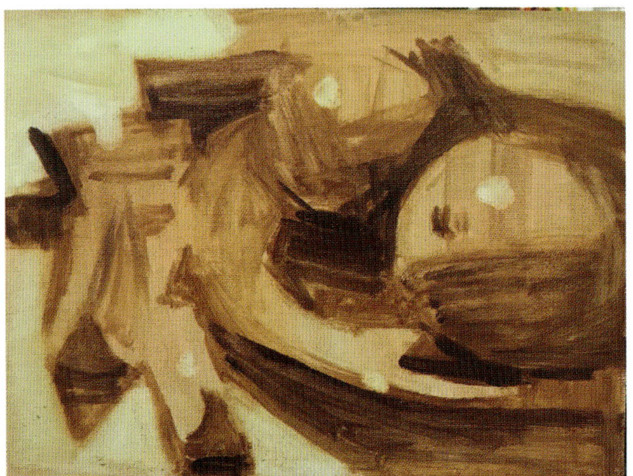

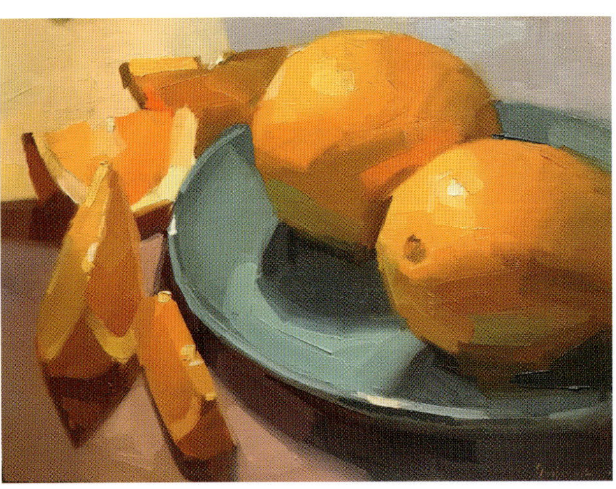

My three steps for alla prima can be practiced simply, with a still life of one or two objects, a background color, and a single light source. The more complex the still life, the greater the challenge, so push yourself—the sky's the limit!

Use your value study still life—or arrange a new one. Keep in mind that the surface you work on will affect your experience, so perhaps try a series of three small paintings on different substrates, like canvas, wood panel, and linen.

You don't need to spend a lot of time to get the feel for the process. Budget an hour or so for the underpainting, keeping it loose, perhaps checking it in a mirror once or twice along the way to catch any drawing issues (like those pesky ellipses).

Next, give yourself fifteen to twenty minutes just to mix paint. You'll be surprised how fast the time goes!

Oranges on a blue plate in three steps—value study, underpainting, finish.

Sarah Sedwick, *Oranges on Teal*, oil on canvas, 9" × 12" | 22.9 × 30.5 cm

This is a good place to pause, if you are breaking the process up into "bites." Stash your palette in the freezer, and it will stay wet for weeks, or store it in an airtight container like the Sta-Wet palette to keep your paint fresh. Some artists use a drop of clove oil on a cotton swab or cotton ball inside their palette box to slow drying. (Note: Do not add clove oil directly to your paint or it may never dry!)

Next, apply that color! Begin with an "easy win" or with a "vulnerable color." Look for the lightest, most saturated color in your still life—the light side of that lemon or the brightest reds on your apple. If there are no intense colors in your still life, choose a starting point that you understand—a color and value that you think you mixed correctly. Any place is a good place to start if you feel relatively confident about it.

Your first strokes will inform the next ones. Wipe off your brush and go back to the palette frequently, reloading it with lots of juicy paint.

Repeat. Enjoy!

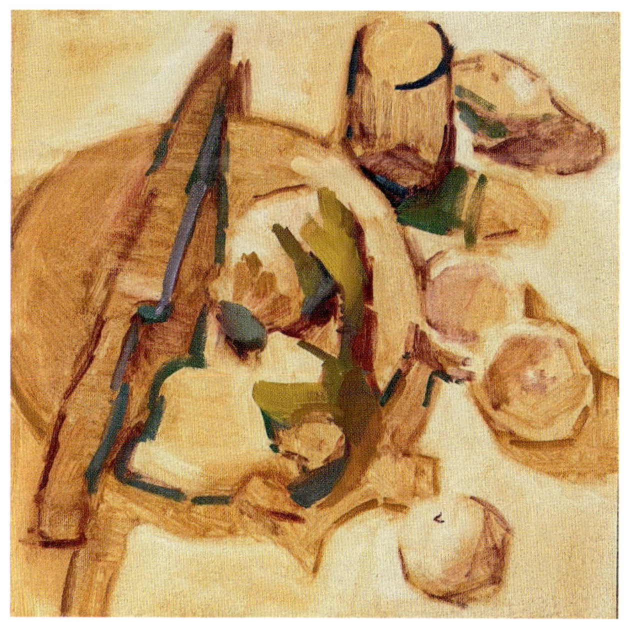

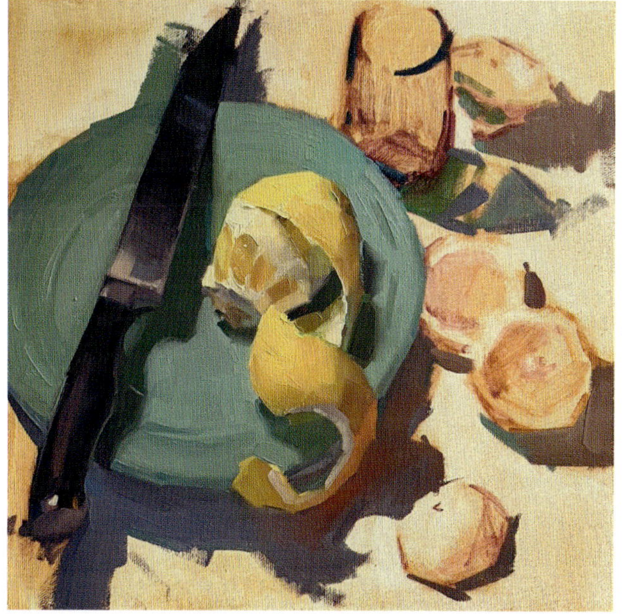

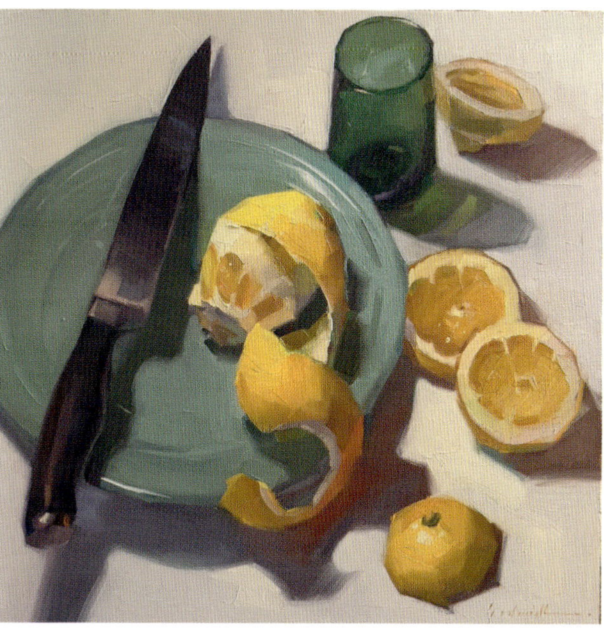

Sarah Sedwick, *Yellow Spiral*, oil on canvas, 12" × 12" | 30.5 × 30.5 cm

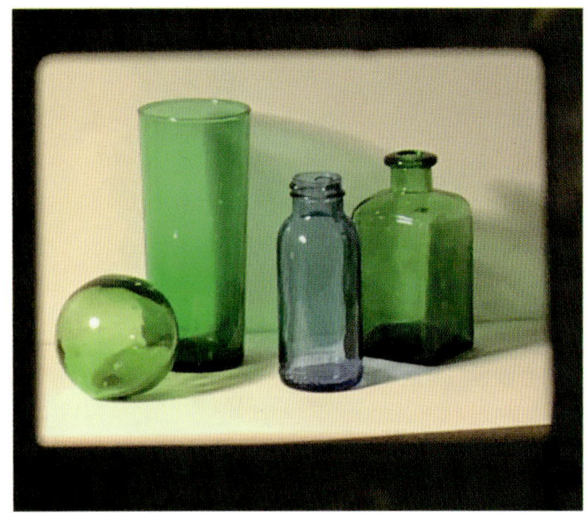

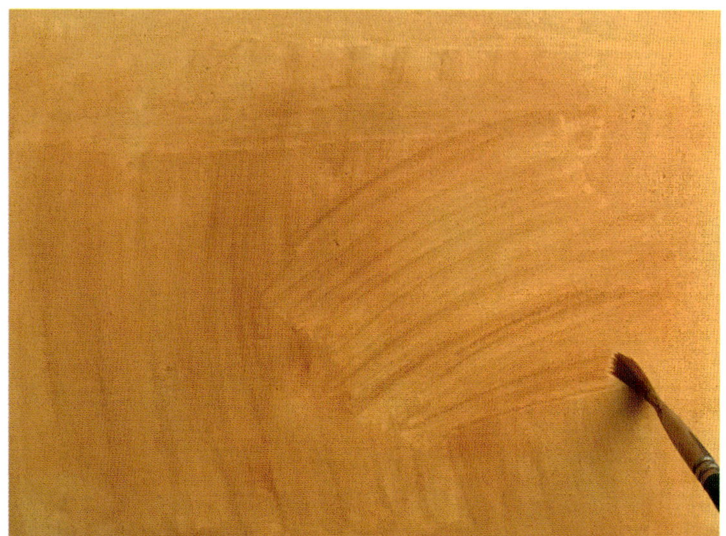

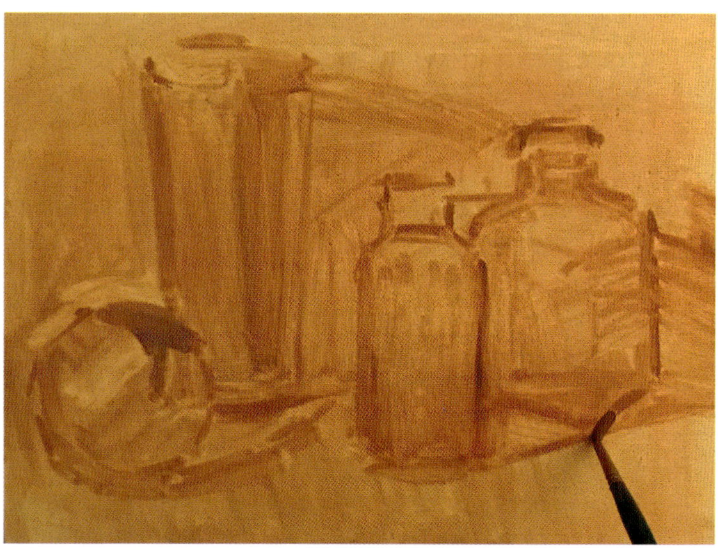

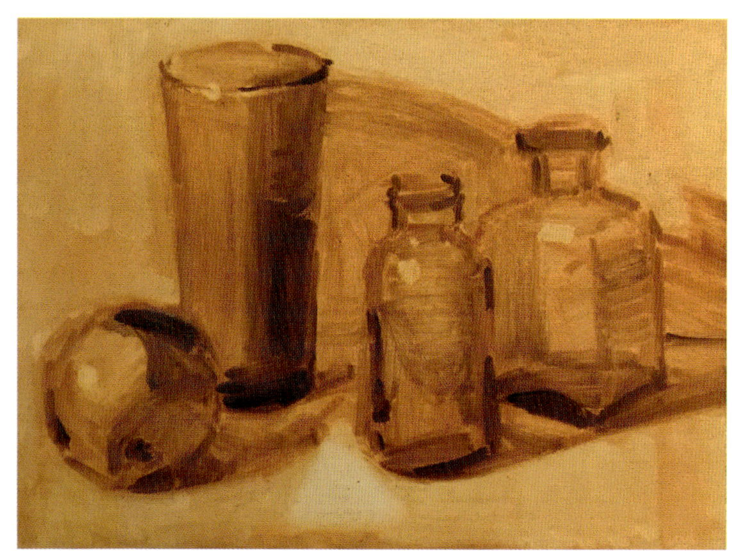

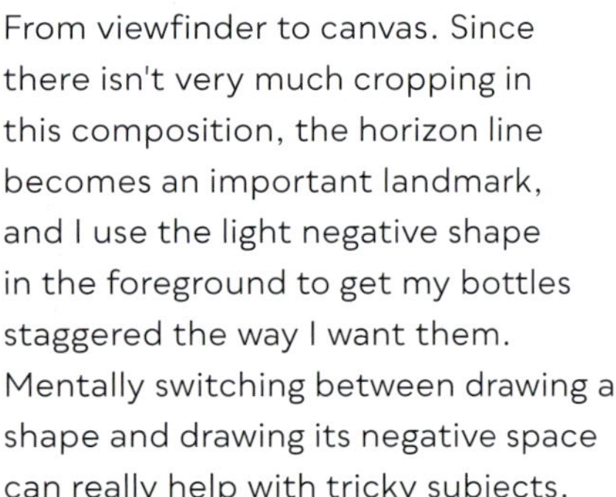

From viewfinder to canvas. Since there isn't very much cropping in this composition, the horizon line becomes an important landmark, and I use the light negative shape in the foreground to get my bottles staggered the way I want them. Mentally switching between drawing a shape and drawing its negative space can really help with tricky subjects.

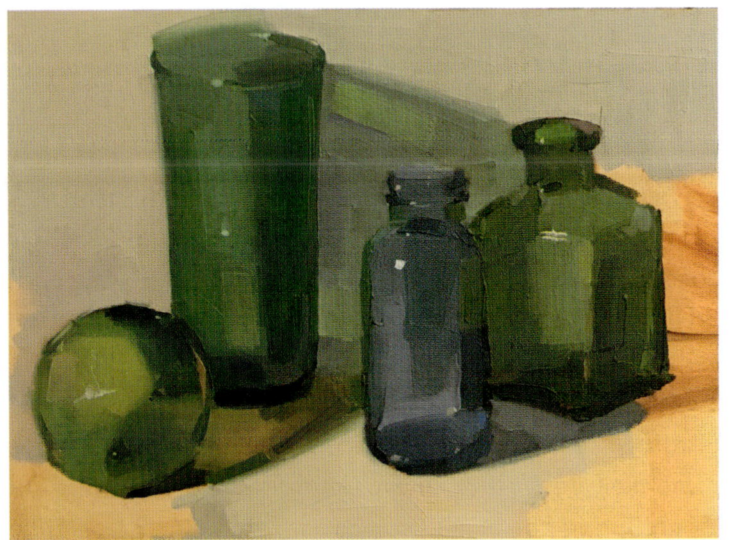

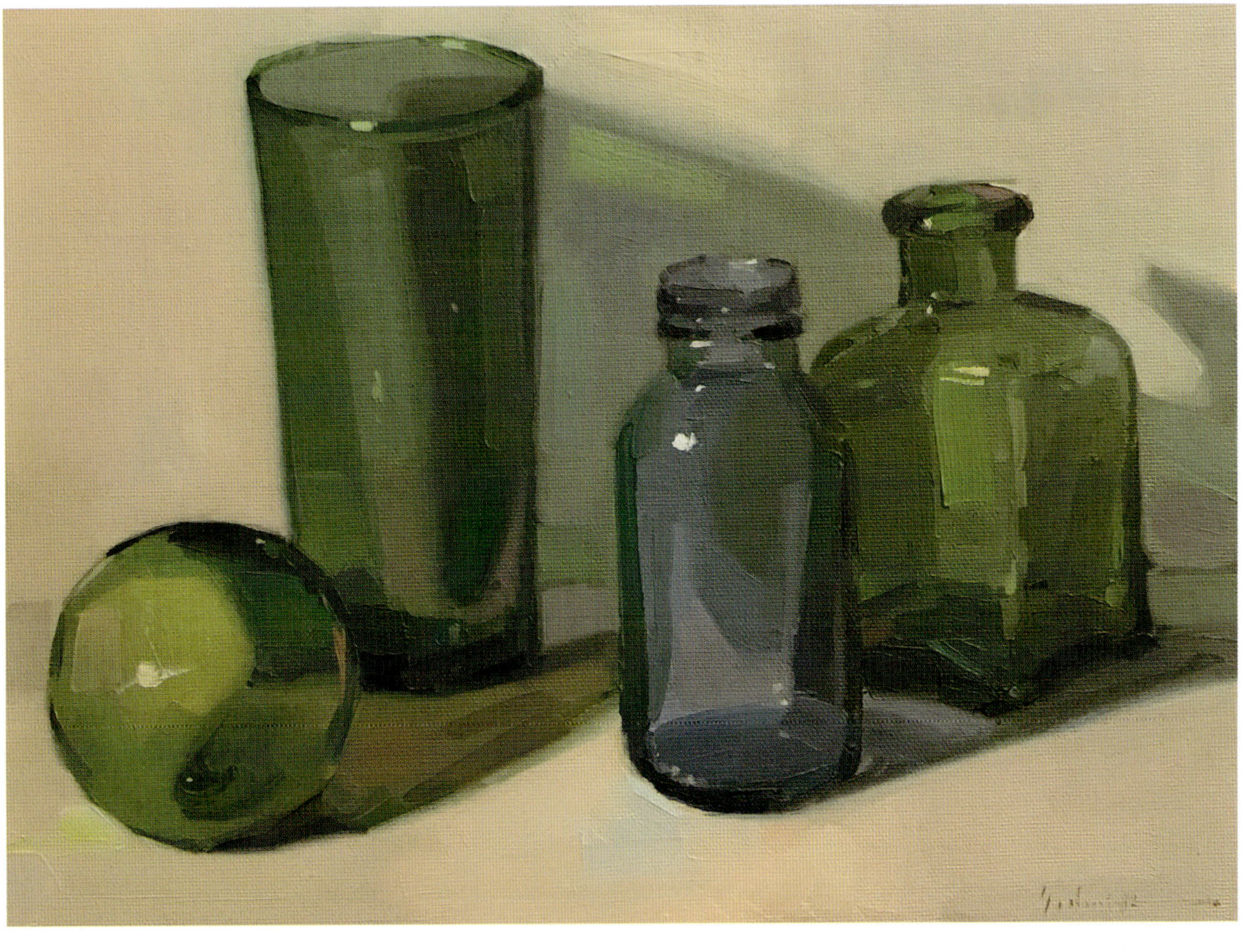

Sarah Sedwick, *Green and Blue Glass*, oil on canvas, 9" × 12" | 22.9 × 30.5 cm

Nothing in a painting is finished until everything is finished! Rather than completing the objects before moving on to the negative space, or working from background to foreground, I try to work all over the painting, letting the colors of my subjects influence each other and crafting my edges by painting back and forth between each object and its negative space.

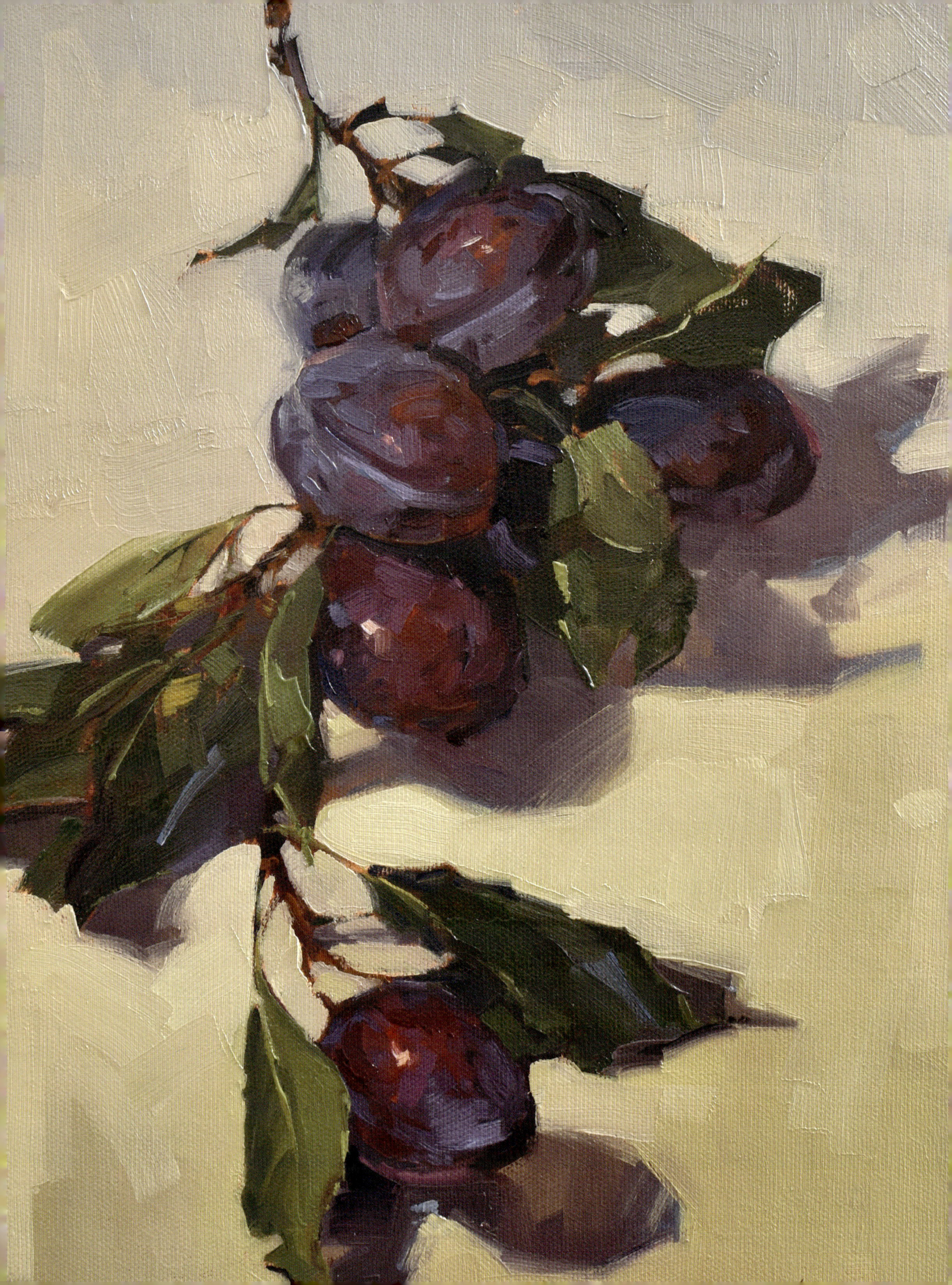

5

YOUR ART JOURNEY CONTINUES

We are artists. We *want* to paint. We want to paint *every day*! So, we ask ourselves: Why has it been three weeks since I've picked up a paintbrush?

Sometimes it feels like the act of painting is not as challenging as the act of *starting to paint*. And this is momentum—starting and then staying connected, forming a practice that keeps us motivated to return to the easel day after day.

Helping artists find their way back to painting after a month or a year away from the easel, after a career, raising a family—or guiding them through the beginning of their art journey—is a fundamental part of my mission as an artist. Let's explore some of the ways that we can all continue, or begin, painting with inspiration and momentum.

◀ Sarah Sedwick, *Ripening*, oil on canvas, 9" × 12" | 22.9 × 30.5 cm

MOMENTUM: THE MOST IMPORTANT THING

Creating art we aren't pleased with is better for us mentally and emotionally than doing nothing, trying nothing, risking nothing, creating nothing. Most, if not all, of us have felt the dull weight of resistance—the pain of procrastination—and it's even more painful because it involves something we love so much.

Whether the problem is that we can't get ourselves physically into the studio or that nothing but disaster seems to be happening once we're in there, it doesn't feel good. A mix of guilt ("I should be doing XYZ, *but*") and terror ("I've forgotten how to paint") adds up to an experience we ALL go through sometimes: artist's block.

The good news is that, like everything else, artist's block doesn't last. When I'm painting a lot, have ideas that cascade one after another, and am feeling strong and confident, then my best hope is to *notice* what is occurring in the moment and acknowledge it. Lulls in inspiration exist to make us appreciate the times when everything just flows.

More good news: If these lulls are particularly painful, it's probably because they're coming on the heels of a period of productivity and growth. If you've been on a roll in the studio but lately feel uninspired, maybe you've reached a plateau and just need a new challenge. At times like these, making paintings is not as important as regaining momentum—the joy of doing, not attachment to the outcome.

So, how do we rekindle that joy?

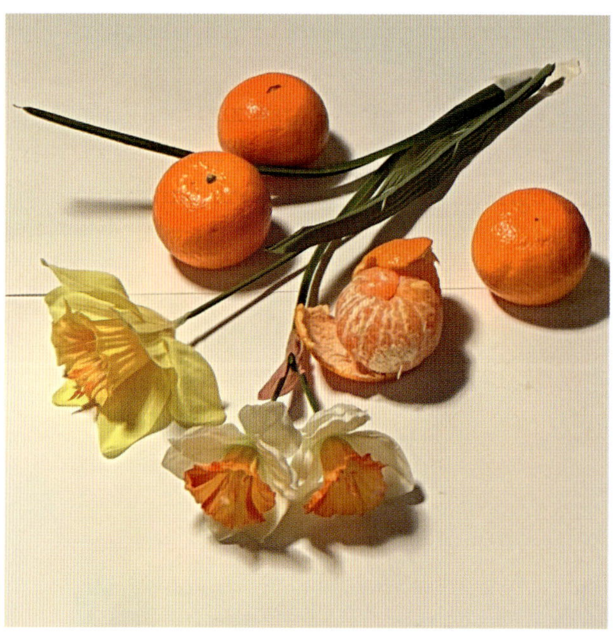

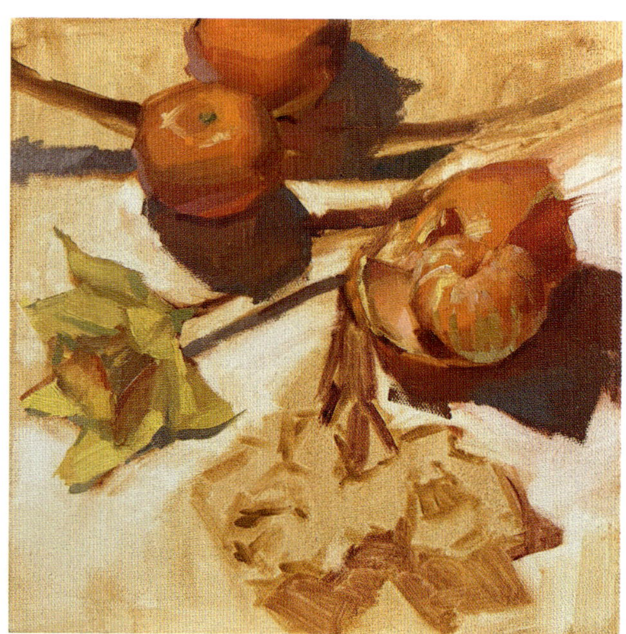

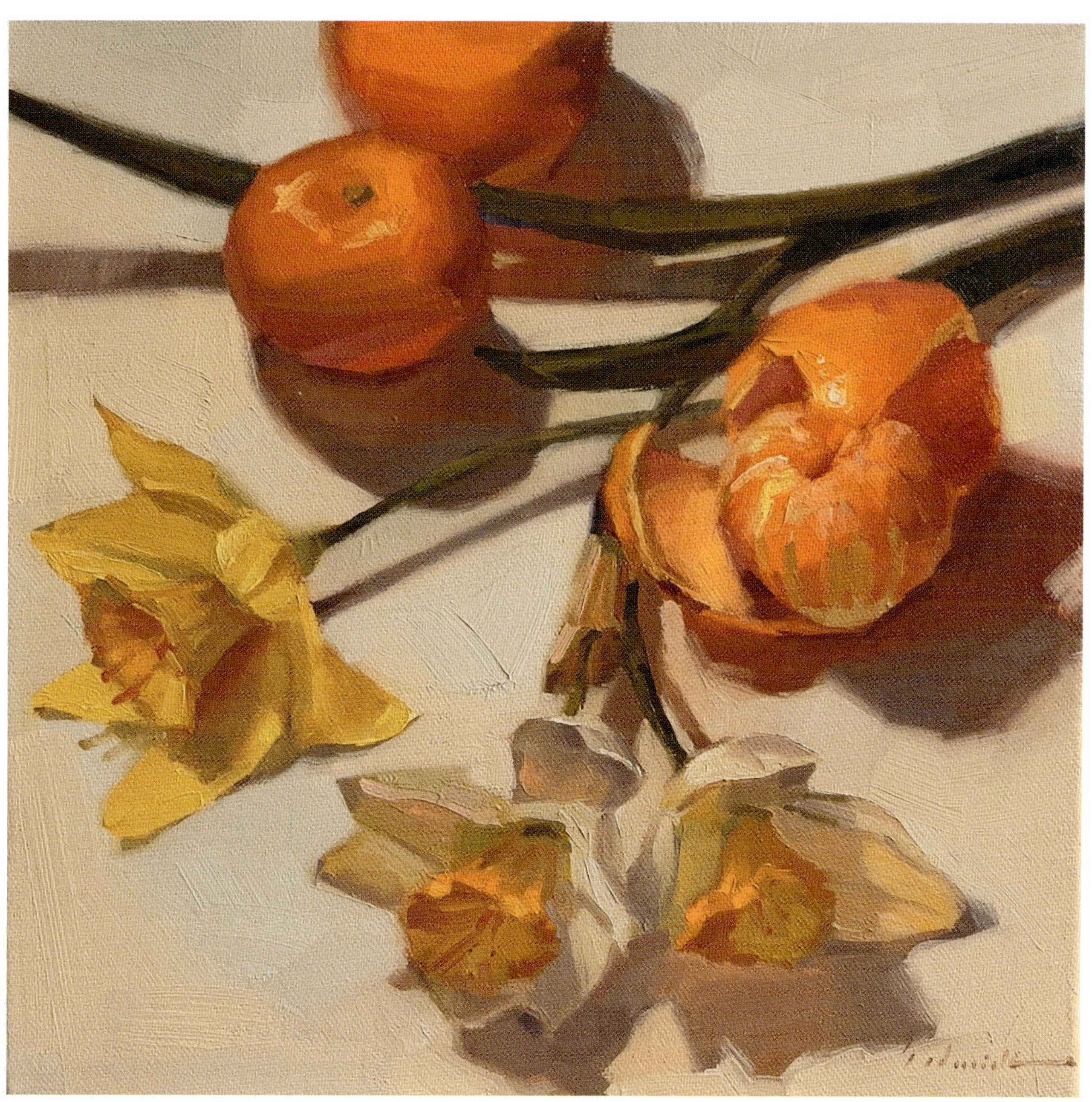

Sarah Sedwick, *Spring on the Way*,
oil on canvas, 10" × 10" | 25.4 × 25.4 cm

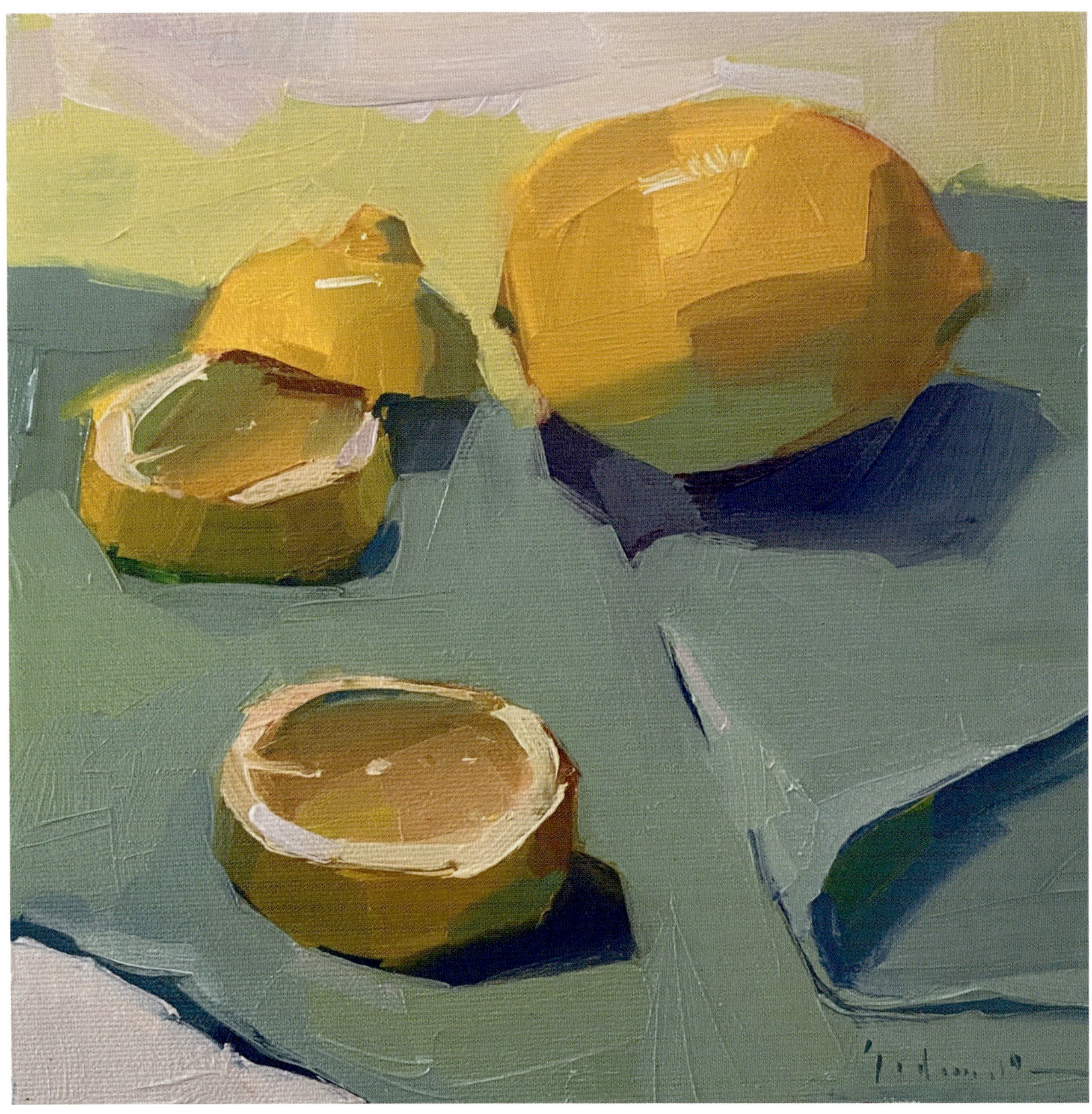

Sarah Sedwick, ***Twenty-Minute Lemons*****,**
oil on Arches oil paper, 8" × 8" | 20.3 × 20.3 cm

You can do anything for 20 minutes! Set a timer and tell yourself, "If it goes off and I want to stop, I will." Chances are you will want to keep going! Hint: I get my still life and canvas set up and mix my colors before I start the timer.

GETTING OUT OF THE STUDIO

Any vacation can be turned into an art retreat by packing along your art supplies. And an art adventure can be created at home simply by painting in a spot we wouldn't normally work. Do you usually paint at the kitchen table? Try setting up a still life in the sun on your patio. Do you have a studio or dedicated room to work in at home? Try painting some objects on your kitchen counter or near a window in another room.

Here I've set up a still life in the kitchen of a vacation rental house, using window light and a few random found objects—a mix of still life, interior, and plein air. This is a *much* better memento than any photograph.

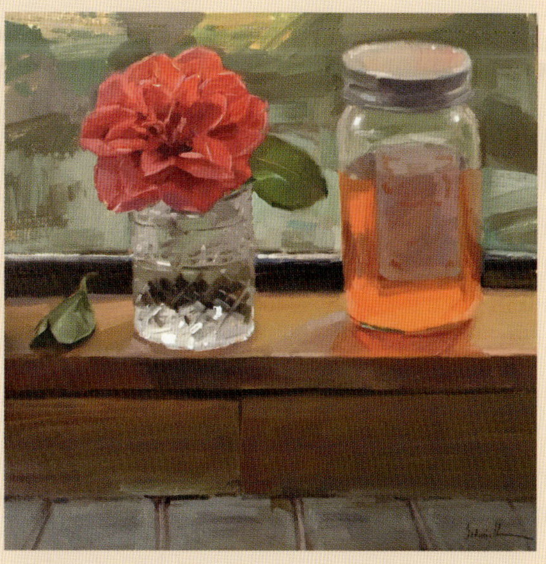

Sarah Sedwick, *Rogue Valley Honey*, oil on canvas, 12" × 12" | 30.5 × 30.5 cm

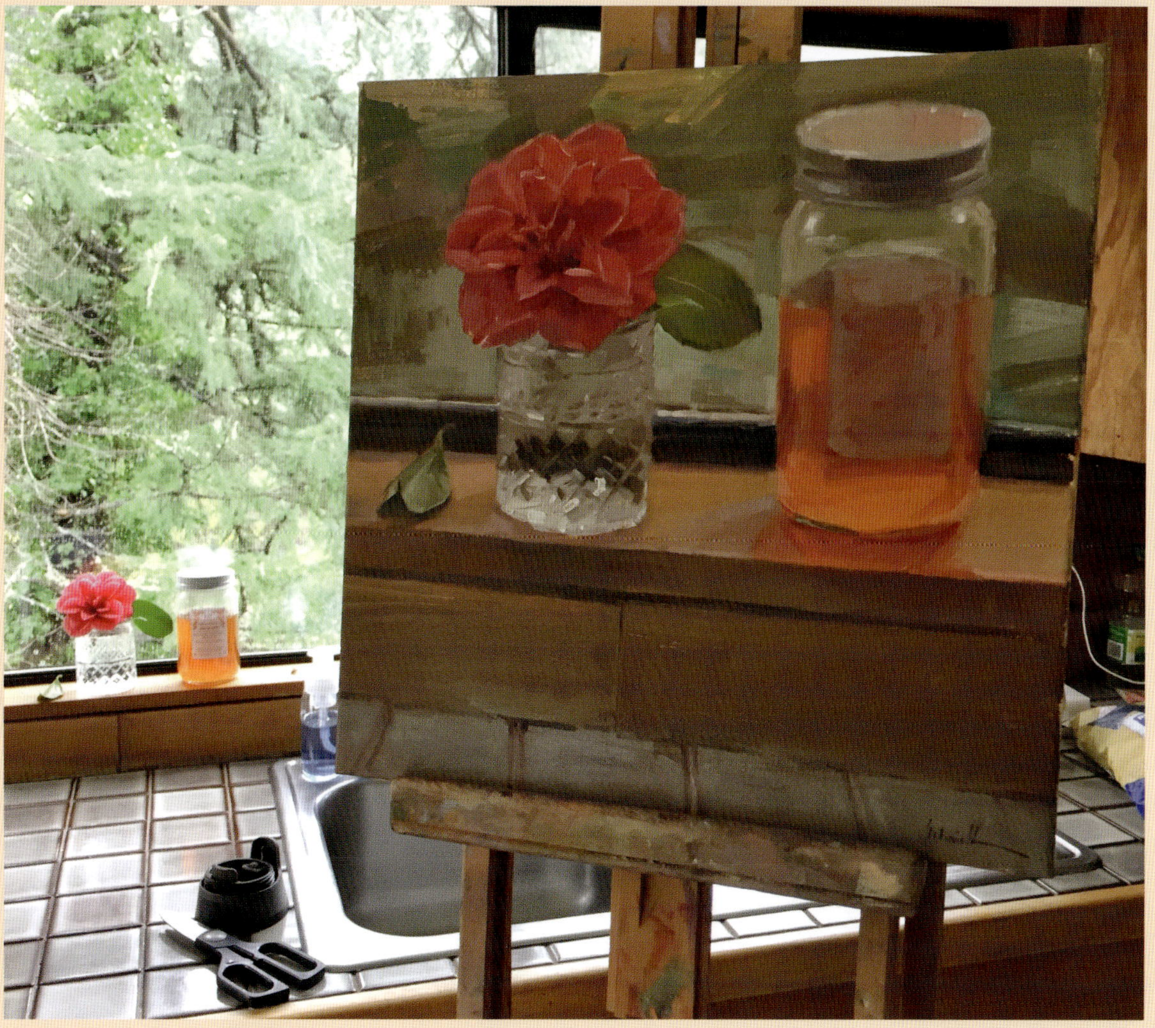

JUMP-STARTING MOMENTUM

Over the years, I've explored lots of ways to "hack" myself, not just for greater productivity but essentially to get myself to do the thing I *want* to do. Personally, I am motivated by accountability: setting a goal, stating that goal, and telling someone else about the goal. My early Daily Painting blog was a great example of this. I committed to a certain number of blog posts per week, and I felt that I'd be letting myself (and some imaginary reader—who really didn't exist at the beginning, let's be honest) down if I didn't post. If I didn't paint, I couldn't post. So, I painted. The truth is—I *wanted* to paint. I wasn't forcing myself; I enjoyed it once I got going. The obligation to post only served to *get me going*.

Other personalities respond to other "hacks." If getting into the studio is feeling impossible, consider a "uniform." Similarly to a person who puts on their gym clothes and then inevitably knows they will walk out the door for the gym, if you have an outfit, such as apron or even a hat, that you ONLY wear to paint, putting it on will make going into the studio seem like the next natural step.

Some of us are motivated by money. And I don't mean spending money on art supplies, which we all do from time to time as a form of "productive" procrastination. Signing up for a workshop, scheduling a session with a mentor, entering a contest with a fee, buying an art instructional video—all of these things require a financial ante, which can be a strong motivator to justify in paint.

Then there are the numbers people. Whether it's signing up for a thirty-day challenge, committing to a certain number of paintings per week/month/year, logging paintings on a spreadsheet, or checking off boxes on a calendar, setting a numerical goal can be a powerful tool.

If pressure is a problem, give yourself permission to keep it simple. For that matter, give yourself permission to make a bad painting. The act of doing leads to more doing, which leads to *better* doing. When I need to go back to basics and stop freaking myself out, painting in black and white is often my go-to, because it feels soothing and "easy."

Lastly, there is the good old-fashioned carrot. Tempt yourself into the studio with a new prop from the antique mall you're itching to paint, a podcast or an audiobook you've been waiting to listen to, or—let's face it—a piece (or bar) of chocolate at the end of a studio session. Whatever works!

Most of us aren't just one kind of self-motivator. A variety pack of hacks—taking a workshop, picking out a studio "uniform," *and* committing to keeping it simple today, perhaps—could be the right recipe for you!

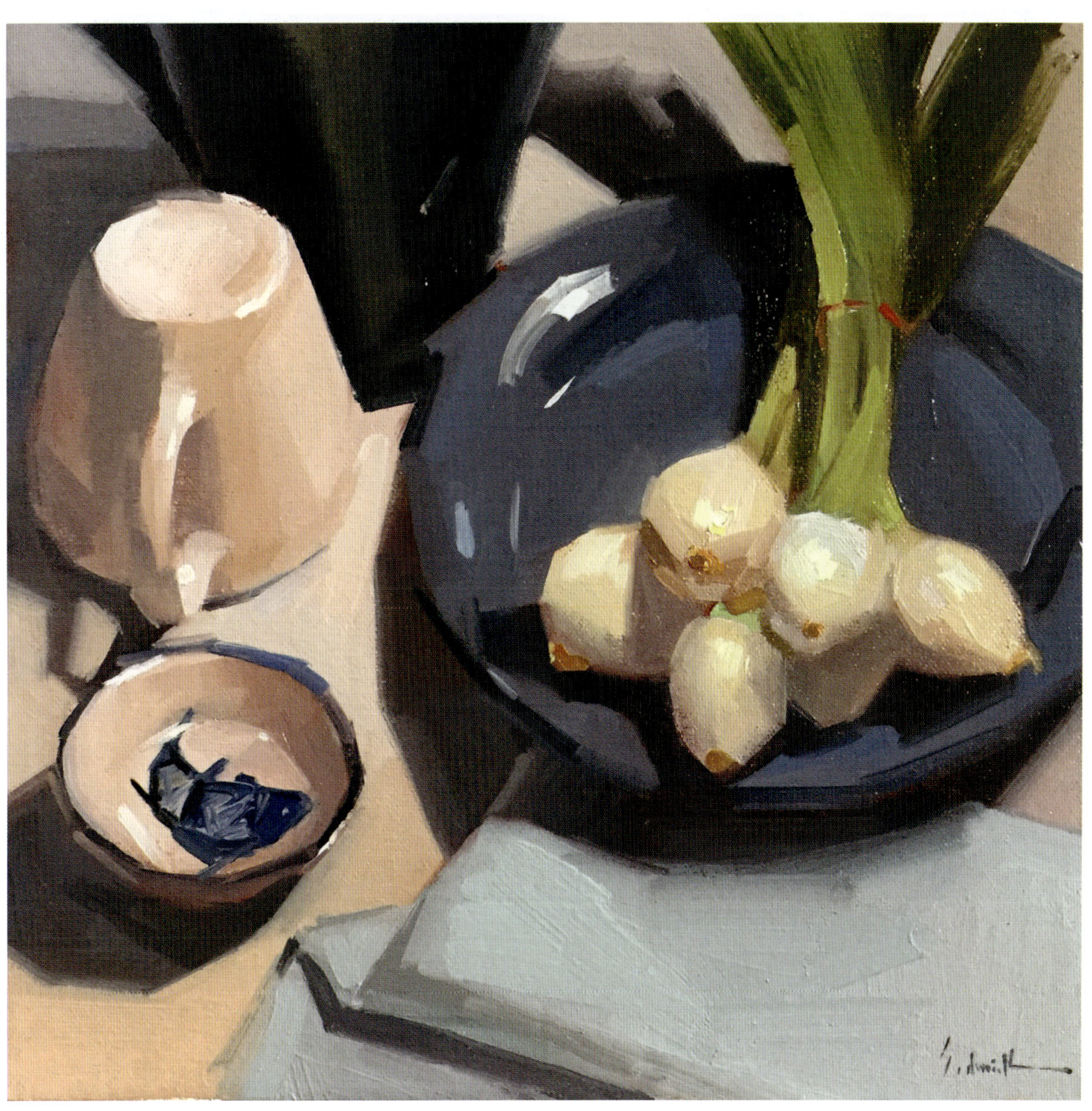

Sarah Sedwick, *Green Onions on Blue*,
oil on canvas, 10" × 10" | 24.5 × 25.4 cm

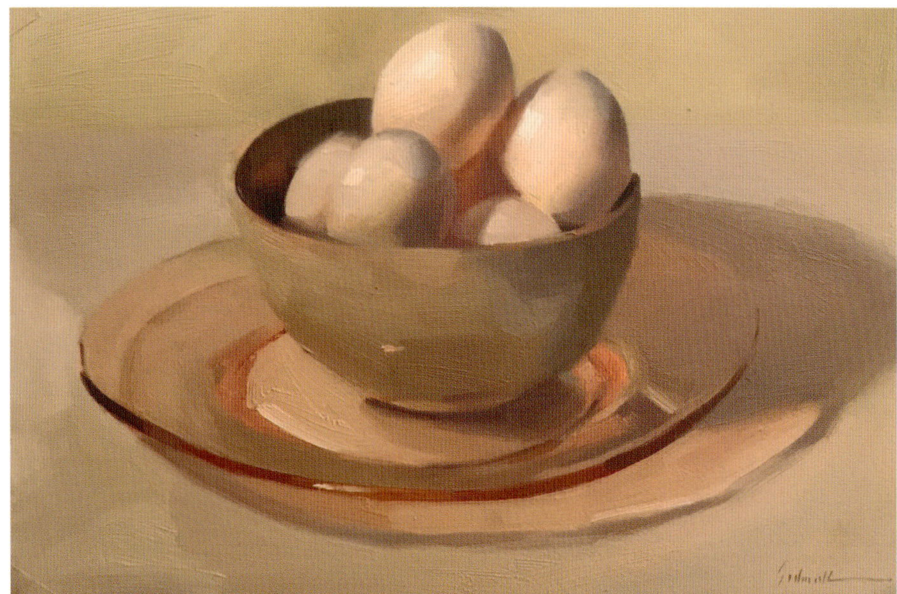

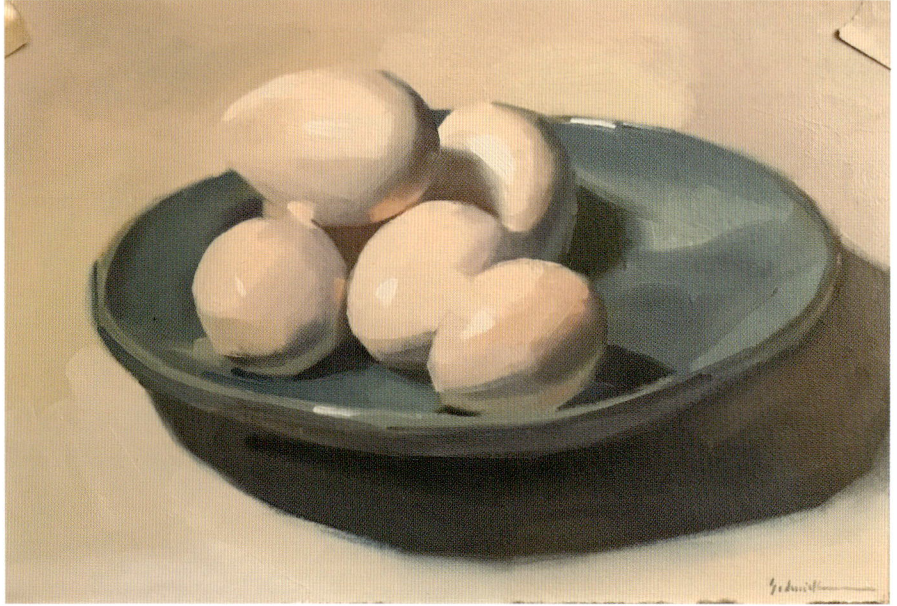

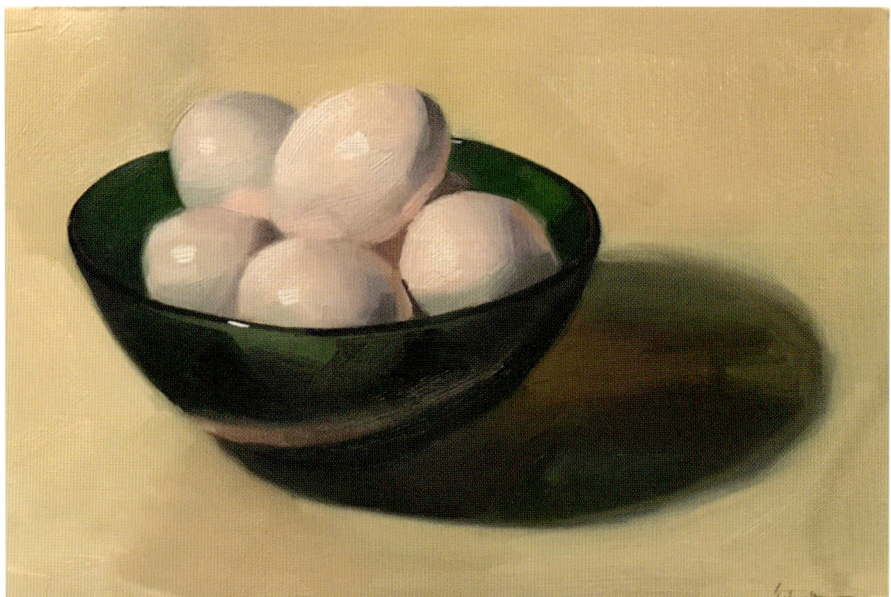

◀ Sarah Sedwick, from top to bottom, *Eggs on Pink*, *Egg Jenga*, *Green Eggs*, oil on Arches oil paper, 9" × 12" | 22.9 × 30.5 cm

Whether working through a 30-day challenge or just trying to keep things simple in the studio, doing a series of variations on a theme can be a big help! Here, I've painted eggs three ways, on three consecutive days, keeping the lighting, size, and substrate the same.

▶ Christina Weaver, *Midday Tomatoes*, oil on linen, 14" × 11" | 35.6 × 28 cm

If you're a painter who loves to garden, you can turn the backyard into your summer studio and paint still life while watching things ripen!

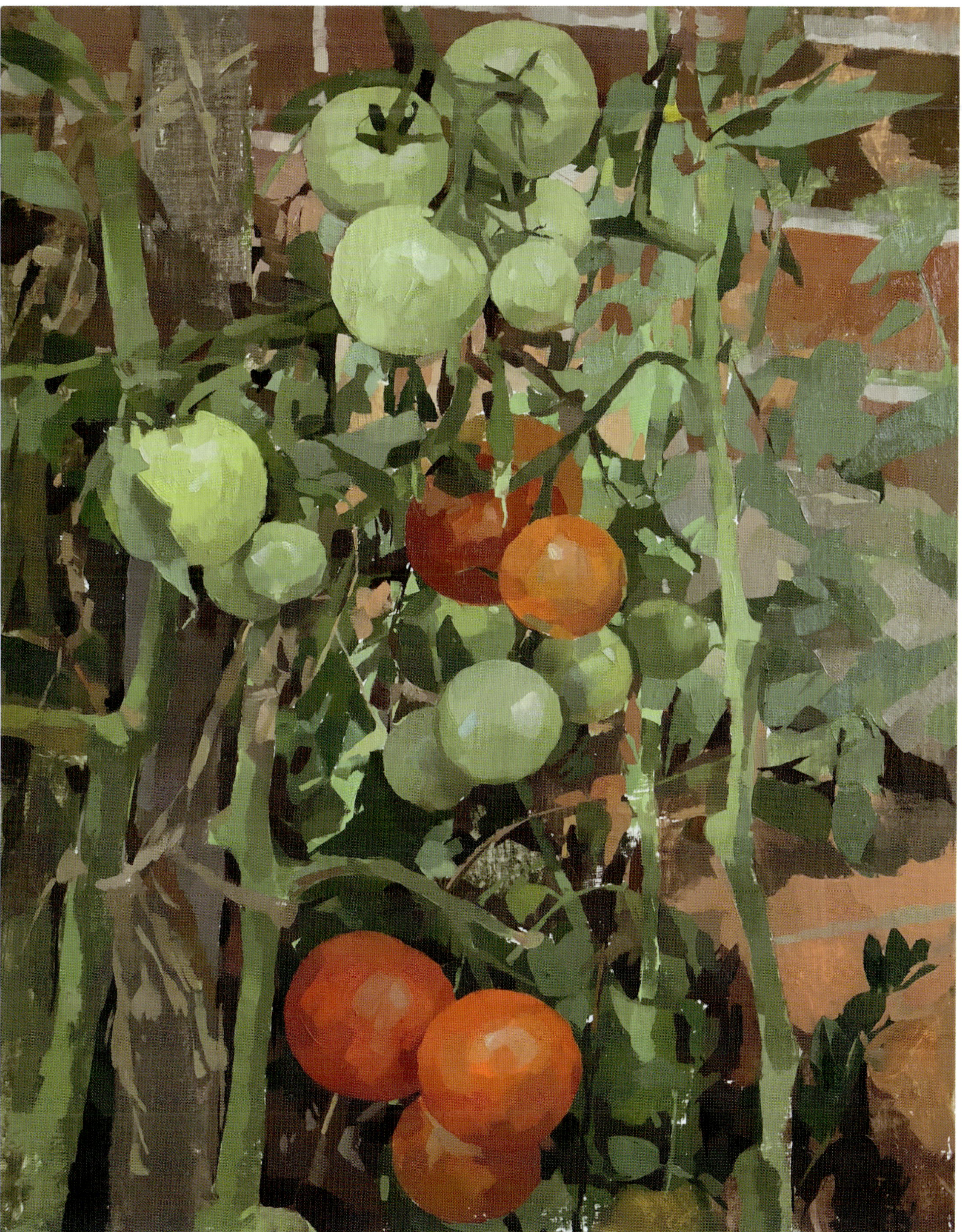

COMPARISON IS THE THIEF OF JOY

Looking at art online is good—until it isn't. We are lucky to live in a time where we have TONS of amazing art at our fingertips! When I hear of a new artist, or encounter one in a gallery, the first thing I do is look them up on Instagram. It can feel like we don't *exist* if we aren't putting our work out there on social media.

The flood of art in our news feeds can be a double-edged sword. On one hand, a treasure trove of inspiration; on the other, a source of self-judgment and seemingly unattainable goals. Recognizing when the enjoyment of all that beautiful art is motivational and when it's time to disconnect and turn inward is key.

Comparing ourselves to others can be useful—helping shape our goals and choose a style of painting to study and practice. After all, most of us don't just pick up a brush for the first time and say, "I'm an impressionist!" or "I'm a photorealist!" We need to see a lot of art to figure out what we like—what we want to *be* like.

When is our work ready to put "out there"? The answer is different for everyone. It's hard to judge our own work. Period. For several reasons. First, we are so close to it, especially as we're making it, both literally and figuratively. The experience we have *making* a painting can really affect how we feel about the outcome. So, if a piece was a struggle from start to finish, we may think it's unsuccessful, when really we're just mentally stuck in the struggle. Second, we may have looked at it for so long that we can't even *see* it anymore, not objectively. Lastly, we may not know *how* to judge it. So much of painting is subjective—what I like versus what you like, the gallery wants, or social media favors. But what about the nitty-gritty, the formal concerns? Is your composition working? Are your values on board? Are there edges that could be softer? Harder? Is there a strong focal point? Are the colors harmonious? This kind of checklist can be used to "self-critique," and it is also wonderful to have another, trusted set of eyes on our work.

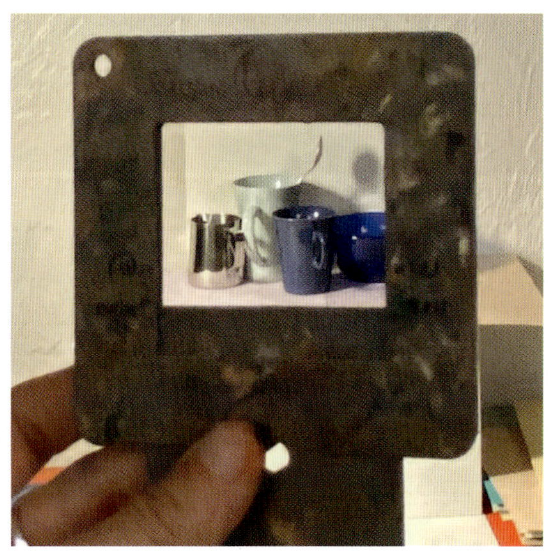

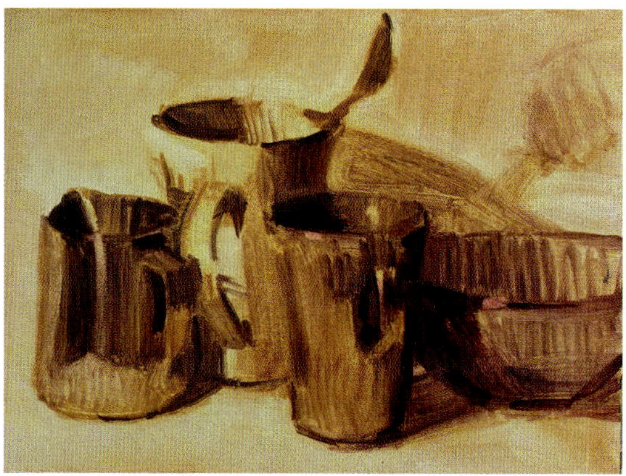

I like to use a viewfinder to visualize my composition before blocking it in on the canvas.

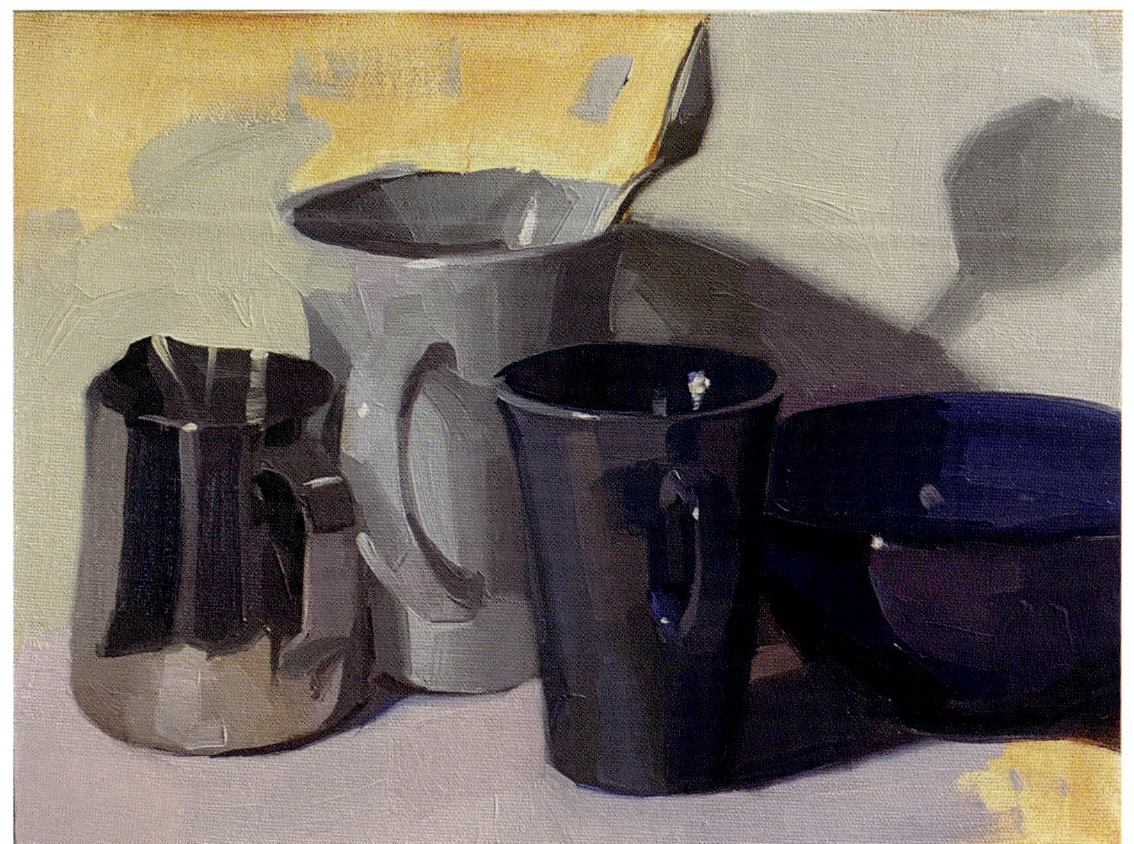

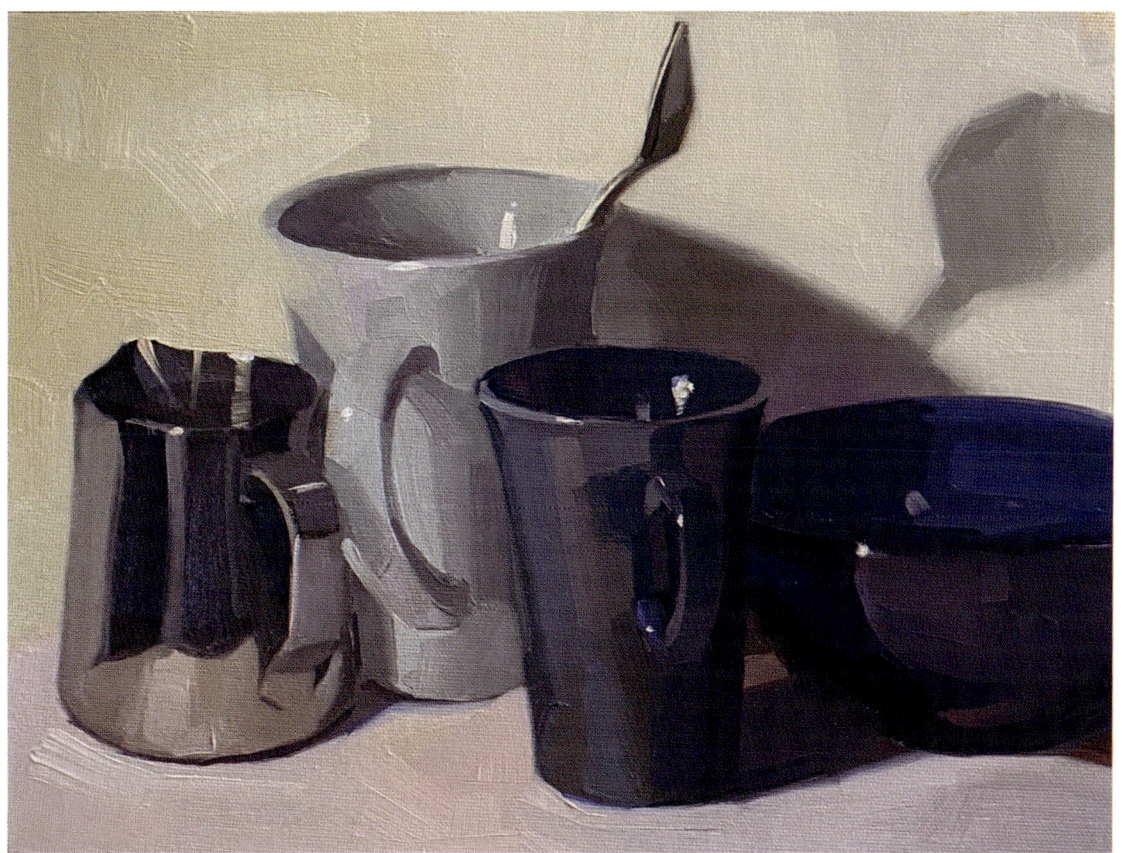

Sarah Sedwick, *February Blues*, oil on canvas, 9" × 12" | 22.9 × 30.5 cm

Working back and forth across my edges is an important part of my process. Here, the rim of the light blue mug was painted out beyond its contour line, then refined by cutting in with the light negative space. Sometimes called "back painting," this is a great technique for crafting both hard and soft edges.

FINDING FRIENDS AND MENTORS

So many of us work in a bubble. If we're not in school or taking a lot of workshops, we may be many miles away from our peers—other painters who share our passion and quest for growth. Being a painter means long hours of (hopefully) contented, focused solitary work. There comes a time, however, when we all need community—for feedback, motivation, new ideas, and a sense that we're not in this alone.

I've mentioned workshops several times in this book, and they are a wonderful way to connect to a new teacher, a new style, a new outlook, and new art friends. Taking a workshop is a wonderful way to jump-start momentum and learn a lot, not just from the instructor, but from the other students as well. Group energy is infectious. If there isn't a venue in your area, consider traveling to a destination workshop in another city. Make an adventure out of getting connected!

If you have a friend who shares your passion, becoming "accountability buddies" could help you both jump-start your momentum. Set a painting date in person, or get "together" online. Nothing will keep you focused like having someone else in the room working alongside you.

The concept of mentorship is popular in many fields right now, and it has been important among painters for centuries, in the form of apprenticeships and private ateliers. Throughout history, whole "schools" of painting have arisen around single teachers. Today, finding a guide for your art journey is easier than ever. There was a time many years ago when I was skeptical that painting could be taught via the internet, and boy was I wrong! A serious student of painting can create their own custom curriculum online today, choosing teachers, demonstrations, and one-on-one mentorship from a wide field of professional artists.

If you love an artist's work, see if they have a page on Patreon. You'll get great content *and* access to a community of other artists who love them too! Daily challenges like the twice-yearly Strada Easel thirty-day challenge, and hashtag challenges—of which there are many on Instagram—can also be a great way to connect with like-minded painters and begin sharing your work online in a supportive environment if you never have before.

If it's not your goal to share your art with the world, *don't*. It doesn't need to be made for anyone's eyes but yours! If you *do* want to share it, and the reason you don't is that you think you're not good enough, or that no one will appreciate it, or worse, that they'll be annoyed by seeing your work online, then it's time for a second opinion. You can borrow mine.

There is so much negativity in the world—from politics to pandemics—and I guarantee you, your family and friends will relish seeing your efforts, however you choose to share them. You may even get a flood of requests for commission paintings!

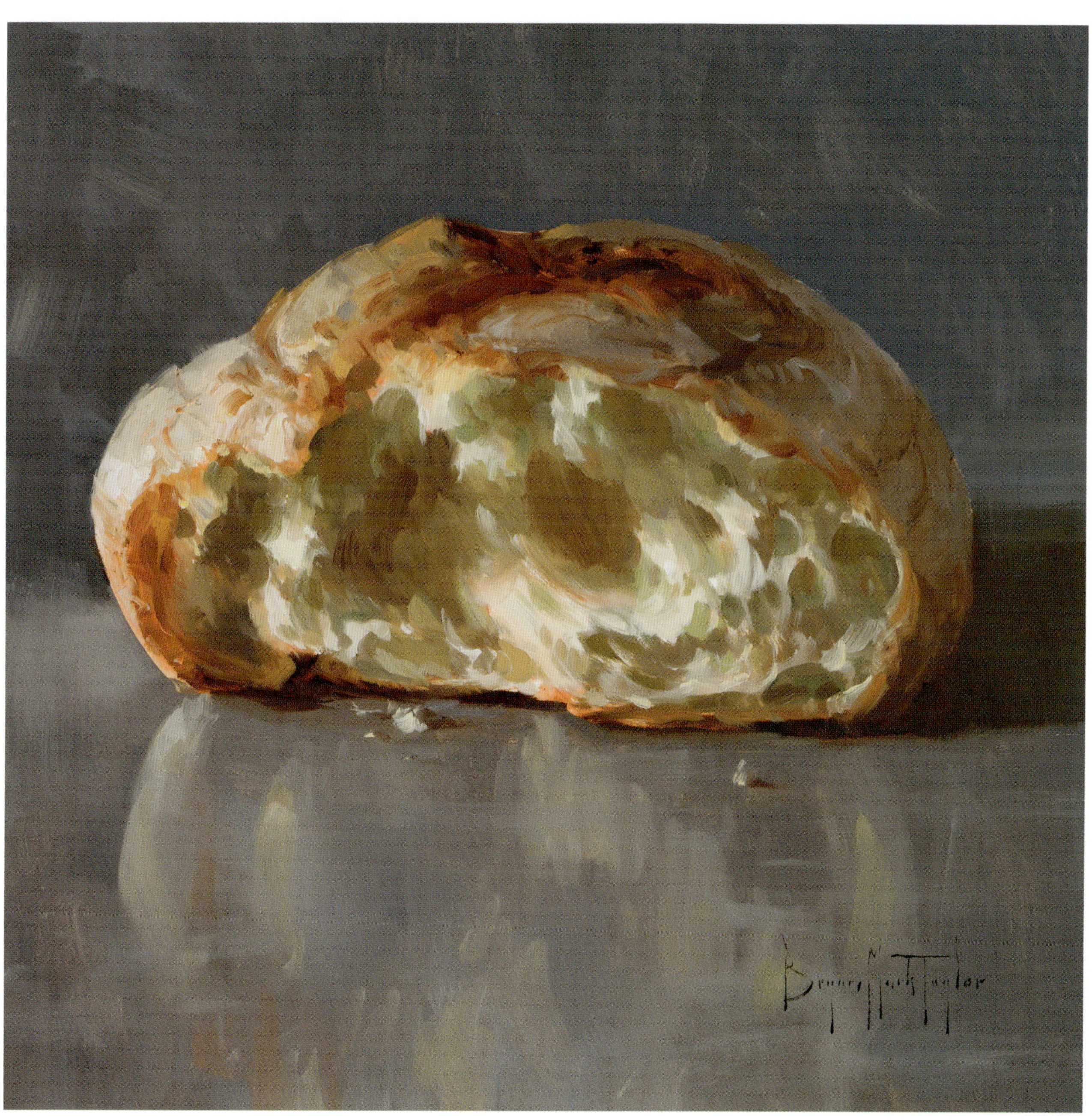

Bryan Mark Taylor, *Sourdough*,
oil on panel, 12" × 12" | 30.5 × 30.5 cm

Bryan Mark Taylor is the inventor of the Strada Easel for plein air painting and creator of the Strada Easel challenge—a twice-yearly 30-day art challenge open to all. Check it out on Facebook and Instagram every January and September!

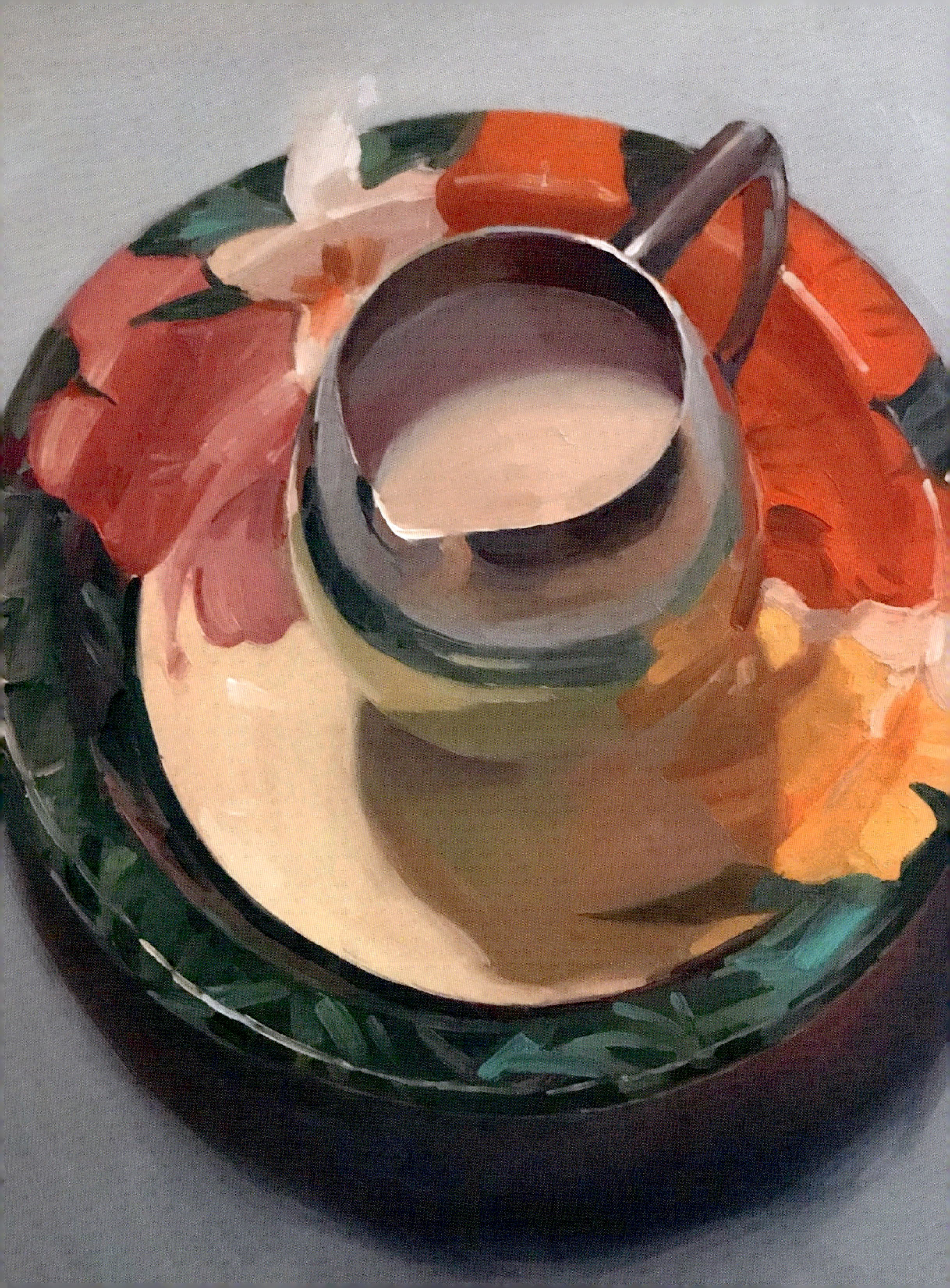

6

CONCLUSION: YOUR UNIQUE ARTISTIC FINGERPRINT

"I want to find my style." It's what almost all artists—brand-new painters, lifelong hobbyists, serious amateurs, emerging professionals—say when they begin working with me. So, I ask them who their favorite artists are. Often many are the same as mine: Sargent, Zorn, Sorolla—the big guns! Then I ask, "What was the last painting you saw that made you just really, really want to *paint*?" Chances are, it was on social media.

We see so much amazing contemporary art online, and we know what we love—but do we know *why* we love it? And can we pinpoint what it is about it that we'd like to see in our own work? Now we are getting somewhere. The art we see has gone from inspirational to aspirational to instructive. I mentioned master copies earlier, and not just of old masters. Any art you love can be studied in this way and is perhaps the best method for incorporating what we love about our favorite painters' work into our own.

◀ Sarah Sedwick, *Blue Hawaii*,
oil on canvas, 14" × 14" | 35.6 × 35.6 cm

But fear not! No matter how many master copies you do—and, perhaps unfortunately, no matter how much you may want to paint like your idols—if you paint consistently, and not even for a very long period of time, you will inevitably paint like YOU.

You cannot outrun your artistic fingerprint. This is great news! The best way to find your style is to paint a whole lot, and then have someone else look at your body of work with you. Chances are, they will see your style emerging long before you do. Another wonderful use of art friends and accountability buddies: They are your eyes and ears on the road to finding your style.

If you want to paint—if you love to paint—then paint and your style will find you. If you have a dream project but don't think you have the skills to tackle it just yet, I gently suggest that rather than going backward to find the missing skills, what's needed can be learned *through the process* of creating the dream project. There is no need to wait to try.

Even if the work is frustrating, even if you have to make several starts, even if you've put something down and not touched it for years, now is a good time to try. The most precious thing we take with us into the studio today is our momentum. And it's the most important thing we create while we're in there. Take the next step. Go do a sketch. Choose a painting you love and begin a master copy, even in pencil. Set up a new still life, or two. Read a chapter of an art book. Write something inspirational on a piece of paper and tape it to your easel. Mix up a palette for tomorrow. You got this. You belong here, and you deserve to give yourself the gift of painting.

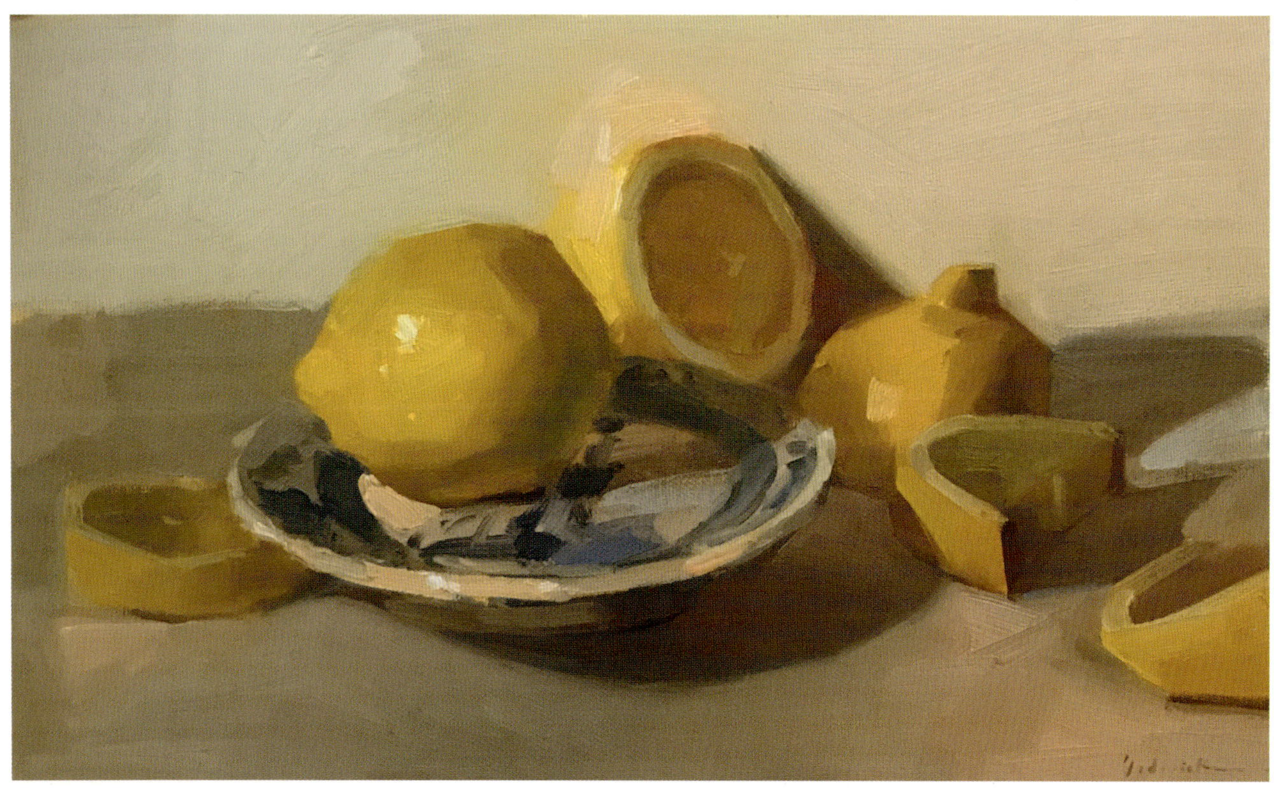

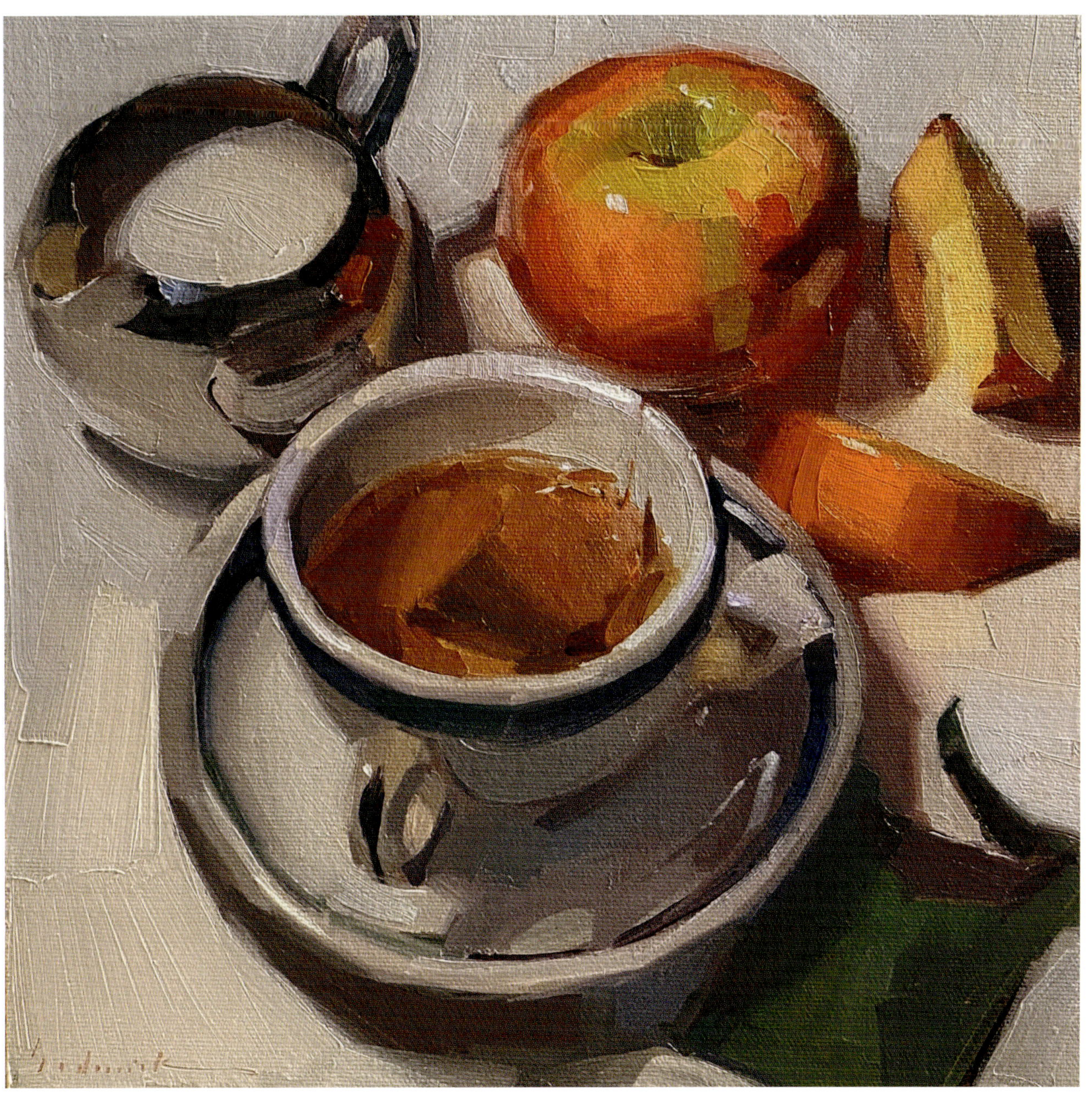

▲ Sarah Sedwick, *Tempting Tea*,
oil on canvas, 10" × 10" | 25.4 × 25.4 cm

◀ Sarah Sedwick, *Slices and Halves*,
oil on canvas, 8" × 13" | 20.3 × 33 cm

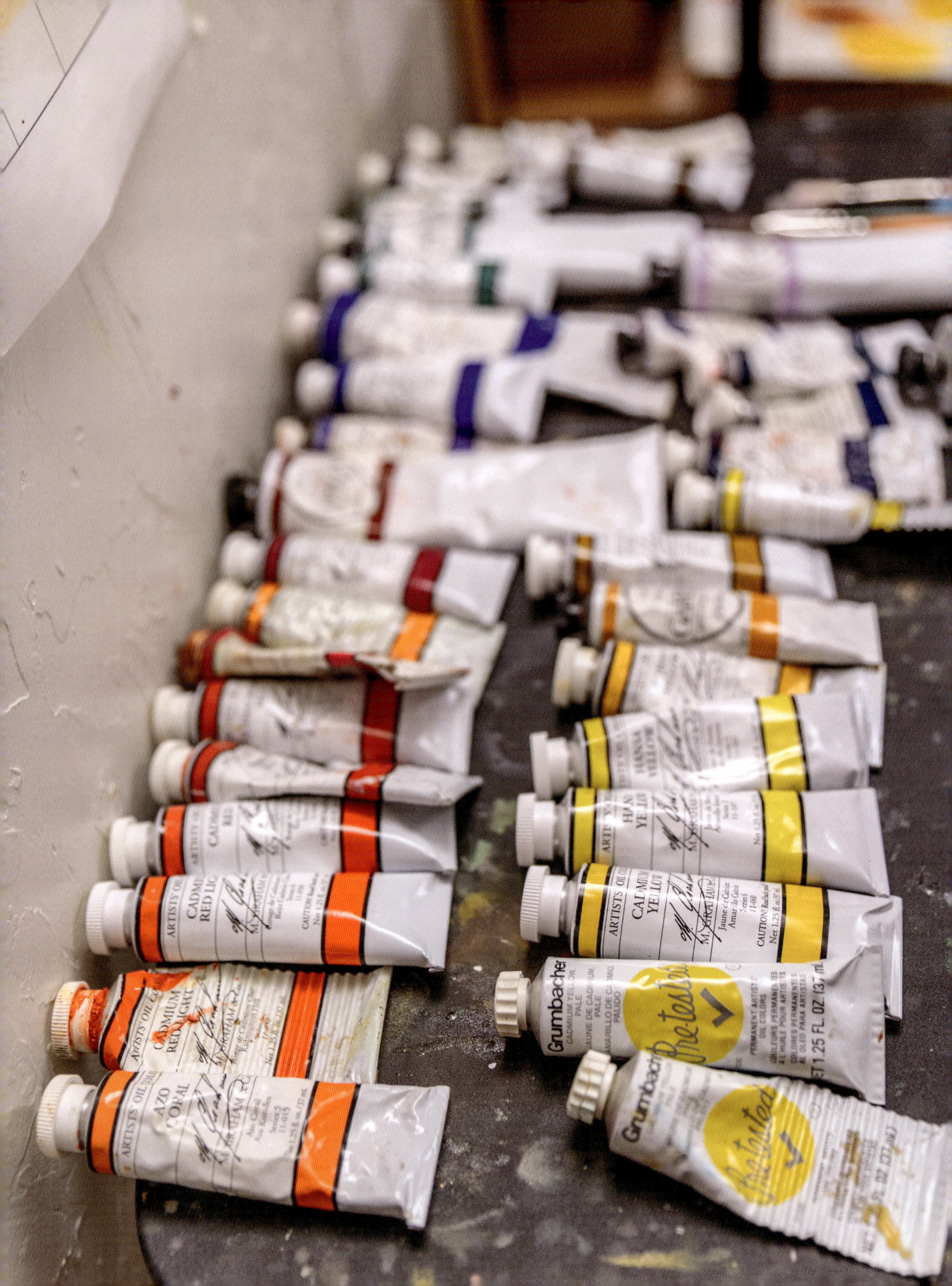
AZO CORAL
CADMIUM RED LIGHT
Grumbacher
Pre-tested
PERMANENT ARTISTS' OIL COLORS
1.25 FL. OZ (37 ml)

RESOURCES

BOOKS

Albert, Greg. *The Simple Secret to Better Painting: How to Immediately Improve Your Art with the One Rule of Composition*. Brattleboro, VT: Echo Point Books & Media, LLC, 2020.

Bayles, David and Ted Orland. *Art & Fear: Observations on the Perils (and Rewards) of Artmaking*. Santa Cruz, CA and Eugene, OR: The Image Continuum, 1993.

Casey, Todd M. *The Art of Still Life: A Contemporary Guide to Classical Techniques, Composition, and Painting in Oil*. Monacelli Studio, 2020.

Edwards, Betty. *Color: A Course in Mastering the Art of Mixing Colors*. New York: Jeremy P. Tarcher/Penguin, 2004.

Henri, Robert. *The Art Spirit*. Overland Park, KS: Digireads.com Publishing: 2019.

Macpherson, Kevin D. *Fill Your Oil Paintings with Light and Color*. Cincinnati, OH: North Light Books, 1997.

Marine, Carol. *Daily Painting: Paint Small and Often To Become a More Creative, Productive, and Successful Artist*. New York: Watson-Guptill Publications, 2014.

INSTRUCTIONAL VIDEOS

karabullockart.com/meet-sarah-sedwick/

PATREON

patreon.com/sedwickstudio

PODCASTS

The Learn to Paint Podcast with Kelly Anne Powers

SELECTED TOOLS

The LederEasel
ledereasel.com/store/p4/ledereasel-sedwick.html#

Raymar Panels
raymarart.com
Use the code SEDWICK15 for 15% off

SmartArt Products Clip-On Brush Holder
etsy.com/shop/SmartArtProducts
Use the code SARAH for 10% off

ACKNOWLEDGMENTS

First, a huge thank you to Duane Keiser, Carol Marine, and all the early Daily Painters for leading my way back to painting. Taking the pressure off creating and setting a strong example of work ethic, you showed me that consistency and momentum are the keys to becoming an artist.

I'll be forever grateful to the people who gave me my first opportunities to teach painting: the staff of the Maude Kerns Art Center and Rebecca Mannheimer of Oregon Art Supply in Eugene, Oregon. Also Leslie Lienau at the Oklahoma Academy of Classical Art, who invited me to lead my first out-of-town workshop. A huge hug and thank you to Kathryn Wilson of Shreveport, Louisiana, for being the first artist to ask me to mentor them online—and to Robin Clawson for introducing us through her fantastic teaching organization.

Thank you to all of my students over the years, both in person and online. You've brought joy and inspiration into my life and taught me as much as—if not more than—I've taught you!

To all of my artist-contributors who helped make this book rich and beautiful with their wonderful works, thank you. I'm honored!

Thank you to the entire team at Rockport Publishers/Quarto Publishing Group for choosing me for this project. It's been a pleasure working with you.

Hugs and thanks to Kara Bullock for her friendship and collaboration and for helping me reach an even wider audience through my video workshops.

Thank you to my parents for raising me in a home where living a creative life was not only accepted, but demonstrated daily, and for your unwavering support and love.

To Roger, thank you for believing from the beginning—and without a shadow of a doubt—that I could do this and encouraging me every step of the way. I love you.

And finally, to you, the reader. Thank you most of all.

ABOUT THE AUTHOR

SARAH SEDWICK began painting in oils at age ten. In 2001, she earned a BFA from Maryland Institute College of Art with a focus on illustration and painting and a minor degree in art history. Her work focuses on still life and portraiture, painting from direct observation. Teaching is an integral part of her creative work. She teaches workshops around the United States and internationally, as well as through an online art mentorship program. Sarah is represented by Tvedten Fine Art in Harbor Springs, Michigan, Cole Gallery in Edmonds, Washington, and Elliott Fouts Gallery in Sacramento, California. She makes her home in Eugene, Oregon. To learn more about Sarah and her work, visit her website sarahsedwick.com, on Patreon at Sarah Sedwick, and on Instagram and Facebook @sedwickstudio.

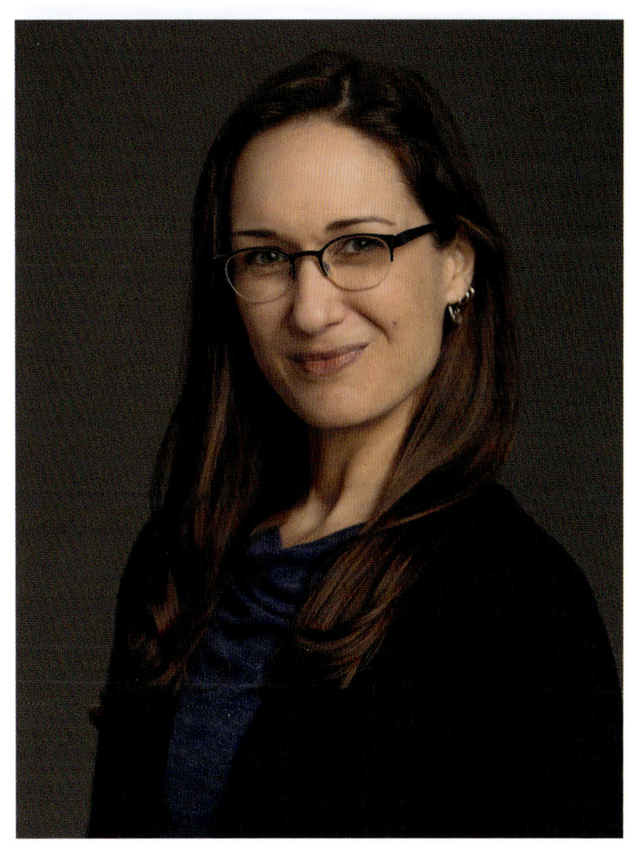

INDEX

OTHER TITLES IN ROCKPORT'S FOR ARTISTS SERIES

The **For Artists series** expertly guides and instructs artists at all skill levels who want to develop their classical drawing and painting skills and create realistic and representational art.

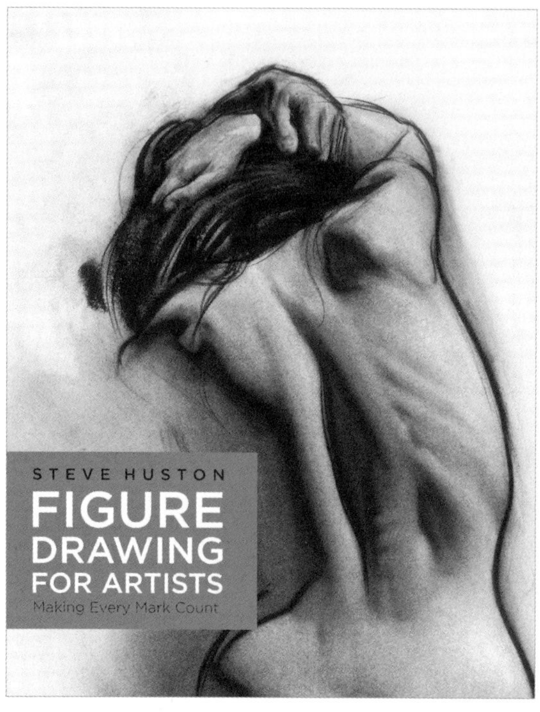

Figure Drawing for Artists
978-1-6315-9065-8

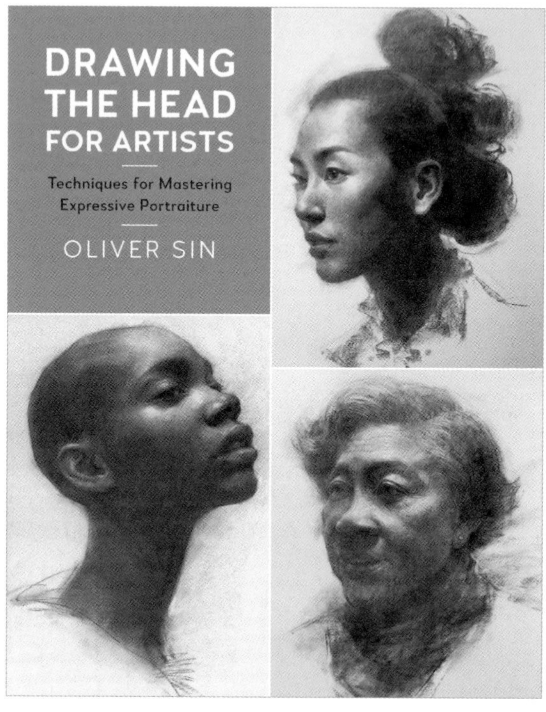

Drawing the Head for Artists
978-1-6315-9692-6

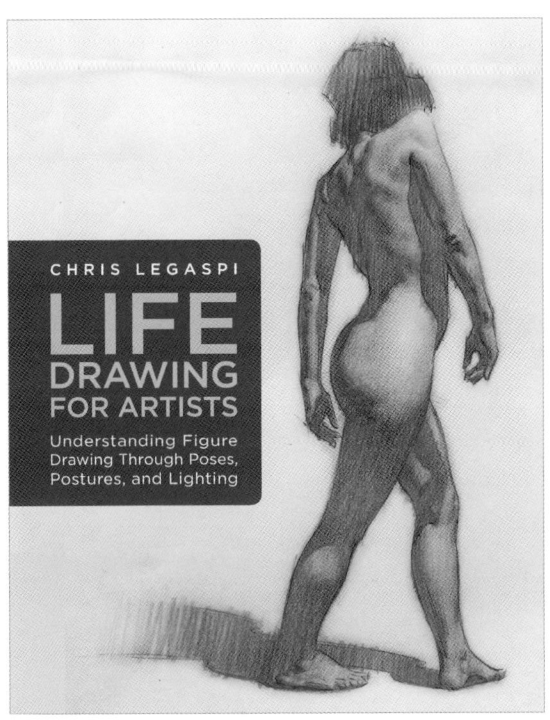

Life Drawing for Artists
978-1-6315-9801-2

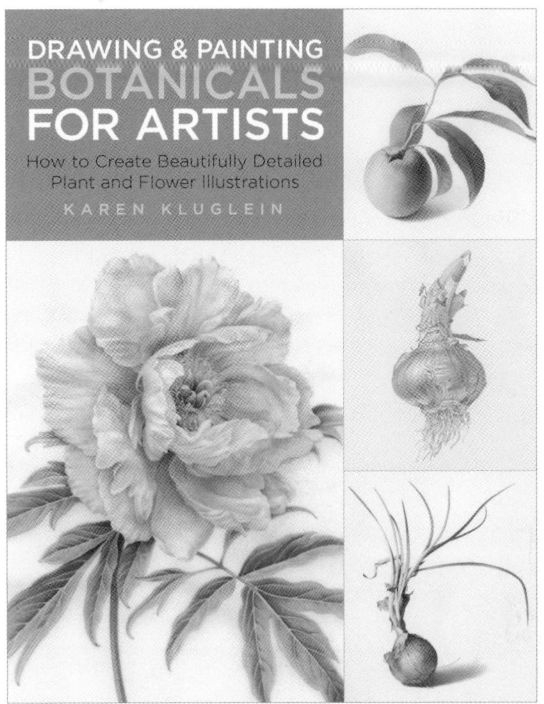

Drawing and Painting Botanicals for Artists
978-1-6315-9857-9

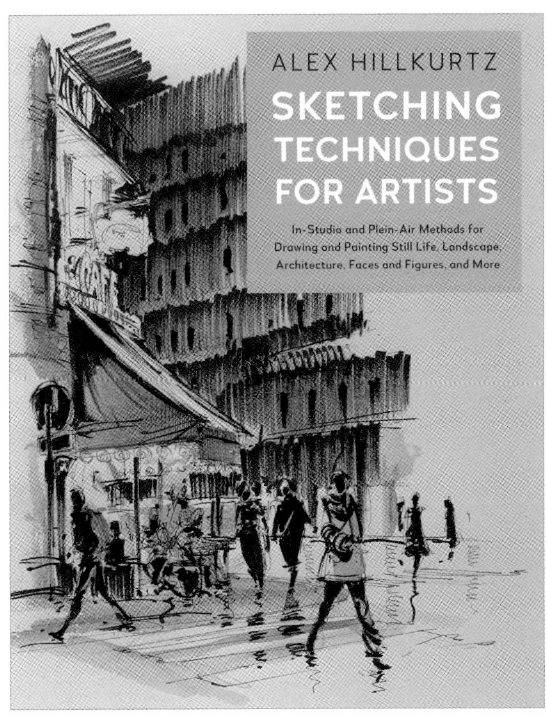

Sketching Techniques for Artists
978-1-6315-9923-1

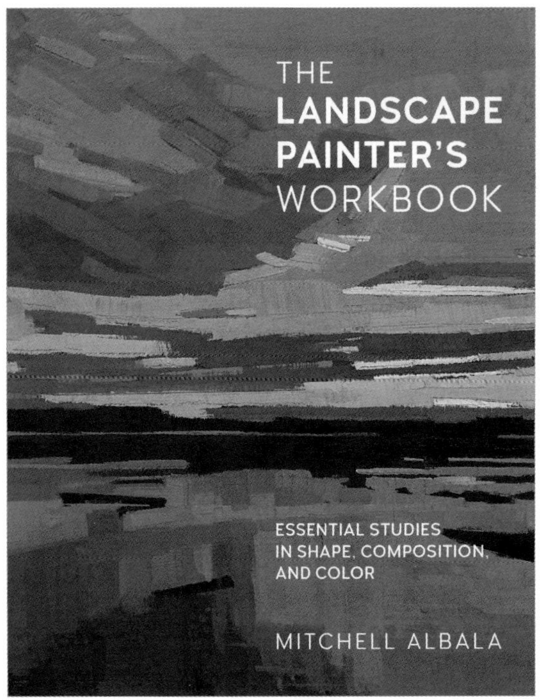

The Landscape Painter's Workbook
978-0-7603-7135-0

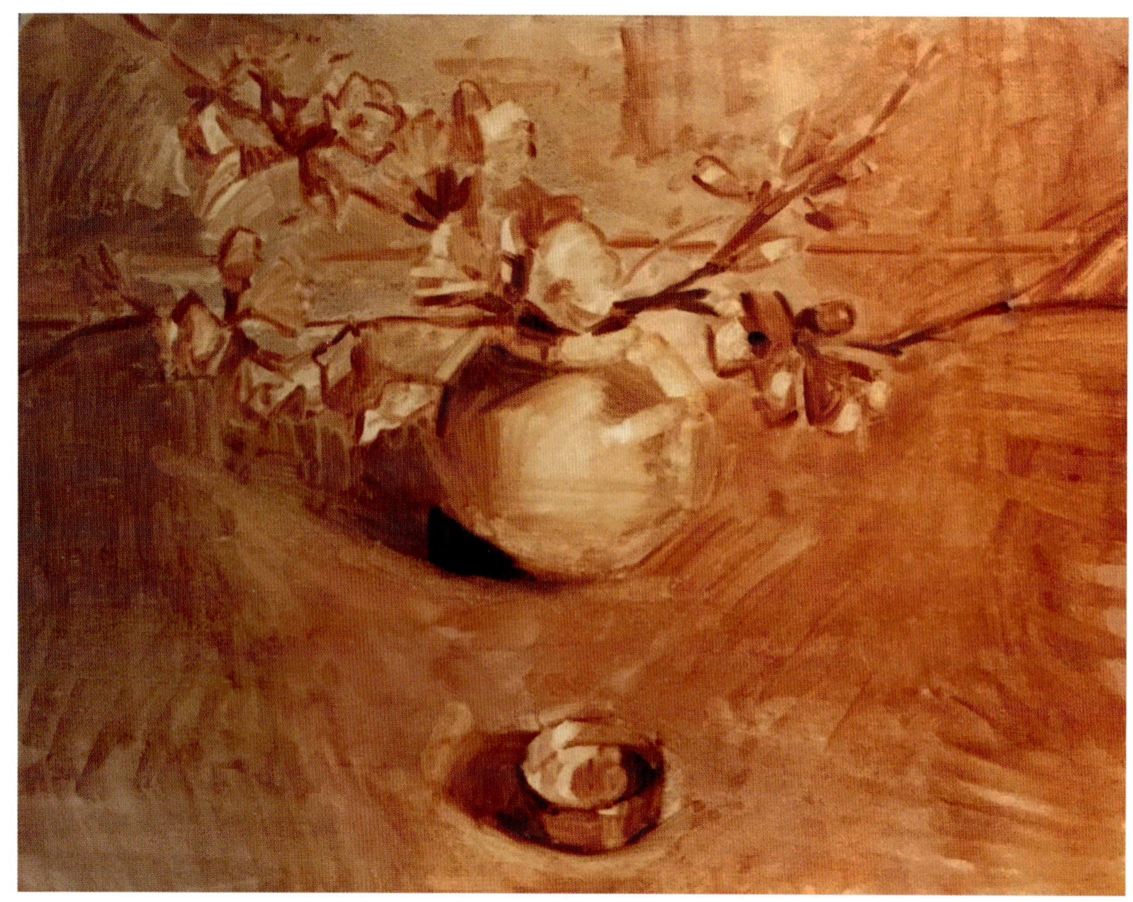

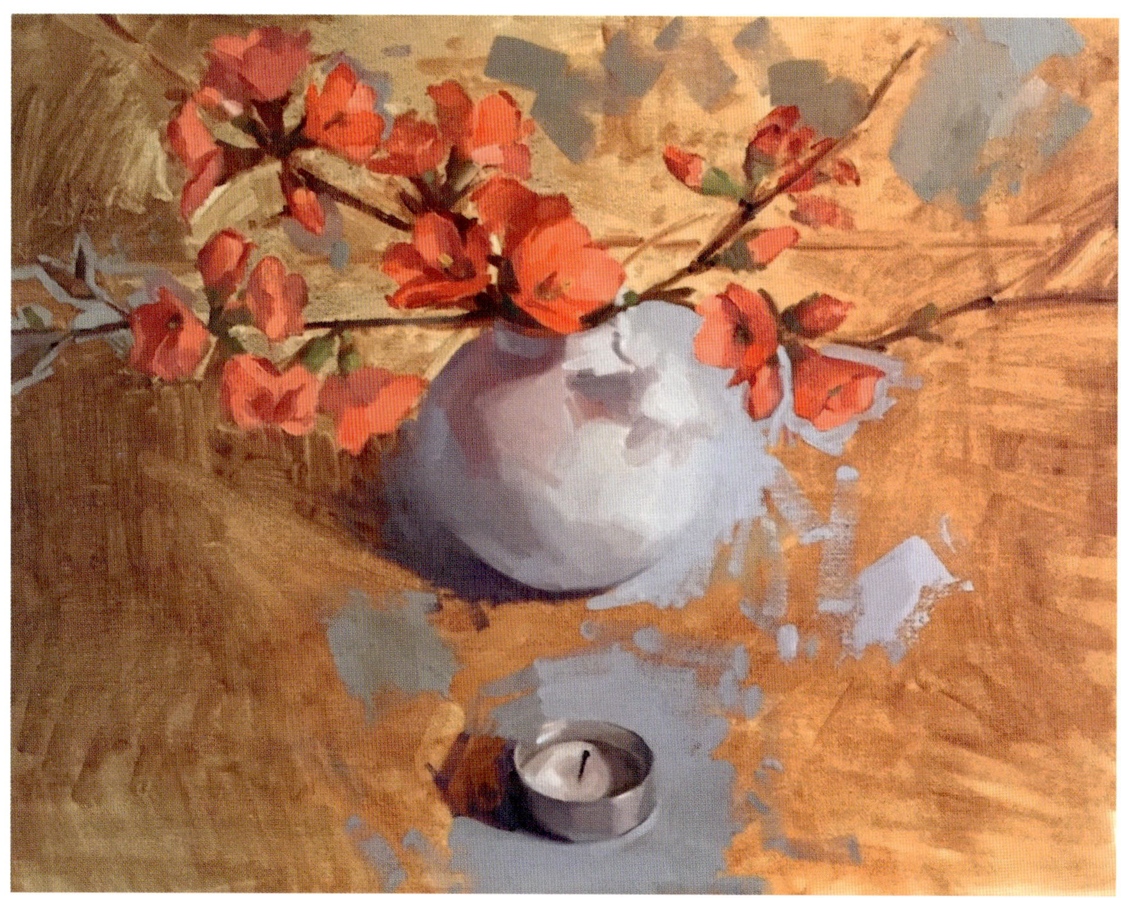